THE KOSHER PALETTE II

Coming Home

the art and simplicity of kosher cooking

JOSEPH KUSHNER HEBREW ACADEMY
RAE KUSHNER YESHIVA HIGH SCHOOL
LIVINGSTON, NEW JERSEY

THE KOSHER PALETTE II
Coming Home

Published by the
Joseph Kushner Hebrew Academy
110 South Orange Avenue
Livingston, New Jersey 07039
973-597-1115

Library of Congress Control Number: 2005935647
ISBN: 0-9676638-1-4

Designed and manufactured by
Favorite Recipes® Press
an imprint of

FRP™

P.O. Box 305142
Nashville, Tennessee 37230
800-358-0560

Art Direction: *Steve Newman*
Book Design: *Dave Malone*
Typography: *Sara Anglin, Jessie Anglin*

Manufactured in China
First Printing 2006
20,000 copies

PROFESSIONAL CREDITS

Todd Aarons, Executive Chef, Tierra Sur at Herzog Wine Cellars, Oxnard, California, Todd's Merguez, page 15, Rosemary Grilled Salmon and Vegetables with Balsamic Syrup, page 141, Roasted Cauliflower and Dill Soup, page 42

Monita Buchwald, Recipe Tester, *Martha Stewart Living* magazine; Recipe Consultant for *Kosher Palette II*

Michele R.B. Friedman, Food Stylist, dairy desserts photo, page 245

George Gellert, President, Tom Gellert, Vice President, Carey Franco, Cheese Department, Atalanta Corporation, Cheese Suppliers and Consultants, cheese photo, page 182

Shelly Golombeck, Morris J. Golombeck Spices, Spice Supplier and Consultant, spice picture, page 20

Suzette Kaminski, Food Stylist

Gitti Samuel, Elegant Touch Caterers, Fresh Fruit Trifle, page 218

Eitan Segal, Royal Wines, Consultant on Wine Pairings and Suggestions

Melissa Singer, Victoria Seasons Florists, Flower Consultant and Supplier, poultry theme page centerpiece, page 89, traditional theme page flowers, page 283

Carole Walter, author, *Great Cookies: Secrets to Sensational Sweets*: Chocolate Chip Peanut Butter Cookies page 252, Chocolate Chocolate Chocolate Biscotti, page 263, Yochevid Hirsch's Passover Mandelbrot, page 289. (From *Great Cookies: Secrets to Sensational Sweets* by Carole Walter, copyright © 2003 by Carole Walter. Photographs copyright © 2003 by Duane Winfield. Used by permission of Clarkson Potter/Publishers, a division of Random House, Inc.)

Duane Winfield, Photographer

Contents

Foreword 4

Dedication 5

About Our School 6

A Note About Kosher Cooking 7

Acknowledgments 8

Sponsors 9

Recipe Testers 10

Recipe Contributors 11

Appetizers 12

Soups 34

Salads 54

Poultry 78

Meats 106

Fish 130

Pasta 152

Brunch and Dairy 168

Side Dishes 188

Desserts 216

Traditional 274

Glossary and Charts 292

Index 295

FOREWORD

Home, family, food: What would life be without them?

Who can't recall the pleasure of coming home from school to find a delectable snack waiting on the table? Who hasn't felt renewed, after a stressful day at work, by sitting down with family to enjoy a delicious homemade supper?

Relatives and friends with momentous news to share invariably make the big announcement in the kitchen or dining room, because those are our favorite places to rejoice; after all, food and drink are close to hand. Whether it's a last-minute brunch or an elaborate cocktail party; a *bris* or a Sweet Sixteen; the Sabbath or the Fourth of July—what we love most about any occasion is celebrating with loved ones at home.

The Kosher Palette II: Coming Home brings this tradition to life with extraordinary recipes and menus that nourish the senses as well as the soul. Every recipe features fresh, flavorful ingredients that evoke the comforts and memories of home. What's more, each one tastes as terrific as it looks—and most take surprisingly little time to prepare.

Planning a Sephardic *meze* feast for Purim? A "Souper Bowl" Sunday night soup extravaganza? Look no further. Here you'll find the sophisticated, international dishes preferred by both gourmet and everyday cooks, along with enduring classics sure to remind your family and guests of treasured meals from the past.

Enlivened by gorgeous photographs and lively anecdotes, *The Kosher Palette II: Coming Home* features menus that will transform every meal into a happy memory. The 300-plus recipes included here will help you prepare elegant, everyday dishes, as well as unforgettable feasts for festive occasions and holidays. Dozens of practical tips—from choosing wines to complement the menu, to creating dazzling tablescapes—will inspire you to entertain family and friends in style.

Every recipe in *The Kosher Palette II: Coming Home* has been double- or triple-tested to ensure accuracy and adherence to *kashrut,* a sampler list on each chapter opener help you identify appropriate dishes for the occasion, whether you need something quick, something for the younger set, or something more sophisticated. This exciting new feature will allow even novice cooks to introduce their children and guests to the joys of Jewish hospitality.

Like the original, groundbreaking *The Kosher Palette,* this book, *The Kosher Palette II: Coming Home,* reflects the experiences, memories, and dedication of hundreds of great cooks from here and abroad. We benefited from the expertise of many professionals, as well as the great home cooks who enjoy entertaining. This feature makes the book so exciting—it is designed for you, by you—and has something for everyone's kitchen. I know you will agree that this newest cache of recipes and menus, heartfelt personal stories, and practical suggestions will not only enrich your cooking repertoire, but also remind you of why *Coming Home* will always be such an important tradition.

Welcome Home!
Sandra Blank
Editor-in-Chief

DEDICATION

We are privileged and honored to dedicate *The Kosher Palette II: Coming Home* to the memory of Rabbi Dr. Steven M. Dworken *z"l*, husband of Mrs. Susan H. Dworken, JKHA head of school. He was known as the "rabbi's rabbi" for his unique ability, in the quietest of ways, to handle many different situations, personalities, and religious issues. His exceptional commitment to *achdut*—bringing people together through love, respect, wisdom, and humor—was his hallmark. Like a chef who blends many different ingredients to create something delicious, so did Rabbi Dworken bring out the best in everyone he met, creating harmony in all that he touched. Rabbi Dworken will always be remembered for his infectious smile, his extraordinary kindness and warmth, and his incredible gift of making all who knew him feel loved and special.

Blessing in the Dough
By Aliza Dworken Frohlich

In the book of Genesis 24:67, following the burial of the matriarch Sarah, her son Isaac takes a wife, Rebecca, "brings her to his mother's tent" and was "comforted." What is the significance of these actions? Rashi's explanation is that "He brought her to his mother's tent and she became the model of his mother Sarah... All the days that Sarah was alive, there was **blessing in the dough**. When she died the blessing stopped. When Rebecca arrived the blessing returned... (Mid. BR 16)." The dough symbolizes sustenance—not just physical, but spiritual as well. The sustenance that Sarah provided throughout her life—through her teachings and the time she spent spreading the word of G-d—that sustenance had blessing from G-d. Dough demands kneading and shaping—it's not a finished product and demands time and effort to develop. Sarah spent her life developing and "kneading" the dough—the sustenance that she was to pass on to others and particularly to her son Isaac. When Sarah passed away, the void was unfillable, the blessing disappeared—until Rebecca arrived and attempted to follow the model of her mother-in-law to sustain others through her life, and the blessing returned.

While our father, Rabbi Dworken *z"l*, was alive, he spent much of his day kneading dough for the Jewish community—and it wasn't always easy. At times, as those of us who bake challah know, the dough has to be beaten down until it forms the shape we want. However, our father never gave up on the Jewish people. He knew that no effort was too great and went to all lengths to spread Torah and encourage Jews to be unified. He helped ensure the future of the rabbinate through his personal guidance of rabbis and his work at the Rabbinical Council of America. And, thank G-d, he saw much blessing in his dough—in the work of his hands. After his death, his family and his community were faced with a void. This is the challenge we face today—to continue the legacy of our father just as Rebecca continued the legacy of Sarah; to continue kneading that dough, spreading Torah and transmitting its values. For we know that when people die, the blessing does not die with them as long as those who follow them transmit their values to the coming generations. The blessing only then flourishes.

And so this dedication to our father is highly appropriate, for it will remind us that as we sustain our physical selves with this sumptuous food, we will also recall the importance of sustaining our spiritual selves—for that is what our father stood for. I would therefore like to end with a blessing for the Joseph Kushner Hebrew Academy and Rae Kushner Yeshiva High School family and this cookbook. May there be much blessing in all the food that it helps create.

Joseph Kushner Hebrew Academy
Rae Kushner Yeshiva High School

From a small house on 13th Street and Clinton Avenue, Newark ...
...to an impressive building on the corner of Seymour and Clinton Avenues, Newark ...
...to a merger with the Hebrew Institute in the Young Israel building on Lyons Avenue, Newark ...
...to a facility on Maple Avenue, Hillside ...to Centre Street, South Orange ...
...to Henderson Drive, West Caldwell ...to its present location on South Orange Avenue, Livingston.

Our first home was a small building on Clinton Avenue in Newark, New Jersey. Today, our state-of-the-art facility is located on a thirty-acre campus in Livingston, New Jersey, and serves eight hundred children from pre-kindergarten through twelfth grade. The values of our founders are the values we remain committed to transmitting to our children: that Jewish continuity and Jewish education go hand in hand; that love of learning encompasses religious studies as well as math, science, and the humanities; that devotion to Torah, the State of Israel and *K'lal Yisrael* are the foundation upon which we build our lives; and that we will always cherish and safeguard the democratic way of life that we enjoy in the United States.

One of the finest Modern Orthodox day schools in the country, we serve communities throughout central and northern New Jersey. Our teachers and administrators are dedicated to meeting the intellectual, emotional, social, and educational needs of *each* child. Our students are encouraged to strive for academic excellence, to reach their individual potential, and to think creatively and critically. Extracurricular programs, clubs, and sports add yet another dimension to the social and educational opportunities we provide. Our children learn to treat others, within and beyond our walls, with respect and wholeheartedly initiate and participate in community service.

Fathers studying *Gemara* and playing basketball with their sons on a Saturday night; mothers poring over sacred texts during weekly classes in the Lower School library; parents and grandparents attending school plays and volunteering for Parent Teacher Council projects— all contribute to the unique atmosphere of JKHA/RKYHS. Our hallways ring with laughter and song; our classrooms with insight; our *Beit Midrash* with prayer; our library with scholarship; and our gyms and playgrounds with camaraderie.

A Note About Kosher Cooking

. . . .

An explosion of kosher products on the market means that almost any dish is within reach of the kosher chef.

Kosher foods fall into three categories: meat, dairy, and parve.

• Kosher meat comes only from animals that both chew their cud and have cloven hooves, such as cows and sheep. Kosher poultry includes chicken, turkey, and duck; birds of prey are forbidden. In order to be kosher, an animal must have been slaughtered by a certified kosher slaughterer in strict compliance with Jewish religious law, and the meat or poultry must have been properly "kashered," soaked (in water) and salted to remove blood. Most kosher butchers sell meat and poultry that have been kashered and are ready to use.

• Dairy foods include milk, cheese, butter, cream, ice cream, and yogurt, as well as all products that contain dairy ingredients.

• Parve foods are neither meat nor dairy and include produce, eggs, and fish.

• All fresh foods, including herbs, vegetables, fruits, nuts, and grains, are parve but should be carefully examined and washed before serving or cooking to remove insects.

• Eggs should be discarded if they contain bloodspots.

• Fish with both fins and scales are kosher; no special kashering is required. Kosher fish include tuna, salmon, flounder, sole, trout, and whitefish. All shellfish are prohibited, as are swordfish, catfish, and eels.

• Meat and dairy foods are never eaten together. They are prepared in separate sets of pots and pans with separate utensils, and are served from and eaten on separate sets of dishes with separate silverware. Parve foods may be served with either meat or dairy dishes.

• Separate meat, dairy, and parve dishes, pots, and utensils are required for Passover use, and packaged or prepared foods must be certified kosher for Passover for use on this holiday.

• Please consult your rabbi about particular kosher certifications or any other questions you have regarding kosher food and its preparation.

• For the purposes of this book, we assume that all margarine and bouillon called for in our recipes are parve. Please note that kosher Worcestershire sauces marked "fish" should not be used when preparing meat dishes.

Icon Key

 Anecdote

 Wine and Beverage: drinks that complement the dish and beverage tips

 Preparation: Hints or shortcuts for an aspect of preparing the dish

 Table settings: Ways to dress up your table

 Accompaniments: Side dishes that go nicely with the recipe

 Garnishing: An extra something to bring your presentation to an extraordinary level

Sampler Key

Family Friendly: Appeals to all ages

Quick and Easy: Simple to make

Freezes Well: See Freezing Chart page 108

Prep Time: Additional preparation time needed

Sophisticated: Appeals to a more cultivated palette

Special Occasions: More elaborate recipes

Acknowledgments

To all of you, who, no matter what we asked, always said yes.
I am so grateful for your time, experience, commitment, and generosity.

Sandra Blank, Editor-in-Chief

Cookbook Committee Chairpersons

Seryl Kushner—You were my motivator and source of encouragement. You are incredibly generous in everything you do. Thank you.

Robin Klatt—Your devotion to this project and our school is a lesson to us all. Thank you.

Sherry Stein—Hearing your calm and rational perspective was always invaluable to me. Thank you.

Recipe Coordinators

Linda Lewinter—Thanks for allowing us to benefit from your many skills and talents.

Barbara Listhaus—Thank you for your energy, hard work, and advice.

Robin Sabbagh—Our Sephardic food expert! Thank you for always going the extra mile and for adding such a special flavor to our book.

Writers

Diane Covkin
Malkie Ratzker
Judy Sandman

Thank you for taking rough images and turning them into a beautifully written text.

Artistic Presentation

Naomi Berg
Dara Orbach

Your fabulous taste helped create the beautiful look of this book. Thank you.

Judaic Advisor

Mrs. Susan Dworken

Your expertise not only helped to influence this cookbook, but is reflected in all of our homes through the education of our children. Thank you.

Fundraising Event Chairperson

Deborah Zuckerman

Nobody throws a party like you. Thanks for all of your time and effort in making it such a successful event.

Corporate Fundraising

Melisa Feldman   *Ari Rosenfeld*
Ariel Nelson   *Naomi Rosenfeld*
Malkie Ratzker

Thanks for taking on this very challenging task and drawing the support of our corporate sponsors.

Business Manager

Giuliana Ross

Thank you for managing all the financial aspects of this project.

Sales Managers

Sharon Kessel
Leah Spielman

Not a book would be received without all of your dedication and support. Thank you.

Copy Editors

Tammy Abramowitz   *Hilary Levin*
Cara Altman   *Ellen Longman*
Ellen Arian   *Lauren Mayer*
Harriet Blank   *Nancy Perlmutter*
Jessica Blank   *Renee Reiser*
Chaya Felzenberg   *Julie Singer*
Fran Glajchen   *Ruth Singer*
Aline Grossman Kahn   *Marisa Stadtmauer*
Barrie Jacob   *Debbie Weintraub*
Alice Klein   *Debra Wenig*

Thank you for undertaking the arduous task of typing, editing, and proofing material for our book.

A special thanks to *Duane Winfield* for making the vision a reality.

Many thanks to *Sid Sayovitz* for his executive seal and to all the *professional staff and lay leadership* of our school for their constant help, support, and dedication.

To my family: *Howie, Jessica, Adam, Joshua,* and *Daniel*—Thank you so much for your love and support during this busy time. Thanks for testing food when you didn't want to, for having patience with endless phone calls and meetings, and for sharing me with this book. I love you all.

Sponsors

Corporate Sponsors

Atalanta Corporation	*IDT*	*Manischewitz Foods*	*Ram Caterers*
Dale & Thomas Popcorn	*Kraft Foods*	*Pepperidge Farms*	*Royal Wines*

Diamond Level

Cheryl and Fred Halpern	Linda and Murray Laulicht	Beth and Martin Statfeld
Robin and Bradford Klatt	Marisa and Richard Stadtmauer	Sherry and Henry Stein
Lee and Murray Kushner		Andrea and Ronald Sultan
Seryl and Charles Kushner		Deborah and Wayne Zuckerman

Gold Level

Hattie and Arthur Dubroff	Marci and Jeffrey Lefkovits	Leah and Joel Spielman
Alice and Jacob Klein		Millie and Abraham Zuckerman

Silver Level

Sandra and Howard Blank	Ruth and Steven Katz	Barbara and Alan Listhaus
Avivah and Michael Gottlieb	Linda and David Lewinter	Gayle and David Newman
Batsheva and Murray Halpern		Ariela and Daniel Spialter

Bronze Level

Bonnie and David Anfang	Maralyn and Isidore Friedman	Malkie and Paul Ratzker
Harvey Bell	Florie and Irwin Gasner	Janet and Sheldon Rosenberg
Sheila and Robert Benrimon	Adena and Leonard Gerstle	Giuliana and Neil Ross
Naomi and Howard Berg	Terri and Michael Goldberg	Chari and Martin Roth
Michelle and Bruce Berger	Eva and Arie Halpern	Randee and Kenneth Rubenstein
Suzanne and Miles Berger	Sharon and David Halpern	Robin and Joseph Sabbagh
Marilyn and Leonard Bielory	Gail and Mark Hausdorff	Jayne and Sidney Sayovitz
Andrea and Bryan Bier	Michele and Gideon Homa	Esther and William Schulder
Harriet and George Blank	Rebecca and Douglas Kuber	Frances and Arie Schwartz
Mirtha and Paul Celler	Marilyn and Leon Moed	Mali and Steven Schwartz
Dawn and Aaron Chevinsky	Lauren and Michael Mayer	Sharon and Henry Sopher
Diane and Richard Covkin	Nicole and Joseph Meyer	Marilyn and Morris Stadtmauer
Dworken Family	Boni and Martin Moskovitz	Sylvia and Arthur Stark
Gwendolyn Francis	Dara and David Orbach	Randee and Brian Stolar
Julie and Fredric Friedman	Mairav and Daniel Pascheles	Jane and Mark Wilf

To the professionals who were so generous in contributing to the success of this book:

Todd Aarons, Executive Chef, Tierra Sur at Herzog Wine Cellars—Your knowledge of food and flavors is incredible. Thank you for sharing your expertise with us.

Monita Buchwald, Recipe Tester of *Martha Stewart Living* magazine—You were a gift to our project, arriving to help at our hour of need. Thank you for your help and guidance in perfecting some of our recipes.

Tom Gellert and *Carey Franco* of Atalanta Corporation—Thank you for your incredibly generous supply of cheese and for all the valuable information.

Shelly Golombeck of Morris J. Golombeck Spices—Thank you for providing such a varied palette of spices and for your expertise.

Melissa Singer of Victoria Seasons—Thank you for your professional guidance and for the donation of a beautiful array of flowers for the book.

Rubenstein Associates—Thank you for your help in generating such great publicity for our book.

Carole Walters, Author of *Great Cookies*—Your "sweet and delightful" temperament made the hours we spent together enjoyable and fascinating. You are truly a dessert expert, and we are so happy to have you in our book. Thank you.

RECIPE TESTERS

The Kosher Palette II: Coming Home gratefully acknowledges the energy and dedicated efforts of the women and men who tested and perfected the recipes in this book. Our sincere gratitude for your time, support, advice, and discerning taste, ensuring our recipes are fabulous. We apologize to anyone whose name was inadvertently omitted.

Tammy Abramowitz
Fran Ackerman
Bluma Acocella
Lee Alexander
Rebecca Alexander
Susie Altas
Robin Amster
Zippy Atlas
Erica Bank
Michelle Bardash
Aaron Bassan
Robin Bellicha
Sheila Benrimon
Naomi Berg ** /▲▲
Caryn Berger
Deborah Berger
Suzanne Berger
Donna Berk
Marilyn Bielory
Debbie Billig
Amy Bitton
Adam Blank
Jessica Blank
Paula Blank
Sandra Blank
Shani Blenden **
Rachel Bliner
Yonna Bliner
Ora Bloom
Robbin Bochner
Cheryl Borenstein
Karen Borger
Frida Braha
Tal Brandwein
Amy Braun
Susan Braverman
Debbie Brody
Gail Bukiet
Michelle Burblin
Rachelle Burghauser
Faigie Cantor
Judy Carmeli
Nurit Chasman
Shari Cherna
Aimee Ciment
Carin Cohen
Faye Cohen
Linda Cohen
Sharon Cohn
Amy Cooper
Jeanette Dadusc
Mindy Davidoff
Michelle Degen **
Cindy Dobrinsky
Jennifer Eichenholz
Ephi Eisenberg
Yael Eisenberg

Mindy Eisenman
Myriam Elefant
Debbie Erdfarb
Emily Faiwiszewski
Steve Faiwiszewski
Sharon Fersel
Debbie Fine
Debbie Finkelstein ▲▲
Richard Finkelstein
Chanalee Fischer
Shira Forman
Gwen Francis
Mina Frank
Laura Frenkel ** /▲▲
Connie Friedman
Fran Friedman
Julie Friedman
Michele Friedman
Leslie-Ann Fromen
Arden Fusman
Florie Gasner
Ilana Gdanski
Jill Geiger
Ellen Gertler
Dianne Gindi
Rachel Ginsberg
Debra Goldberg
Jay Goldberg
Elissa Gorkowitz
Avivah Gottlieb
Jennifer Gozlan
Ilana Greenberg
Miriam Greenberg
Deborah Greenfield
Dolores Greenfiel
Toba Leah Grossbaum
Rachel Grosser
Tsila Grossman
Ashera Haar
Eti Hagag
Valerie Harris
Gail Hausdorff
Faige Helprin
Eilene Herzfeld
Abby Hirschmann ▲▲
Pamela Hirt **
Laura Holland
Michele Homa
Beth Indyk
Judy Israeli
Larry Jacobs
Shelly Jacobs
Sharon Joshowitz
Vivian Kandel
Donna Karp
Sheryl Kaye
Stephanie Keiser

Sharon Kessel
Jacqui Kimmel
Anna Kirschblum
Debbie Klahr
Robin Klatt
Lisa Klein
Ellen Kleinhaus
Nicole Koppel
Nancy Kornblum
Esther Kosoffsky
Doug Kuber
Rebecca Kuber
Seryl Kushner
Chani Laifer
Debra Lando
Sandy Lang
Ellie Langer
Loraine Langer
Shari Lasher
Ruth Borgen Lauer
Marci Lefkovits
Nancy Lefkovitz
Sallie Levi
Louise Levine
Debby Levitt
Rebecca Levy **
David Lewinter
Linda Lewinter
Cindy Lichtbroun ** /▲▲
Lisa Lifshitz
Adina Lipson
Barbara Listhaus ▲▲
Jessica Listhaus
Marsha Loeb
Bobbi Luxenberg
Karen Lyman
Fariba Mahgerefteh
Martha Maik
Lori Mann
Lea Marcus
Yaffa Markovich
Shira Mathias
Jay Matthew
Liat Matthew
Lauren Mayer **
Toby Mayer
Michelle Meiner
Jennifer Mendelson
Keith Mendelson
Nicole Meyer
Valerie Meyers
Edith Michaely
Julie Miller
Cheryl Minkoff **
Nancy Mond
Boni Moskowitz **
Suri Moskowitz

Susan Moskowitz
Sarah Naus
Ina Nelson
Sharon Niman
Dara Orbach ** /▲▲
David Orbach
Bobbie Ostrow
Janet Paniri
Mairav Pascheles
Janet Peleg
Aliza Poleyeff
Abbie Prince
Darbie Rabinowitz **
Robert Rabinowitz
Anne Rand
Helen Ratzker
Malkie Ratzker
Andrea Reichel
Shira Reiz
Shelley Ridner
Riki Rimberg
Deborah Rinn
Naomi Rosenfeld
Debbie Rosenwein **
Giuliana Ross
Chari Roth
Marcia Roth
Deena Rubin
Joeseph Sabbagh
Robin Sabbagh ▲▲
Sharon Sacks
Judy Sandman **
Erica Sassoon
Josh Savitz
Naomi Savitz
Rena Appel Schanholz
Lisa Schechder
Amanda Schechter
Lisa Schechter
Rena Appel Schlanger
Karen Schlussel
Sharon Schlusselberg **
Vickie Schulman
Dasi Schwalbe
Fran Schwartz
Roberta Schwartz
Monica Schwartzbach
Judy Schwartzberg
Dina Schwartzman
Yael Schwartzman
Sari Shalom
Miriam Shamsian
Ilene Sheris
Robin Shimoff
Hinda Shriky
Shana Shua
Elana Silber

Randi Silvermintz
Elana Singer
Ruth Singer
Anina Slonim
David Small
Sandy Small
Hedy Smith
Rena Appel Soclof
Sari Solomon
Serena Solomon
Howard Sragow
Caren Srulovitz
Marisa Stadtmauer
Sylvia Stark ** /▲▲
Sherry Stein ▲▲
Esther Steinberg
Julie Stiel
Phylis Stier
Ellen Stokar
Suzanne Stokar
Blimie Strauss
Andrea Sultan
Jane Sutton
Avri Szafranski
Gavriel Szafranski
Sherri Szafranski ** /▲▲
Hope Tafet
Lilli Tammam
Sondra Tammam
Elissa Titen
Karine Turetsky
Aimee Turner
Sandy Ungar
Sue Wagner
Karen Wasserman
Debbie Weintraub
Pearla Lulinski Weisman
Joanie Weissman **
Helene Wengrofsky ** /▲▲
Micahel Wengrofsky
Debra Wenig
Suri Winograd
Susie Wolf
Cecille Wollman
Michael Wollman
Betsy Yarkony
Raizy Strahl Zakheim
Chana Erbst Ziment
Deborah Zuckerman
Sharon Zughaft

Section chairs–**
Host for Testing–▲▲

10

RECIPE CONTRIBUTORS

. . . .

The Kosher Palette II: Coming Home thanks all of the cooks and storytellers who generously contributed their treasured recipes and food memories to this book. We regret that we were unable to include all of the stories and recipes which were submitted due to similarity or availability of space. We also hope that we have not inadvertently overlooked any contributors.

Tammy Abramowitz
Shari Alter
Gitti Altman
Beth Aron
Susie Atlas
Shira Baruch
Naomi Berg
Harriet Blank
Paula Blank
Sandra Blank
Shani Blenden
Ora Bloom
Mark A. Bloomberg
Ruth Borgen Lauer
Judy Botnick
Rochelle Brand
Gertrude Brenner
Debbie Buechler
Shari Cherna
Eileen David
Michelle Degen
Susan Degen
Barbara Deutsch
Hope Dickter
Donna Dinson
Yael Eisenberg
Blanche Eisenstark
Myriam Elefant
Judi Epstein
Gail Feingold
Bernita Feldman
Julie Feldman
Melissa Feldman
Esther Felsen
Sandra Fiori
Susie Fishbein
Cheryl Freidman
Debby Klein Friedman
Michele R. B. Friedman
Elisa Freilich
Kaye Freireich
Estie Fried
Caryn Friedman
Dolly Friedman
Fran Friedman
Jill Friedman
Karen Friedman
Margery Friedman
Marjorie Friedman
Leslie Ann Fromen
Rebecca Frommer Klein
Arden Fusman

James Geller
Adena Gerstle
Sarah Gerstley
Dianne Gindi
Rachel Ginsberg
Fran Glajchen
Rachel Glatt
Carl Goldberg
Mary Ellen Goldberg
Stephanie Goldenberg
Lauren Goldman
Anne Golombeck
Aviva Golombeck
Lisa Golombeck
Shelly Golombeck
Yonina Gomberg
Avivah Gottlieb
Rosalyn Grad
Susan Gross
Toba Leah Grossbaum
Ashera Haar
Batshevah Halpern
Cheryl Halpern
Laurie Hasten
Sue Hausdorff
Abby Herschmann
Deborah Hiller
Dvora Hirschey
Pamela Hirt
Anne Homa
Michele Homa
Aline Kahn
Ilana Kahn
Orlee Kahn
Jamie Katz
Jill Kirsch
Debbie Klahr
Robin Klatt
Alice Klein
Chani Klein
Chaya Kleiner
Ellen Koller
Gladys Koppelman
Seryl Kushner
Zanna Lantzman
Banji Latkin-Ganchrow
Aleeza Lauer
Ilse Lauer Klirsfeld
Sally Lefkofsky
Lillian Leiderman
Rebecca Levy
Frieda Lewinter

Linda Lewinter
Dena Lieblich
Rita Lifton
Barbara Listhaus
Audrey Lookstein
Robin Luchins
Channie Lundner
Karen Lyman
Gabrielle Mahler
Martha Maik
Edit Masuelli
Nissah Mattenson
Pearl Mattenson
Jay Matthew
Etie Mayer
Lauren Mayer
Karen Mazurek
Michelle Meiner
Emma Mendelson
Jennifer Mendelson
Joan Meyer
Nicole Meyer
Valerie Meyers
Edith Michaely
Julie Miller
Risa Milman
Cheryl Minkoff
Debbie Moed
Leon Moed
Marilyn Moed
Pnina Moed Kass
Boni Moskovitz
Rachel Neufeld
Gail Shulman Newman
Lynd Novick
Yocheved Orabach
Dara Orbach
Leslie Ostrin
Bobbie Ostrow
Deena Ottensoser
Mairav Pascheles
Janet Peleg
Darbie Rabinowitz
Rachel Rabinowitz
Drorit Ratzker
Helen Ratzker
Malkie Ratzker
Malkie Rosen
Debbie Rosenwein
Giuliana Ross
Chari Roth
Randee Rubenstein

Deena Rubin
Robin Sabbagh
Judy Sandman
Jayne Sayovitz
Bonnie Schertz
Linda Schiffman
Esther Schulder
Janie Schwalbe
Mali Schwartz
Toby Schwartz
Monica Schwartzbach
Nicole Sebbag
Shana Shua
Robin Shulman
Ruth Singer
Ilene Siscovick
Amy Sklar
Sandy Small
Janet Spector
Howard Sragow
Davida Stadtmauer
Marilyn Stadtmauer
Marisa Stadtmauer
Sylvia Stark
Beth Statfeld
Sherry Stein
Ellen Stokar
Andrea Sultan
Bonita Sussman
Jane Sutton
Hope Tafet
Sondra Tammam
Jordan Tepp
Terri Trieger
Yael Weil
Joyce Weinberger
Esther Weinstein
Lauryn Weiser
Karen Weiss
Susan Wellish
Helene Wengrofsky
Debra Wenig
Suri Winograd
Jill Wohlfarth
Shoshana Wolf-Mehlman
Rayzel Yaish
Michael Yakount
Betsy Yarkony
Chana Erbst Ziment
Shaindy Zudick

APPETIZERS

SAMPLER
. . . .

FAMILY FRIENDLY
Far Eastern Short Ribs 14 • Sicilian Stuffed Rice Balls 16
Tortilla Shells with Meat Taco Filling 17
Lahamagine 18 • Bubbie's Fricassee 19
Spicy Turkey Wontons 24 • Stuffed Wrappers with Meat and Rice 25
Chicken Spinach Rolls 26 • Chopped Chicken with Dill en Croûte 27
Glazed Garlic Chicken Wings 28 • Colorful Fish Pâté 29
Artichoke and Spinach Swirls 30 • Avocado Dip 32

QUICK AND EASY
Far Eastern Short Ribs 14 • Glazed Garlic Chicken Wings 28
Chicken en Papillote 28 • Artichoke and Spinach Swirls 30
Greek Garlic Dip 30 • Avocado Dip 32
California Strawberry Salsa 33 • Barzargan 33

SOPHISTICATED
Veal Pâté 14 • Todd's Merguez 15
Yebra 22, 23 • Chicken en Papillote 28
Seared Tuna and Avocado Tartare 31
Smoked Salmon Rolls 32 • Barzargan 33

HORS D'OEUVRE
Sicilian Stuffed Rice Balls 16
Lahamagine 18 • Yebra 22, 23
Glazed Garlic Chicken Wings 28
Artichoke and Spinach Swirls 30 • Greek Garlic Dip 30
Smoked Salmon Rolls 32 • Avocado Dip 32
California Strawberry Salsa 33 • Barzargan 33

QUICK MUSTARD SAUCE

Combine 1 cup mayonnaise, 2 tablespoons fresh lemon juice, $1/3$ cup Dijon mustard and 1 tablespoon horseradish in a small bowl and mix well. Serve with the Veal Pâté.

LEMON CUPS

For a great look on the plate, scoop out lemon halves and fill them with the mustard sauce.

VEAL PÂTÉ

Meat

2 tablespoons olive oil	1 pound ground veal
1 onion, minced	1 pound chopped meat
$1^{1}/_{2}$ teaspoons rosemary	$3/4$ cup seasoned bread crumbs
1 (10-ounce) package frozen chopped spinach, thawed and well drained	2 eggs
	$1^{1}/_{2}$ teaspoons salt
	$1/2$ teaspoon pepper

Preheat oven to 350 degrees. Heat olive oil in a skillet and sauté onion and rosemary until tender; remove from heat. Combine spinach, ground veal, chopped meat, bread crumbs, eggs, salt, pepper and onion mixture in a large bowl and mix well. Press veal mixture into one large or two small loaf pans. Bake, uncovered, for 1 hour and 20 minutes or until cooked through and the top is brown. Serve on leaf lettuce with Quick Mustard Sauce (at left). *Makes 12 servings.*

FAR EASTERN SHORT RIBS

Meat

1 cup soy sauce	$1/4$ cup minced garlic (about 15 cloves)
$1/2$ cup sweet sherry	2 large scallions, chopped
$1/2$ cup packed dark brown sugar	5 pounds flanken short ribs, cut $1^{1}/_{2}$ inches thick
$1/4$ cup unseasoned rice vinegar	Scallions for garnish
$1/4$ cup toasted sesame oil	

Whisk soy sauce, sherry, brown sugar, vinegar, sesame oil, garlic and chopped scallions in a medium bowl and mix well. Pour into a large sealable plastic bag. Add ribs; seal the bag. Turn the bag over several times to coat ribs evenly. Marinate in the refrigerator 8 to 12 hours, turning bag occasionally.

Preheat oven to 350 degrees. Place ribs and marinade in a large baking dish. Roast, uncoverd, for 1 hour 15 minutes or until tender, basting and turning occasionally. Cool slightly; cut into chunks. Serve warm topped with sauce and garnished with scallions. Serve over prepared couscous. *Makes 10 to 12 servings.*

TODD'S MERGUEZ

Meat

" I was asked by many in our area to try and get this recipe. Todd was so kind in giving it to us. It is wonderful, though very spicy. You may also serve merguez with salad or in your favorite bread as a sandwich."

2 pounds ground lamb shoulder
1/4 cup harissa (Tunisian chile pepper mix)
1 small Spanish onion, or 1/2 large Spanish onion, minced
1/4 bunch fresh cilantro, chopped
2 tablespoons cumin seeds, toasted and ground
1 tablespoon ground ginger
1 tablespoon ground coriander
2 garlic cloves, minced
   Salt and pepper to taste

Combine lamb, harissa, onion, cilantro, cumin, ginger, coriander, garlic and salt and pepper to taste in a large bowl. Refrigerate lamb mixture, covered, for at least one day.

Shape lamb mixture into small oval meatballs or flat patties. Grill or brown on all sides in a skillet until cooked through; drain. Serve with tahini sauce, if desired. *Makes 6 appetizer or 4 main-dish servings.*

Note: Sausage is a strange term in the kosher world, as it usually suggests the addition of some kind of nonkosher fat and meat. In North Africa where Judeo-Arabic cooking traditions prevail, lamb is the predominant choice of meat. Spicy balls of ground lamb are transformed into sausages, usually without casings, for grilling or frying. Harissa, a North African chili paste, is the main flavoring in merguez.

Photograph for this recipe is on page 21.

CREATING A BUFFET TABLESCAPE

Color is paramount for eye appeal on any plate, whether individual plates or buffet platters. And eye appeal is the first thing that entices a person to taste something.

For a buffet, visit a home decor store and look for glass blocks, mirrored or other glass pieces, and marble or granite odds and ends. Keep your eyes open for anything unusually attractive. Or, imagine a theme and dress the table accordingly. For example, a fall Sukkot table might be decorated with gourds, squash and Indian corn. A meal of Israeli or Italian foods might include table accents of olive oil bottles filled with multi-colored pasta shapes or other colorful foods.

When garnishing a plate, use edible flowers and leaves or carved whole vegetables, such as bell pepper flowers, lemon cups, and tomato rosettes.

DAIRY VARIATION

For a dairy filling, substitute 6 to 8 ounces of mozzarella cheese, cut into 1-inch cubes, for the meat filling ingredients. Prepare risotto as directed, substituting 5 to 6 cups of water for the chicken broth. Prepare rice balls as directed, filling each cavity with a cheese cube.

TO MAKE AHEAD

Rice balls may be prepared one day ahead. Cool; refrigerate loosely covered. Reheat, uncovered, on a baking pan at 350 degrees for about 15 minutes or until heated through.

SICILIAN STUFFED RICE BALLS

Meat or Dairy

*T*here are two ways to make these rice balls—with meat or dairy. The risotto is basically prepared the same way in both versions (using either chicken broth or water), but there are different filling options.

RISOTTO
- 3 tablespoons olive oil
- 2 cups arborio rice
- 5 to 6 cups MANISCHEWITZ® Chicken Broth or bouillon
- 1½ teaspoons salt
- 2 eggs, lightly beaten
- Pepper to taste

MEAT FILLING
- 2 tablespoons olive oil
- 1 onion, chopped
- 2 large garlic cloves, finely chopped
- 4 ounces mushrooms, cut into halves and thinly sliced
- ½ pound ground beef
- 1 (8-ounce) can tomato sauce
- Oregano to taste (optional)
- Salt and pepper to taste
- ½ cup frozen baby peas
- 1 to 1½ cups plain bread crumbs
- Vegetable oil for deep-frying

For the risotto, heat olive oil in a large saucepan. Add rice and stir for about 2 minutes or until well coated. Stir in 1½ cups of broth and salt. Cook and stir until broth is absorbed. Continue adding broth 1 to 1½ cups at a time, simmering and stirring after each addition until broth is absorbed. Cook for 18 to 20 minutes total or until risotto is sticky and tender. Spoon into a large bowl. Cool. Add eggs and pepper to taste and mix until well blended; set aside.

For the meat filling, heat olive oil in a large skillet over medium heat and sauté the onion and garlic for 4 minutes or until slightly softened. Add mushrooms. Cook about 5 minutes or until light brown and the liquid is evaporated. Add ground beef. Cook until ground beef is brown and crumbly, stirring; drain. Stir in tomato sauce and oregano. Add salt and pepper to taste. Boil for about 3 minutes or until slightly thickened. Stir in peas.

Place bread crumbs in a bowl. For each rice ball, shape about 2 tablespoons of the risotto mixture into a 2-inch ball. Make a cavity in each ball and fill with 1 teaspoon of the meat mixture. Press rice around filling to enclose. Roll rice balls in bread crumbs to coat. Place on a waxed paper-lined baking sheet. Heat vegetable oil in a large deep skillet or stockpot over medium-high heat until hot (350 degrees). Fry rice balls 1½ to 2 minutes or until golden brown on all sides. Drain on paper towels. *Makes 10 to 12 servings.*

TORTILLA SHELLS WITH MEAT TACO FILLING

Meat

This is a fun-filled appetizer that the whole family will enjoy.

1 pound ground beef
1 large onion, chopped
4 tablespoons vegetable oil, divided
2 to 3 tablespoons taco seasoning mix
6 (10-inch) corn tortillas
1 (15-ounce) can kidney beans, drained and rinsed

1 green bell pepper, diced (optional)
2 plum tomatoes, diced
4 scallions, chopped
1 cup salsa
Lettuce for serving
Salsa and guacamole (optional)

Brown ground beef with onion in 2 tablespoons oil in a large skillet, stirring until ground beef is crumbly; drain. Stir in taco seasoning mix. Set aside; cool.

Heat remaining 2 tablespoons oil in a clean skillet until hot. Add tortillas one at a time, frying until toasted on both sides. Immediately place each tortilla in a small bowl to form a shell.

Toss beans, bell pepper, tomatoes and scallions with beef mixture. Add salsa and mix well. Spoon taco filling evenly into tortilla shells. Serve on a bed of lettuce along with spoonfuls of salsa and guacamole, if desired. *Makes 6 servings.*

**RAMON CORDOVA
RIOJA (RED, SPAIN)**
Dark berry, oak
and nutmeg aromas
with a delicious
spicy and fruity flavor
that matches well
with seasoned or
spicy dishes.

LAHAMAGINE
. . . .
Meat

Though these pies are labor intensive, they have a very refreshing, unique flavor that will broaden your palette. They freeze very well.

DOUGH

- 1/4 envelope dry yeast
- 1/2 cup plus 2 tablespoons warm water, divided
- 2 cups flour
- 1/2 teaspoon salt
- 1 tablespoon vegetable oil

MEAT TOPPING

- 1 pound ground beef
- 1 onion, grated and drained
- Juice of 1 lemon
- 1/4 to 1/3 cup tamerhindi or prune butter
- 1 tablespoon (heaping) tomato paste
- 1/2 teaspoon ground allspice
- Salt to taste
- Pine nuts for garnish

For the dough, dissolve yeast in 2 tablespoons water. Combine flour and salt in a bowl. Add yeast mixture and mix well. Stir in oil. Add remaining 1/2 cup warm water gradually. Knead on a floured surface until a soft dough forms. Place in a greased bowl, turning to coat the surface. Let rise, covered with a clean linen towel, in a warm place for 1 hour.

For the meat topping, combine ground beef, onion, lemon juice, tamerhindi, tomato paste, allspice and salt to taste in a bowl and mix well.

Preheat oven to 350 degrees. Divide dough into quarters and roll out as thinly as possible. Cut into circles: 1¹/₂-inch for bite size or 3-inch for appetizer size. Place slightly apart on well-greased baking sheets. Spoon meat topping onto each circle, spreading a thin layer to cover dough; press topping firmly into dough. Garnish center of each pie with three pine nuts. Bake for about 25 minutes or until dough is light brown. *Makes 10 servings.*

Photograph for this recipe is on page 21.

BUBBIE'S FRICASSEE

Meat

"When I mentioned the possibility of including Fricassee in this cookbook, I encountered the same response from everyone, 'I love that and haven't eaten it in so long.' So here it is. Everyone has their own version, so adjust this recipe to suit your taste."

1/4	cup vegetable oil	1 1/2	pounds chicken necks
4	onions, chopped	1 1/2	pounds giblets
4	to 5 ribs celery, cut into 1-inch slices		Pepper, garlic powder, paprika and salt to taste
4	to 5 carrots, peeled and cut into 1/2-inch slices	3	pounds chopped meat
2	pounds chicken wings or legs	2	eggs, lightly beaten
		1/4	cup matzo meal

Heat oil in a large stockpot over medium heat and sauté onions until golden brown. Add celery, carrots and all the chicken. Season generously with pepper, garlic powder, paprika and salt to taste. Add water to cover (do not fill the pot more than halfway). Simmer, uncovered, while preparing the meatballs.

Combine meat, eggs and matzo meal in a large bowl. Season with pepper, garlic powder and paprika to taste; mix well. Shape into small meatballs with moistened hands; add to stockpot on top of chicken and vegetables. Lightly sprinkle paprika over the surface of meatballs. Simmer, covered, for 2 hours or until the meatballs are tender, stirring once after 45 minutes to separate the meatballs. *Makes 12 to 14 servings.*

The Flavors of Spices and Herbs

ALLSPICE: woody, cinnamon-like flavor that blends the tastes of cinnamon and cloves

BASIL: fragrantly sweet

BAY LEAF: slightly bitter and strongly aromatic

CARDAMOM: grapefruit-like flavor with a menthol undertone; similar to ginger

CHERVIL: sweet, aromatic flavor similar to anise and parsley

CINNAMON: woody, musty, earthy flavor and aroma; warming to taste

CORIANDER: minty, sweet, and citrus-like flavor

CUMIN: strong musty, earthy flavor; often used in Middle Eastern food

DILL: subtle, fresh flavor used for pickling and dressings

GINGER: unique combination of citrus and earthy flavors; often used in Asian food

PAPRIKA: common variety is mild with a slightly sweet flavor and pleasantly fragrant aroma

PEPPER, BLACK: sharp, penetrating aroma; hot, biting taste

PEPPER, RED (CAYENNE): hot, sharp, pungent flavor

TURMERIC: yellow in color with a musky, earthy aroma and pungent, slightly bitter flavor

Storage of Spices and Herbs

Spices and herbs lose their color and aroma over time. To preserve the oils that give spices and herbs their peak flavor and color, place them in airtight containers, such as glass jars, plastic containers, or tins. Store the containers in a cool, dry place away from bright light, heat, moisture, and air. If possible, avoid storing spices and herbs too close to the stove, oven, dishwasher, or refrigerator, where rising steam or heat may come in contact with them. It's also better to store them on a lower rather than upper pantry shelf. Dampness may cause ground spices to cake or clump.

The shelf life of each spice and herb differs according to variety, form, and plant part. Check homegrown spices and herbs—and those you purchase—to see if they look fresh, not faded, and have a distinct aroma. Cut and ground forms have more surface area exposed to the air and lose their flavor more rapidly than whole leaves and seeds.

To avoid storing spices and herbs too long, it's a good idea to set an annual date as a time each year to review spice inventories. It may seem wasteful to discard those that are diminished in flavor and color but not spoiled. However, keep in mind that while spices and herbs represent a small percentage of the cost of any dish, they are often responsible for most of the flavor.

Shelf Life

Whole Spices and Herbs
Leaves and flowers: 1 year
Seeds and barks: over 2 years
Roots: over 2 years

Ground Spices and Herbs
Leaves: 6 months
Seeds and barks: 6 months
Roots: 1 year

Meze Notes

A Syrian meze spread. Clockwise from top right: Barzargan 33
Yebra Sweet or Simple 22 • Lahamagine 18
Todd's Merguez 15 • Yebra with Chick-Peas 23

**BARON HERZOG
SAUVIGNON BLANC
(WHITE, CALIFORNIA)**
Fresh, herbal, crisp,
lemony, and pear
character; velvety-
smooth, medium-bodied
and ideal with
appetizers that
include vegetables.

VARIATION
Yebra can also be
baked in two 9×13-inch
pans. Line the pans
with the stuffed grape
leaves and pour over
the preferred sauce.
Add enough water to
just cover the grape
leaves. Bake, covered
tightly with foil,
at 350 degrees
for 1½ hours.

YEBRA SWEET OR SIMPLE
(MEAT-STUFFED GRAPE LEAVES)

Meat

GRAPE LEAVES

1⅓   cups water
⅔   cup uncooked rice, rinsed
2   tablespoons vegetable oil, divided
1   teaspoon kosher salt
1   (1-pound) jar grape leaves
2   pounds chopped meat
2   teaspoons ground allspice
½   teaspoon ground cinnamon
   Salt to taste

SWEET SAUCE

1   (6-ounce) can prune juice
6   ounces water
1   cup dried apricots
¼   cup prune butter
   Juice of 1 lemon (or more)
2   tablespoons brown sugar

SIMPLE SAUCE

1   cup water
¼   cup vegetable oil
   Juice of 1 lemon (or more)
6   to 7 garlic cloves, minced
2   tablespoons crushed dried mint
   Salt to taste

For the leaves, combine water, rice, 1 tablespoon oil and 1 teaspoon salt in a saucepan. Bring to a boil. Reduce heat to low. Simmer, covered, until rice is cooked and water is absorbed. Let cool. Soak grape leaves in a large bowl of water for about 1 hour. Combine rice, meat, allspice, remaining 1 tablespoon oil, cinnamon and salt to taste with your hands in a large bowl.

Open each leaf gently while it is under water. Place one open grape leaf at a time on a flat surface, vein side up. Cut off and discard stem and tough section where stem and veins meet. Overlap bottom two ends of leaf, forming a circle. For each grape leaf, shape 1 heaping teaspoon rice mixture into a small log. Place log in center of leaf about ⅓ from bottom. Fold bottom of leaf over log; fold in left and right sides. Roll up filled end toward remaining corner. Place filled grape leaves in a stockpot, fitting them in tightly.

For the sweet sauce, combine prune juice, water, apricots, prune butter, lemon juice and brown sugar in a bowl and mix well.

For the simple sauce, combine water, oil, lemon juice, garlic and mint in a bowl and mix well. Pour desired sauce over filled grape leaves.

Add enough water to just cover grape leaves. Bring to a boil. Reduce heat to low. Simmer for 1½ hours. Season with salt. Remove one at a time to a serving platter. *Makes about 6 servings.*

Photograph for this recipe is on page 21.

Yebra with Chick-Peas
(Cold Stuffed Grape Leaves)

Parve

4 cups water	1/4 cup chopped fresh parsley
2 cups uncooked rice	Juice of 2 lemons
1/2 cup plus 1 tablespoon olive oil, divided	8 garlic cloves, minced
1 teaspoon kosher salt	3 tablespoons crushed dried mint
1 (1-pound) jar grape leaves	Salt to taste
1 (15-ounce) can Israeli chick-peas, drained	

Bring water to a boil in a large saucepan. Add rice, 1 tablespoon olive oil and 1 teaspoon salt and simmer for 20 minutes. Let cool.

Soak grape leaves in a large bowl of water for about 1 hour. Open each leaf gently while it is under water. Combine rice, chick-peas and parsley in a large bowl. Place one open grape leaf at a time on a flat surface, vein side up. Cut off and discard stem and tough section where stem and veins meet. Overlap bottom two ends of leaf, forming a circle. For each grape leaf, shape 1 heaping teaspoon rice mixture into a small log. Place log in center of leaf about 1/3 from bottom. Fold bottom of leaf over log; fold in left and right sides. Roll up filled end toward remaining corner. Place filled grape leaves in a stockpot, fitting them in tightly.

Combine remaining 1/2 cup olive oil, lemon juice, garlic, mint and salt to taste in a bowl and mix well. Pour over filled grape leaves. Add enough water to the pot to just cover grape leaves. Bring to a boil. Reduce heat to low. Simmer for about 1 hour. Season with salt to taste. Let cool before serving. Remove one at a time to a serving platter.
Makes about 6 servings.

Note: You may also bake the stuffed grape leaves in two 9×13-inch baking pans. Line the pans with the stuffed leaves and pour lemon juice mixture over the leaves. Add enough water to just cover grape leaves. Bake, covered tightly with foil, at 350 degrees for 1 1/2 hours.

Photograph for this recipe is on page 21.

Photograph for this recipe is on page 21.

Purim
Celebrate with Middle Eastern Food
Purim celebrates the survival of the Jewish people despite the evil plans of Haman in ancient Persia. Esther and Mordecai helped the Jewish people overcome a plot calling for their destruction. Food, fun and celebration now rule the day. We can celebrate the geographical origins of this holiday with these delicious middle eastern foods. These unique recipes open up avenues of taste and smell that are perhaps new to you and your family but are sure to entice and intrigue.

SESAME NOODLES
Parve

Cook 1 pound linguini or spaghetti according to the package directions until al dente; drain. Rinse under cold water; drain. Place in a large bowl. Combine 3¹/2 tablespoons sesame oil, 3¹/2 tablespoons soy sauce, 2 tablespoons sugar, 1¹/2 tablespoons balsamic vinegar, ¹/2 to 1 tablespoon chili oil and ¹/2 teaspoon ginger in a small bowl. Pour over pasta, using a handful of pasta to wipe all sauce from the bowl. Toss gently with your hands, separating pasta. Add ¹/4 cup chopped scallions; toss again. Chill, covered, for at least 1 day to allow flavors to blend. Serve at room temperature sprinkled with sesame seeds. *Makes 10 servings.*

Note: Be sparing when adding chili oil; its heat and flavor become more pronounced with time.

SPICY TURKEY WONTONS
Meat

"We worked hard to make this recipe just right. You can plate the wontons over Sesame Noodles (see sidebar) and drizzle the sauce on top."

WONTONS

1 pound ground turkey
2 tablespoons finely chopped scallions
1 tablespoon hoisin sauce
1 tablespoon teriyaki sauce
1 teaspoon salt
1 teaspoon finely chopped fresh ginger, or ¹/2 teaspoon ground ginger
¹/2 to 1 teaspoon chili oil
1 (12-ounce) package wonton wrappers

SPICY DIPPING SAUCE

¹/3 cup soy sauce
¹/3 cup rice vinegar
2 garlic cloves, minced
2 teaspoons dark sesame oil
1 teaspoon chili oil
¹/2 teaspoon sugar
¹/2 teaspoon ground ginger
Chopped scallions for garnish

For the wontons, combine turkey, scallions, hoisin sauce, teriyaki sauce, salt, ginger and chili oil in a medium bowl. Chill, covered, for at least 1 hour.

Spoon about 1 teaspoon turkey mixture in the center of each wonton wrapper. Moisten edges of wrapper with water. Bring both sets of opposite corners up over filling to form a tepee shape.

Bring 1 inch water to a boil in a large pot, then reduce heat to simmer. Coat a collapsible metal steamer rack with nonstick cooking spray and set in the water. Arrange filled wontons about 1 inch apart on rack (there will be several batches). Steam, covered, for 6 to 7 minutes. Repeat with remaining wontons, adding more water to pot as needed. While wontons are steaming, prepare dipping sauce.

For the dipping sauce, combine soy sauce, vinegar, garlic, sesame oil, chili oil, sugar and ginger in a small bowl. Let stand for at least 10 minutes before serving.

Serve wontons warm with dipping sauce. Garnish with chopped scallions. *Makes 18 servings.*

STUFFED WRAPPERS WITH MEAT AND RICE

Meat

S erve with salsa, and your whole table will enjoy this dish.

HERZOG SPECIAL RESERVE ALEXANDER VALLEY CABERNET SAUVIGNON (RED, CALIFORNIA) Wonderful complexity, finesse, and depth of flavor, with layers of earthy currant, plum, wild berry, spice, and cedar that pair well with meat-based appetizers.

2   cups water

1   cup uncooked rice

2   to 3 tablespoons vegetable oil plus additional for frying, divided

1   large onion, diced

2   pounds ground beef or turkey

Garlic powder to taste

Chili powder to taste

Salt and pepper to taste

2   cups marinara sauce

2   (1-pound) packages wonton or egg roll wrappers

Salsa (optional)

Combine water and rice in a saucepan and cook according to the package directions.

Heat 2 to 3 tablespoons oil in a large skillet and sauté onion until translucent. Add ground beef, garlic powder and chili powder. Season with salt and pepper. Cook and stir until ground beef is brown and crumbly; drain. Add marinara sauce and rice and mix well.

If using wonton wrappers, place 1 tablespoon meat filling in center of each wrapper. Moisten edges of wrapper with water. Fold wrapper in half diagonally forming triangle; press to seal. If using egg roll wrappers, place 3 to 4 tablespoons meat filling in center of each wrapper. Fold bottom corner of wrapper over filling, tucking tip of corner under filling; fold left and right corners over filling. Moisten remaining corner with water; tightly roll filled end toward remaining corner; press to seal.

Fry wrappers in about 1 inch oil for 3 to 5 minutes per side or until golden brown. Serve with salsa.

Makes about 48 small or 24 large servings.

Note: While the wrappers are best served immediately, they may be assembled in advance and fried just before serving. Or if reheating, heat uncovered.

CHICKEN SPINACH ROLLS
. . . .
Meat

T̲his recipe is a winner. If you slice the rolls into ¹/₂-inch rounds and serve them over couscous or rice drizzled with the sauce, you're sure to have everyone at the table wowed.

4   tablespoons olive oil, divided
2   tablespoons minced shallot, divided
1   garlic clove, minced
1   (10-ounce) package frozen chopped spinach, thawed and drained
2   tablespoons ground walnuts
¹/₂   teaspoon sage

Salt and pepper to taste
2   pounds chicken cutlets, cut into halves and pounded (8 to 10 pieces)
3   tablespoons all-purpose flour
1   cup WEINSTOCK CABERNET SAUVIGNON® (red)
1   tablespoon balsamic vinegar

Heat 2 tablespoons olive oil in a large skillet over medium-high heat and sauté 1 tablespoon shallot and garlic until tender. Add spinach and mix well. Remove to a food processor fitted with a steel blade. Add walnuts, sage, salt and pepper and process until puréed.

Spread 1 tablespoon spinach mixture in center of each chicken piece. Roll up chicken; secure with wooden toothpick. Spread flour on a plate; coat each chicken roll with flour.

Brown chicken rolls in remaining 2 tablespoons oil over medium-high heat. Remove chicken from skillet; set aside.

Sauté remaining 1 tablespoon shallot in the skillet until tender. Add wine and chicken to the skillet. Baste chicken with pan juices. Cook, covered, over low heat for 15 minutes or until cooked through, turning once and basting twice. Remove from heat; stir in vinegar. Season with salt and pepper, if desired. *Makes 8 to 10 servings.*

CHOPPED CHICKEN WITH DILL EN CROÛTE

Meat

For years, people have come to the home of one of our contributors requesting to eat this dish.

3	tablespoons margarine	1	small onion, chopped
3	tablespoons flour	3	tablespoons chopped fresh
1/2	cup nondairy creamer		dill weed
1/2	cup BARON HERZOG	3	egg yolks, beaten, divided
	SAUVIGNON BLANC® wine	1/8	teaspoon white pepper
1	tablespoon soy sauce	3	egg whites, stiffly beaten
	Salt and pepper to taste	1	(17-ounce) package frozen
	Garlic powder to taste		PEPPERIDGE FARM® Puff
4	cups soup chicken,		Pastry, thawed
	boned and chopped	1	tablespoon water
8	ounces mushrooms, sliced		

Preheat oven to 350 degrees. Melt margarine in a saucepan. Add flour and whisk until well blended. Add creamer and wine. Cook, stirring constantly, until thickened. Stir in soy sauce, salt, pepper and garlic powder; set aside.

Combine chicken, mushrooms, onion and dill weed in a food processor fitted with a steel blade. (Do not purée; mixture should be chunky.) Add 2 egg yolks, white pepper and wine sauce and process until well blended. Remove to a bowl; fold in egg whites.

Roll out one puff pastry sheet on a lightly floured surface to a 9×15-inch rectangle. Place half the chicken mixture in center of pastry. Lift each side over filling, overlapping pastry; seal pastry around filling. Place in a 9×13-inch baking dish. Combine remaining egg yolk and water; brush over surface of pastry. Repeat with remaining puff pastry, chicken filling and egg wash. Bake for about 45 minutes to 1 hour or until golden brown. *Makes 2 loaves, 14 to 16 servings.*

MAKING YOUR OWN STOCK

If you don't have soup chicken, make your own stock and use the chicken for this recipe, reserving the stock for another use. Prepare the sauce for the recipe while the chicken is cooking.

Combine 2 pounds chicken, 1 onion, 3 carrots, cut into chunks, 3 ribs celery, cut into chunks, fresh parsley sprigs to taste, dill weed to taste, salt and pepper to taste in a large pot. Add enough water to generously cover all ingredients. Bring to a boil. Reduce heat to low. Simmer for 2 hours or until chicken is cooked and vegetables are tender.

GLAZED GARLIC CHICKEN WINGS

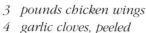

Meat

3 *pounds chicken wings*	2 *cups packed dark*
4 *garlic cloves, peeled*	*brown sugar*
1 *piece fresh ginger*	$^1/_2$ *cup red wine vinegar*
(1×1$^1/_2$ inches), peeled	2 *teaspoons dry mustard*
$^1/_2$ *cup soy sauce*	

Preheat oven to 350 degrees. Rinse chicken wings and pat dry. Disjoint wings and discard tips. Place on a rack in a roasting pan. Bake for 45 minutes. Remove from the oven; set aside. Finely chop garlic and ginger in a food processor fitted with a steel blade. Add soy sauce, brown sugar, vinegar and dry mustard and process until smooth. Pour into a saucepan. Cook for 3 to 5 minutes. Pour over chicken wings. Bake for 15 minutes. *Makes about 15 servings.*

CHICKEN EN PAPILLOTE

Meat

The term "en papillote" means "in parchment paper," but aluminum foil is easier to handle. Purists can use greased baking parchment instead of foil to make this wonderful, light, healthy appetizer.

2 *tablespoons minced fresh*	1 *tablespoon olive oil*
dill weed	4 *boneless skinless chicken*
1 *to 2 teaspoons grated*	*breast halves, sliced*
orange zest	*thinly crosswise*
1 *teaspoon minced garlic*	4 *cups (about 8 ounces)*
$^3/_4$ *teaspoon salt*	*firmly packed fresh*
Pepper to taste	*spinach leaves*
1 *cup cherry tomatoes,*	
cut into halves	

Preheat oven to 400 degrees. Combine dill weed, orange zest, garlic, salt and pepper to taste in a large bowl. Combine tomatoes, olive oil and 1 teaspoon of the dill mixture in a small bowl. Add chicken to the remaining dill mixture; toss to coat.

Cut four 20-inch-long foil pieces. Arrange 1 cup spinach on each foil piece; top with $^1/_4$ of the chicken pieces and $^1/_4$ of the tomato mixture. Fold foil to form four individual packets, sealing tightly. Bake for about 10 minutes or until chicken is cooked through. *Makes 8 servings.*

ZESTING FRUIT

To zest fruits, you should always use a fresh firm fruit because the peel will grate much easier than on a soft fruit. To zest the whole fruit, a wonderful tool to use is a microplane. Use it like a larger grater and you will have a fine zest. The zest can also be removed in larger strips by using a vegetable peeler. Cut the pieces of zest into julienne strips or chop them. Use only the colored part of the rind because the white pith is bitter.

COLORFUL FISH PÂTÉ

Parve

An updated recipe enhanced by color and flavor.

1   (22-ounce) package frozen gefilte fish, thawed
1   (22-ounce) package frozen salmon gefilte fish, thawed
1/4 cup sugar
    Pepper to taste
2   tablespoons vegetable oil
1   onion, chopped
2   garlic cloves, minced
1   (10-ounce) package frozen chopped spinach, thawed
    and drained
    Salt to taste
1   pound baby carrots

Preheat oven to 375 degrees. Lightly grease two loaf pans or line with parchment paper. Place each gefilte fish loaf in a separate bowl. Sprinkle salmon gefilte with sugar and both loaves with pepper to taste.

Heat oil in a skillet and sauté onion for 3 to 5 minutes or until tender. Add garlic. Sauté for 2 minutes. Add spinach. Sauté for 2 to 3 minutes; season with salt and pepper. Taste and set aside. Steam carrots over boiling water for 15 to 20 minutes or until very soft. Cool slightly; mash with a fork.

Layer 1/2 each of the carrots, plain gefilte fish, spinach mixture and salmon gefilte fish in each of the prepared pans. Bake for 1 hour. Cool completely. Refrigerate, covered, until chilled. To serve, invert onto a serving platter and slice. *Makes 20 servings.*

Photograph for this recipe is on page 283.

ARTICHOKE AND SPINACH SWIRLS

Dairy

1 (14-ounce) can artichoke hearts, drained and chopped	1/2 cup grated Parmesan cheese
1 (10-ounce) package frozen chopped spinach, thawed and squeezed dry	1 teaspoon onion powder
	1 teaspoon garlic powder
	1/2 teaspoon pepper
1/2 cup mayonnaise	1 (17-ounce) package frozen PEPPERIDGE FARM® Puff Pastry sheets, thawed

Combine artichoke hearts, spinach, mayonnaise, cheese, onion powder, garlic powder and pepper in a medium bowl. Unfold puff pastry sheets and place each on a piece of plastic wrap. Spread half the artichoke mixture evenly on each pastry sheet. Roll up both sides of each pastry to center, starting at long sides and making sure pastry is even and tight. Wrap each roll with the plastic wrap. Freeze for 30 minutes so pastry is firm enough to cut neatly. (Rolls may be frozen at this point for up to one month. When ready to bake, let stand at room temperature for about 10 minutes or until a sharp knife can slice through roll without compressing shape.)

Preheat oven to 400 degrees. Line a baking sheet with baking parchment paper. Cut rolls crosswise into 1/2-inch-thick slices with a sharp knife. Place on the baking sheet. Bake for 20 minutes or until puffed and golden. *Makes 2 dozen.*

GREEK GARLIC DIP

Parve

- 2 cups mayonnaise
- 5 tablespoons fresh bread crumbs
- 1/4 cup ground almonds
- 2 tablespoons chopped fresh parsley
- 3 garlic cloves, chopped
  Salt and pepper to taste

Combine mayonnaise, bread crumbs, almonds, parsley, garlic, and salt and pepper to taste in a bowl and mix well. Chill, covered, for 2 hours before serving. *Makes about 2 1/2 cups.*

SEARED TUNA AND AVOCADO TARTARE

Parve

*S*erve in stemmed glasses garnished with chips or lime slices.

1 (6-ounce) tuna steak	1/3 cup chopped red onion
3 1/2 tablespoons extra-virgin olive oil, divided	1/3 cup chopped fresh cilantro
Salt and pepper to taste	1/4 cup fresh lime juice
1 large avocado, pitted, peeled and diced	1 serrano chile or jalapeño chile, seeded, deveined and minced

Heat a small heavy skillet for 2 minutes over high heat. Brush tuna with 1/2 tablespoon olive oil; sprinkle with salt and pepper to taste. Place in the skillet. Sear about 3 minutes on each side or until brown outside and almost opaque in the center. Cool completely. Dice tuna and place in a medium bowl. Add avocado, onion, cilantro, lime juice, remaining olive oil and serrano chile. Mix with a fork just until combined. Season to taste with salt and pepper. Refrigerate, covered, until chilled. *Makes 4 servings*.

PRESENTING HORS D'OEUVRE

For imaginative serving pieces, collect plates in different sizes, colors, shapes, and patterns.

STORING FOODS THAT DISCOLOR

When storing foods that discolor, such as guacamole, pour a small amount of olive oil on top. Place plastic wrap directly on top of the food, forming a seal. The less the food is exposed to air, the less it will discolor.

CHOPPING HARD-COOKED EGGS

To easily chop hard-cooked eggs, use an egg slicer to first cut them horizontally and then rotate the egg slices to cut them vertically.

SMOKED SALMON ROLLS

Parve

If you like sushi, you'll relish this refreshing appetizer or hors d'oeuvre.

4 kirby cucumbers, or 1 English cucumber, peeled and julienned	2 teaspoons finely grated fresh ginger
1/4 cup rice vinegar	1/2 teaspoon sesame oil
3 tablespoons toasted sesame seeds (reserve some for garnish)	Pinch of sugar
	Salt and pepper to taste
4 scallions, chopped	1 pound smoked salmon, thinly sliced

Combine the cucumbers, vinegar, sesame seeds, scallions, ginger, sesame oil, sugar, and salt and pepper to taste in a bowl. Refrigerate, covered, until chilled.

Place a bundle of cucumbers on one end of each salmon slice. Roll up and place seam side down on a serving platter. Chill, covered, until ready to serve. Garnish with reserved sesame seeds. *Makes 10 servings.*

AVOCADO DIP

Parve

If you are a guacamole fan, you will love this dip. The hard-cooked eggs add a wonderful creamy texture. The seasoning amounts are just a guide and should be adjusted to your own tastes.

5 Hass avocados, pitted, peeled and chopped	Juice of 2 limes
	1 teaspoon kosher salt
4 hard-cooked eggs, peeled and chopped	1/2 teaspoon onion powder
	1/2 teaspoon garlic powder
5 scallions, chopped	1/4 teaspoon pepper

Combine avocados, eggs, scallions, lime juice, salt, onion powder, garlic powder and pepper in a bowl and mix well. Do not overmix or dip will be mushy. *Makes about 6 cups.*

CALIFORNIA STRAWBERRY SALSA

Parve

This is a different spin on salsa that was a huge success at our taste testing. Hope you enjoy it also!

1 cup strawberries, minced	1 jalapeño chile, seeded
1/4 cup finely chopped onion	and chopped
2 tablespoons finely chopped	2 ripe avocados, pitted,
fresh cilantro	peeled and halved
1/2 teaspoon salt	Tortilla chips for serving

Combine strawberries, onion, cilantro, salt and jalapeño chile in a bowl and mix well. (Salsa can be made ahead and chilled until ready to serve.) Cut each avocado half into six wedges. Place around the edge of a platter, fanning out wedges. Spoon salsa in center of avocados. Or, fan out each avocado half on an individual plate and spoon salsa evenly on top. Serve with tortilla chips. *Makes 4 servings.*

HOT HANDS

Wear disposable gloves while handling jalapeño and other hot chiles. May substitute 1/2 teaspoon red pepper flakes and 1/2 teaspoon hot red pepper sauce for the jalapeño chile.

BARZARGAN (CRACKED BULGUR SALAD)

Parve

"When I was asked to taste bulgur salad, I was very skeptical even though I was told it was delicious. Keeping an open mind, I gave it a try and shocked myself by LOVING it! Everyone I serve it to has this same reaction. The only difference is I don't tell them what it is until after they try it. Be brave and give it a try, too!"

1 cup fine bulgur wheat	2 tablespoons lemon juice
3 tablespoons vegetable oil	2 tablespoons ketchup
1/2 cup walnuts or almonds,	Dash of cayenne pepper,
finely chopped	or black pepper to taste
4 to 6 tablespoons tamarind	Salt to taste
or prune butter	Parsley for garnish
1 small onion, grated	

Soak bulgur in warm water to cover for 30 minutes; drain well. Let stand for 1 hour. Stir in oil. Add walnuts, tamarind, onion, lemon juice, ketchup, cayenne pepper and salt to taste and mix well. Garnish with parsley. *Makes 6 servings.*

Photograph for this recipe is on page 21.

BULGUR TALK

If fine bulgur is unavailable, use regular bulgur and grind it in a coffee grinder or food processor.

Soups

SAMPLER

QUICK AND EASY
Artichoke Soup 36
Cream of Asparagus Soup 36
Pureé of Carrot and Dill Soup 39
Mediterranean Chick-Pea Soup 43
Refreshing Summer Minted Honeydew Soup 45
Velvety Broccoli Soup 48
Tomato and Spinach Bisque 52
Garden Verde Soup 53
Zucchini and Spinach Soup 53

SOPHISTICATED
Artichoke Soup 36
Cream of Asparagus Soup 36
Chilled Avocado-Cucumber Soup 37
Creamy White Bean Soup 38
Ratatouille Soup 43 • Hearty Lentil Soup 44
Exotic Mushroom Soup 48

FREEZES WELL
Cream of Asparagus Soup 36
Creamy White Bean Soup 38
Pureé of Carrot and Dill Soup 39
Roasted Cauliflower and Dill Soup 42
Hearty Lentil Soup 44 • Velvety Broccoli Soup 48
Lentil Minestrone Soup 49
Roasted Root Vegetable Soup 50
Sweet Potato and Leek Soup with Pecan Garni 51
Tomato and Spinach Bisque 52
Zucchini and Spinach Soup 53

ARTICHOKE SOUP

Parve or Meat

1/4 cup (1/2 stick) margarine
4 (13-ounce) cans artichoke
   bottoms, drained
1 leek, white and light green
   parts, sliced and rinsed
1/2 cup sliced yellow onion
3 shallots, sliced
6 garlic cloves, chopped

1 large Yukon gold potato,
   chopped or cubed
3 quarts vegetable stock or
   chicken stock
1/4 cup fresh parsley, chopped
1 teaspoon thyme
1 bay leaf
1/2 teaspoon black peppercorns
   Salt to taste

Heat margarine in a large pot over medium heat and sauté artichokes, leek, onion, shallots and garlic until tender but not brown. Add potato and stock. Tie up parsley, thyme, bay leaf and peppercorns in cheesecloth for a bouquet garni; add to pot. Bring to a boil. Reduce heat to low. Simmer, covered, for 1 hour.

Remove and discard bouquet garni. Purée soup in a food processor or blender. Season with salt to taste. *Makes 6 to 8 servings.*

CREAM OF ASPARAGUS SOUP

Parve, Meat or Dairy

1/4 cup (1/2 stick) margarine
   or butter
1 onion, chopped
3 cups asparagus pieces
1/4 cup all-purpose flour
1/4 teaspoon salt

1/8 teaspoon white pepper
4 cups MANISCHEWITZ®
   Chicken Broth or bouillon
1/2 cup soy milk, nondairy
   creamer or half-and-half

Heat margarine in a 3-quart saucepan over medium heat and sauté the onion until tender, stirring occasionally. Stir in asparagus. Cook for 1 minute. Add flour, salt and white pepper and mix well. Stir in broth gradually. Cook until thickened, stirring constantly. Reduce heat to low. Simmer, covered, for 15 to 20 minutes or until asparagus is tender. Stir in soy milk.

Purée soup in a food processor or blender. Return puréed soup to the saucepan. Cook until heated through. Serve hot or refrigerate, covered, until chilled and serve cold. (If chilled soup becomes too thick, thin with additional soy milk.) *Makes 6 servings.*

CHILLED AVOCADO-CUCUMBER SOUP

Dairy

*S*erve this soup in bowls or goblets and garnish with alternating lime and lemon slices and a sprinkling of chopped scallions in the center.

2   ripe Hass avocados, pitted, peeled and cut into chunks
1   seedless cucumber, peeled and cut into chunks
1½   cups orange juice
½   cup yogurt
¼   cup chopped scallions
¼   cup buttermilk
     Juice of 1 lime
2   tablespoons fresh dill weed, finely chopped
2   garlic cloves, sliced
2   teaspoons salt
½   teaspoon hot red pepper sauce
     Pepper to taste

Combine avocados, cucumber, orange juice, yogurt, scallions, buttermilk, lime juice, dill weed, garlic, salt, red pepper sauce and black pepper to taste in a blender or food processor and process until smooth. (Do this in two batches if necessary.) Taste and adjust the seasonings. Refrigerate, covered, until chilled. Serve cold.
Makes 6 servings.

SALT, SALT, SALT

Table salt, also called granular salt, is the most common salt. It is mined and processed to become so fine.

Kosher salt is made by compacting granular salt between rollers which produces large and irregular shapes. Unlike table salt, kosher salt contains no additives.

Sea salt is created when the ocean waters flood shallow beds along coastlines. The flavor is also influenced by the different waters and minerals and surrounding lands.

Table salt and sea salt are not interchangeable, measure for measure. To use table salt rather than coarse sea salt or kosher salt, use a third less table salt than called for by the recipe.

CREAMY WHITE BEAN SOUP

. . . .

Parve or Meat

W*hite beans create a thick, creamy consistency when puréed.*

8 ounces dried cannellini beans	1 (6- to 7-inch) sprig of fresh rosemary plus additional sprigs for garnish
8 ounces dried small white beans	
1/4 cup olive oil	2 teaspoons kosher salt
4 cups diced onions (about 3 large)	1/2 teaspoon pepper
2 garlic cloves, minced	1 bay leaf
2 quarts MANISCHEWITZ® Chicken Broth or bouillon	

Sort and rinse beans. Place in a large bowl and add enough water to cover by 1 inch. Soak for 8 to 12 hours. Drain beans.

Heat olive oil in stockpot over medium-high heat and sauté onions for 10 minutes or until translucent. Add garlic. Sauté for 3 minutes. Stir in beans, broth, rosemary sprig, salt, pepper and bay leaf. Bring to a boil. Reduce heat to low. Simmer, covered, for 30 to 40 minutes or until beans are tender. Remove and discard rosemary and bay leaf. Purée soup in a food processor or with an immersion blender, until desired consistency. Serve warm garnished with additional rosemary sprigs. *Makes 6 to 8 servings.*

Photograph for this recipe is on front cover and on page 41.

PURÉE OF CARROT AND DILL SOUP

Parve, Meat or Dairy

"When a friend gave me this soup recipe and told me it was delicious, I was reluctant to try it, knowing how much we love the carrot soup in The Kosher Palette I. *I'm so glad I listened and tried it! The combination of flavors and textures produces a wonderful soup."*

1	tablespoon margarine or butter
1	tablespoon olive oil
1	large onion, chopped
2	pounds carrots, peeled and coarsely chopped
2	large Yukon gold potatoes, peeled and diced
5	to 6 cups MANISCHEWITZ® Chicken Broth or vegetable stock
1/2	cup milk, soy milk or nondairy creamer (optional)
1/4	cup chopped fresh dill weed plus additional fresh dill weed for garnish
1	teaspoon salt
1/4	teaspoon pepper

Heat margarine and olive oil in a large pot over medium-high heat and sauté onion for 5 to 10 minutes or until translucent, stirring occasionally. (Reduce heat if onion browns too quickly.) Add carrots and potatoes. Cook for 15 to 20 minutes. Add 5 cups broth. Bring to a boil. Reduce heat to low. Simmer, covered, for 30 to 40 minutes or until carrots are tender. Remove from heat. Purée soup in a food processor or with an immersion blender. Stir in milk, 1/4 cup dill weed, salt and pepper. Simmer for 5 minutes. (Soup should be thick, but if too thick, thin with additional broth.) Serve warm garnished with additional dill weed. *Makes 8 to 10 servings.*

THE BREAD SPREAD

A bowl of hot, hearty soup and warm, freshly baked bread are the perfect ingredients for a casual winter evening with family and friends.

GARLIC BREAD

Parve or Dairy

1/2 cup (1 stick) margarine or butter, softened
1/4 cup grated Parmesan cheese (optional)
  2 tablespoons chopped fresh parsley
  4 garlic cloves, chopped Kosher salt to taste
  1 (8-ounce) loaf Italian bread

Preheat oven to 350 degrees. Combine margarine, cheese, parsley, garlic and salt in a small bowl. Partially cut bread lengthwise into halves; do not cut all the way through. Spread garlic mixture generously on both cut sides. Close bread; place on a baking sheet. Bake for 10 minutes or until margarine is melted. *Makes 6 to 8 servings.*

SAVORY OLIVE BREAD

Dairy

  1 cup warm (105- to 110-degree) water
  1 envelope dry yeast
  2 teaspoons sugar
1/2 cup warm (105- to 110-degree) milk
1/4 cup olive oil
1/4 teaspoon salt plus additional for sprinkling
2 3/4 to 3 cups bread flour
1/4 cup black olives, chopped

Pour 1 cup water in a large mixing bowl. Add yeast and sugar; do not stir. Let stand for 5 minutes or until foamy. Stir in milk, 3 tablespoons of the olive oil and 1/4 teaspoon salt. Add flour 1 cup at a time, beating with an electric mixer until dough is elastic and pulls away from side of bowl. Add olives and beat until dough is soft. Turn out onto a lightly floured surface and knead for 10 minutes or until dough is smooth and elastic, adding more flour as needed to prevent sticking. Place dough in a large oiled bowl.

Let rise, covered, in a warm place until doubled in bulk.

Spray a 9×13-inch baking pan with nonstick cooking spray. Punch dough down. Remove to prepared pan. Let rise, covered, in a warm place for 1 hour.

Preheat oven to 425 degrees. Stretch dough into a rectangle, leaving space around edge of pan. Cut 6 to 8 evenly spaced oval holes into dough with a sharp knife. Brush with remaining 1 tablespoon oil; sprinkle lightly with salt. Let stand for 15 minutes or until puffy. Bake for 20 minutes or until golden brown. *Makes 12 servings.*

OLIVE BUTTER

Dairy

1/2 cup (1 stick) butter, softened
  2 tablespoons to 1/4 cup chopped black olives

Combine butter and olives and mix well. Serve with Savory Olive Bread. *Makes about 2/3 cup.*

A Souper Bowl Party

A tasty palette of soups. From bottom:
Sweet Potato and Leek Soup with Pecan Garni 51 • Zucchini and Spinach Soup 53
Creamy White Bean Soup 38 • Lentil Minestrone Soup 49

ROASTED CAULIFLOWER AND DILL SOUP
. . . .
Parve or Meat

"This recipe is an adaptation of two cauliflower soup recipes: a submitted one that was a favorite at the taste testing and one from Todd Aaron's restaurant that roasts the cauliflower for wonderful flavor. When roasted, cauliflower tastes reminiscent of toasted almonds. I serve this soup with either a drizzle of lemon-infused oil or toasted walnut oil."

1 large head cauliflower
1/4 cup olive oil
Salt and pepper to taste
15 baby carrots, or 4 to 5 large carrots, cut into chunks (about 8 ounces)
1 yellow onion, diced
2 ribs celery, diced (about 1/2 cup)
1 parsnip, cut into small pieces
3 to 4 garlic cloves, sliced
7 to 8 cups MANISCHEWITZ® Chicken Broth or bouillon
1/4 cup chopped fresh dill weed

Preheat oven to 350 degrees. Cut cauliflower into 1 1/2- to 2-inch pieces. (Do not cut pieces too small or they will burn during roasting.) Toss with 2 tablespoons of olive oil, salt and pepper. Place on a baking sheet or in a roasting pan. Roast 35 to 40 minutes until golden brown and very tender. Meanwhile, heat remaining 2 tablespoons olive oil in large heavy pot. Add carrots, onion, celery, parsnip and garlic. Sauté until onion is translucent. Add roasted cauliflower, broth and dill weed. Bring to a boil. Reduce heat to low. Simmer, covered, for about 45 minutes. Remove from heat; cool slightly. Purée soup in a food processor or with an immersion blender. Season with salt and pepper. *Makes 4 to 6 servings.*

Note: If you prefer, sauté the cauliflower with the other vegetables rather than roasting it.

RATATOUILLE SOUP

Parve or Meat

3   tablespoons olive oil
1   eggplant, peeled and
    chopped
1   large onion, chopped
1   large red bell
    pepper, chopped
1   zucchini, chopped
2   garlic cloves, minced

2   large tomatoes, chopped
2   tablespoons chopped fresh
    thyme, or 2 teaspoons
    dried thyme
1½ to 2 cups MANISCHEWITZ®
    Chicken Broth or bouillon
    Salt and pepper to taste
    Croutons for garnish

Heat 2 tablespoons of the olive oil in a large deep skillet over medium heat and sauté eggplant, onion, bell pepper, zucchini and garlic for 15 minutes or until tender, stirring occasionally. Add remaining 1 tablespoon olive oil, tomatoes and thyme. Reduce heat to medium-low. Cook, covered, until vegetables are very tender, stirring about every 20 minutes. Purée vegetables with 1 cup of the broth, in batches, in a food processor or blender. Pour into a saucepan. Season with salt and pepper. Cook for about 5 minutes or until heated through, thinning soup with additional broth if desired. Ladle into bowls. Garnish with croutons. *Makes 4 to 6 servings.*

Photograph for this recipe is on page 35.

MEDITERRANEAN CHICK-PEA SOUP

Parve or Meat

This recipe was a winner at the testing with kids and adults alike. If you prefer, you can cook pasta separately and add it just before serving.

2   teaspoons olive oil
1   cup diced onion
2   cups MANISCHEWITZ®
    Chicken Broth or bouillon
1   (15-ounce) can
    chick-peas, drained
1   (14-ounce) can diced
    tomatoes, undrained

1½ cups water
½   teaspoon cumin
¼   teaspoon each ground
    cinnamon and pepper
½   cup uncooked ditalini
    pasta
2   tablespoons chopped
    fresh parsley

Heat olive oil in a large saucepan and sauté onion for 3 minutes. Add broth, chick-peas, tomatoes, water, cumin, cinnamon and pepper. Bring to a boil. Reduce heat to low. Simmer, covered, for 5 minutes. Add pasta. Cook for 9 minutes. Stir in parsley. *Makes 4 to 6 servings.*

BELL PEPPER TIPS
To cut a bell pepper, slice off the top and bottom. Cut through one side and go around the inside of the pepper with the knife. The seeds will come out attached to the core and the pepper will be a rectangular piece that can then be cut into julienne strips, chopped, or grilled whole.

HEARTY LENTIL SOUP

. . . .

Parve or Meat

*S*oaking the lentils makes all the difference in this recipe. The amount of liquid will be incorrect if you skip this step.

3 cups lentils, sorted and rinsed	2 tablespoons lemon juice
3 tablespoons margarine	1¹/₂ tablespoons dark brown sugar
1¹/₂ cups chopped fresh or canned tomatoes	1 tablespoon red wine vinegar
1 cup chopped onion	1 to 2 teaspoons salt
1 cup chopped celery	Pepper to taste
1 cup chopped carrots	Fresh dill weed for garnish
3 garlic cloves, chopped	
8 to 9 cups MANISCHEWITZ® Chicken Broth or bouillon	

Soak the lentils in water to cover for at least 3 hours; drain. Heat margarine in a large skillet over medium-high heat and sauté tomatoes, onion, celery, carrots and garlic for 10 minutes or until tender. Add broth. Bring to a boil. Add lentils and reduce heat to low. Simmer, covered, for 2¹/₂ hours, stirring occasionally. Stir in lemon juice, brown sugar, vinegar, salt and pepper to taste. Simmer for 30 minutes, stirring frequently. Garnish with dill weed. *Makes 6 to 8 servings.*

REFRESHING SUMMER
MINTED HONEYDEW SOUP

Parve

or a special presentation, serve this soup in wine goblets. Place mint sprigs in the center of the soup and lemon slices on the goblet rims.

1 large ripe honeydew melon (about 4 pounds), peeled, seeded, cut into chunks

$^1/_2$ cup loosely packed fresh mint leaves (about $1^1/_2$ ounces) plus additional sprigs for garnish

6 tablespoons fresh lime juice (about 2 limes)

2 tablespoons honey

1 lemon, cut lengthwise into halves and thinly sliced for garnish

Working in batches, process melon, mint leaves, lime juice and honey in a blender at high speed for 2 minutes or until smooth and light. Pour into a container. Chill, covered, for at least 1 hour. Adjust flavor with additional lime juice if necessary before serving. Ladle into soup bowls and garnish with additional mint sprigs and lemon slices. *Makes 6 servings.*

GARLIC-MUSHROOM SOUP

Parve, Meat or Dairy

1/4 cup (1/2 stick) plus 2 tablespoons margarine or butter, divided
4 to 5 potatoes, peeled and cut into cubes
2 leeks, white parts only, cleaned and coarsely chopped
10 garlic cloves
2 quarts MANISCHEWITZ® Chicken Broth or bouillon
12 ounces mushrooms, thinly sliced
1 cup nondairy creamer, soy milk or heavy cream (optional)
Salt and freshly ground pepper to taste
2 tablespoons chopped fresh parsley for garnish
Croutons for garnish

Heat 1/4 cup margarine in a large heavy saucepan over medium heat and sauté potatoes, leeks and garlic for 10 minutes, stirring frequently. Add broth. Bring to a boil. Reduce heat to low. Simmer, covered, for 1 hour, stirring occasionally.

Melt remaining 2 tablespoons margarine in skillet over medium heat. Add mushrooms. Sauté for 2 minutes; set aside.

Process soup in batches in a food processor or with an immersion blender until smooth. Return to saucepan. Add mushrooms and milk. Cook over medium heat until heated through, stirring occasionally. Season with salt and freshly ground pepper. Garnish with parsley and croutons. *Makes 8 servings.*

Cold Roasted Red Gazpacho with Tortilla Strips

Parve

E*ight gazpacho recipes were tested and this one was the winner.*

4 pounds plum tomatoes,
   cut into halves
5 large red bell peppers
4 red onions
1/2 cup extra-virgin olive
   oil plus additional
   for drizzling
3 cups water

3 tablespoons red
   wine vinegar
1 teaspoon hot red
   pepper sauce
   Salt to taste
1 English cucumber, peeled
   and finely chopped (2 cups)
   Tortilla Strips for garnish
   (at right)

Tortilla Strips

This is a wonderful garnish for gazpacho. Preheat oven to 350 degrees. Cut one 7-ounce package tortillas into 1/2-inch strips. Place in single layer on a baking sheet. Spray with olive oil nonstick cooking spray. Bake for 10 minutes or until crisp. Sprinkle with salt to taste.

Preheat oven to 450 degrees. Place tomatoes on a baking sheet. Cut 4 of the bell peppers into 1-inch pieces; place on another baking sheet. Cut 3 of the onions into 1-inch pieces; add to bell peppers. Drizzle 1/2 cup olive oil over vegetables. Roast for about 50 minutes or until tender and slightly charred, rotating the pans in the oven after 25 minutes. Purée half the vegetables with pan juices in a food processor. Add 1 cup of the water. Process until very smooth. Pour into a large bowl. Repeat with remaining vegetables and another 1 cup of the water. Chill, covered, for 8 to 12 hours.

Add remaining 1 cup water, vinegar and pepper sauce to gazpacho. Season with salt. Finely dice remaining bell pepper and onion. Combine with cucumber in a small bowl. Pour soup into a serving bowl; top with diced vegetables and drizzle with additional oil. Break Tortilla Strips into 1-inch pieces. Sprinkle over top of soup.
Makes 10 servings.

THE BEST BROCCOLI

Broccoli is at its peak from October to April. Look for heads with tightly clustered, deep green florets (tinged with purple in some varieties). The stalks should be firm. Broccoli can be stored in the refrigerator for up to four days. Wash and trim just before using.

To trim, remove the leaves and cut off the thick end of the stalk. Using a vegetable peeler or small sharp knife, peel away the outer layer from the stalk and cut into desired pieces.

To steam: Bring 1 inch water to boil in a steamer basket. Add broccoli in a single layer and steam about 5 minutes, or until tender.

VELVETY BROCCOLI SOUP

Parve or Meat

This is a very healthy and easy soup. The oats add nice flavor and texture.

2	tablespoons olive oil	1	large bunch broccoli
1	onion, chopped		(about 1¹/2 pounds),
2	garlic cloves, minced		trimmed and chopped
1	quart MANISCHEWITZ®	1	cup water
	Chicken Broth or bouillon	¹/2	cup quick-cooking oats
			Salt and pepper to taste

Heat olive oil in a stockpot over medium-high heat and sauté onion and garlic for about 5 minutes or until tender. Add broth, broccoli, water, oats and salt and pepper to taste. Bring to a boil. Reduce heat to low. Simmer for 20 to 30 minutes or until broccoli is tender. Purée soup in a food processor or with an immersion blender. Adjust seasoning before serving. *Makes 4 to 6 servings.*

EXOTIC MUSHROOM SOUP

Parve or Meat

¹/2	ounce dried porcini	4	ounces chanterelle
	mushrooms		mushrooms, diced
	White wine	¹/2	cup all-purpose flour
¹/4	cup olive oil	2	quarts MANISCHEWITZ®
¹/2	cup chopped onion		Chicken Broth or bouillon
²/3	cup chopped celery root		Salt and freshly ground
4	ounces portobello		pepper to taste
	mushrooms, chopped		Chopped fresh chives
4	ounces shiitake		for garnish
	mushrooms, diced		

Soak porcini mushrooms in wine to cover for 30 minutes. Strain wine to remove any debris; reserve mushrooms and wine separately.

Heat olive oil in a 6-quart pot and sauté onion until tender. Add celery root and portobello, shiitake and chanterelle mushrooms. Sauté for 5 minutes. Stir in porcini mushrooms and flour and mix well. Add broth and reserved wine gradually, stirring constantly. Bring to a boil. Reduce heat to low. Simmer for 35 to 40 minutes. Season with salt and freshly ground pepper. Garnish with chives. *Makes 6 to 8 servings.*

LENTIL MINESTRONE SOUP

Parve

This soup tastes better a day or two after it is prepared. This soup will thicken and may need an adjustment of the liquid.

10	cups water
2	Vidalia or Spanish onions, diced
1	(15-ounce) can cannellini beans, drained and liquid reserved
1	(10-ounce) can tomato soup
1/2	large turnip, coarsely chopped (optional)
2	garlic cloves, cut lengthwise into halves
2 3/4	to 3 tablespoons kosher salt
3/4	teaspoon freshly ground pepper
3/4	cup lentils, sorted and rinsed
3	ribs celery hearts, chopped
2	ripe plum tomatoes, peeled and diced
1/2	teaspoon herbes de Provence
1/2	to 3/4 cup uncooked rotini pasta
	Chopped fresh parsley and dill weed (optional)

Bring water to a boil in a stockpot over high heat. Add onions, liquid from beans, tomato soup, turnip, garlic, salt and pepper. Reduce heat to low. Simmer for 15 to 20 minutes. Add lentils. Simmer for 10 to 15 minutes. Stir in cannellini beans, celery, tomatoes and herbes de Provence. Simmer for 30 to 45 minutes or until vegetables are tender. Add pasta. Bring to a boil. Cook for 8 minutes. Remove from heat. Stir in parsley and dill weed. *Makes 8 to 10 servings.*

Photograph for this recipe is on front cover and on page 41.

ROASTED ROOT VEGETABLE SOUP

Parve or Meat

*T*his is a perfect winter's night soup. The combination of root vegetables
with their beautiful colors produces a stunning contrast to the green
spinach and white pasta.

SOUP
    Olive oil
3 pounds butternut squash,
    cut lengthwise into
    halves and seeded
5 large sweet potatoes, cut
    into halves
12 ounces carrots, peeled and
    cut into ¹/₂-inch chunks
6 shallots, peeled
6 garlic cloves, peeled

2 quarts MANISCHEWITZ®
    Chicken Broth or bouillon
    Salt and pepper to taste

GARNISH
2 teaspoons olive oil
2 garlic cloves, minced
1 (10-ounce) package fresh
    spinach, chopped
1 cup tubettini pasta,
    cooked and drained

For the soup, preheat oven to 375 degrees. Coat a baking sheet with olive oil. Place squash, sweet potatoes, carrots, shallots and garlic cut sides down on pan. Roast for 40 minutes or until vegetables are tender. Let stand until cool. Scoop flesh from squash and sweet potatoes into a stockpot; discard skins. Add remaining roasted vegetables, broth and salt and pepper to taste. Bring to a boil. Reduce heat to low. Simmer for 30 minutes. Purée soup in a food processor or with an immersion blender. Taste and adjust seasonings; set aside.

For the garnish, heat olive oil in a skillet over medium heat and sauté garlic for about 1 minute. Add spinach. Sauté for 2 minutes or until spinach is wilted and heated through. Pour soup into bowls. Top with a scoop of spinach and spoonful of pasta. *Makes 8 servings.*

Note: For a shortcut, instead of roasting the vegetables you can sauté them in oil for about 10 to 15 minutes and add remaining ingredients. Follow the directions above. You may need to adjust the cooking time until vegetables are tender.

Sweet Potato and Leek Soup with Pecan Garni

Parve, Meat or Dairy

Long cooking gives leeks a sweet flavor, and the wine adds a subtle touch that you will enjoy.

3	tablespoons vegetable oil	2	russet potatoes, peeled and cut into cubes
1	large onion, finely chopped	6	cups (or more) MANISCHEWITZ® Chicken Broth or bouillon
1	cup chopped leeks		
3	large carrots, cut into chunks (about 1 1/2 cups)	1 1/2	cups water
2	large garlic cloves, minced	3/4	cup dry white wine
3	pounds sweet potatoes, peeled and cut into cubes (about 3 large)	1	bay leaf
			Salt and pepper to taste
			Pecan Garni (see sidebar)

Heat oil in a stockpot over medium-high heat and cook onion, leeks, carrots and garlic for about 10 minutes or until vegetables are tender, stirring occasionally. Add sweet potatoes, russet potatoes, broth, water, wine, bay leaf and salt and pepper to taste. Bring to a boil. Reduce heat to low. Simmer, covered, for 1 hour or until potatoes are very tender. Remove and discard bay leaf. Purée soup in a food processor or blender until very smooth. (If soup is too thick, thin with additional broth.) Serve hot, ladled into bowls with Pecan Garni sprinkled in center. *Makes 8 to 10 servings.*

Photograph for this recipe is on front cover and on page 41.

PECAN GARNI

Melt 2 tablespoons unsalted butter or margarine in a skillet over low to medium heat. Add 3/4 cup pecans, chopped, and salt to taste. Cook for about 10 minutes or until pecans are golden brown, stirring often. Drain on paper towels. May be made in advance and stored in an airtight container or sealable plastic bag.

**DON'T WASTE
THE PASTE**

When recipes call for a
tablespoon or two of
tomato paste, don't let
the rest of the can go
to waste. Line an ice
cube tray with plastic
wrap and drop one
tablespoon of tomato
paste into each section.
When the cubes are
frozen, remove to a
sealable plastic bag.
Store them in the
freezer for up
to six months and use
as needed.

TOMATO AND SPINACH BISQUE

Parve or Meat

The whole family will enjoy this soup.

 2 tablespoons vegetable oil
 1 tablespoon extra-virgin olive oil
 1 cup chopped Spanish onion
 1 cup diced carrots
 ¹/₂ cup diced celery
 2 bay leaves
 1 tablespoon minced garlic
 1 cup uncooked rice
 2 (6-ounce) cans tomato paste
 3¹/₂ quarts MANISCHEWITZ® Chicken Broth or bouillon
 1 (46-ounce) can tomato juice
    Salt and cayenne pepper to taste
 1 (10-ounce) package frozen chopped spinach,
    thawed and drained

Heat vegetable oil and olive oil in a heavy stockpot over medium-high heat and sauté onion, carrots, celery and bay leaves until vegetables are golden brown. Add garlic. Cook until fragrant. Add rice and stir until well coated with oil. Stir in tomato paste. Add broth and stir well to remove any lumps. Add tomato juice. Bring to simmer. Cook until rice is tender and breaks down, stirring frequently. Remove from heat. Remove and discard bay leaves. Pass soup through a food mill. Spoon into a clean stockpot. Bring to a simmer. Season with salt and cayenne pepper. Just before serving, stir in spinach. Serve immediately. *Makes 10 servings.*

GARDEN VERDE SOUP

Parve or Meat

" I had this soup at a friend's house over Sukkot and immediately asked for the recipe. It's a very simple soup both in preparation and flavor. While it can be served warm, I think it's even better at room temperature."

3 tablespoons vegetable oil	3 cucumbers, peeled and cut into $1/2$-inch cubes
3 onions, minced	
3 cups MANISCHEWITZ® Chicken Broth or bouillon	$1/4$ cup fresh dill weed, minced
4 medium zucchini, peeled and cut into $1/2$-inch cubes	Salt and pepper to taste

Heat oil in a stockpot over high heat and sauté onions for 12 to 15 minutes or until golden brown. Add broth, zucchini, cucumbers, dill weed and salt and pepper to taste. Bring to a boil. Reduce heat to low. Simmer, covered, for 35 to 45 minutes or until vegetables are tender.
Makes 6 servings.

ZUCCHINI AND SPINACH SOUP

Parve or Meat

$1/4$ cup extra-virgin olive oil	1 quart MANISCHEWITZ® Chicken Broth or bouillon
2 onions, diced	Salt and pepper to taste
$1^1/2$ pounds zucchini, trimmed and cut into $1/2$-inch slices	1 (10-ounce) package fresh spinach, or 1 (10-ounce) package frozen chopped spinach, thawed and drained
2 Yukon gold potatoes, peeled and cut into cubes	

Heat olive oil in a stockpot and sauté onions until tender. Add zucchini and potatoes. Sauté for 5 minutes. Stir in broth and salt and pepper to taste. Bring to a boil. Reduce heat to medium-low. Simmer, covered, for 30 minutes or until potatoes are tender. Remove from heat. Add spinach. Let stand, covered, for 15 minutes. Purée soup in a food processor or with an immersion blender until smooth.
Makes 6 servings.

Photograph for this recipe is on front cover and on page 41.

SALADS

SAMPLER

FAMILY FRIENDLY
Avocado and Hearts of Palm Salad with Pesto Vinaigrette 57
Mexican Salad 59 • Autumn Salad with Walnut Vinaigrette 60
Mediterranean Chicken Salad 61
Simply Delicious Beet Salad (sidebar) 64 • Greek Tortellini Salad 65
Mushroom Salad 68 • Crunchy Nutty Salad 70
Strawberry Brie Salad with Poppy Seed Dressing 72 • Asian Salad 74

QUICK AND EASY
Artichoke, Fennel and Edamame Salad 56
Black Bean and Quinoa Salad 58 • Mexican Salad 59
Autumn Salad with Walnut Vinaigrette 60 • Simply Delicious Beet Salad (sidebar) 64
Deli Meat Salad 64 • Greek Tortellini Salad 65
Crunchy Nutty Salad 70 • Asian Salad 74 • Turkey Caesar Salad 77

SOPHISTICATED
Artichoke, Fennel and Edamame Salad 56
Green Bean, Watercress and Beet Salad 57 • Spicy Bean Salad 58
Black Bean and Quinoa Salad 58 • Chopped Greek Salad 59
Chicken Salad with Roasted Garlic Mayonnaise 63 • Salad Niçoise 69
Pear, Arugula and Endive Salad with Spiced Walnuts 71
Summertime Couscous Salad 76

GREAT FOR A BARBECUE
Avocado and Hearts of Palm Salad with Pesto Vinaigrette 57
Spicy Bean Salad 58 • Mexican Salad 59 • Roasted Corn Salad 61
Veggie Slaw 68 • Crunchy Nutty Salad 70
Strawberry Brie Salad with Poppy Seed Dressing (made parve) 72
Very Wild Basmati Salad 73 • Summertime Couscous Salad 76

Artichoke, Fennel and Edamame Salad

Parve

"When I was testing this salad, I made it for good friends who joined us for Shabbat lunch. I was a little concerned how it would be received since fennel has such a distinct flavor. I was pleasantly surprised when it was the hit of the meal."

FENNEL
Trim the base from the fennel bulb and remove and discard the upper stalks. Slice the bulb lengthwise into halves. Separate the fennel layers in each half and cut them into thin strips.

4 (15-ounce) cans artichoke hearts, well drained
$^1/_2$ cup plus 3 tablespoons olive oil, divided
    Salt and pepper to taste
6 tablespoons fresh lemon juice
$^1/_4$ cup chopped shallots
1 teaspoon grated lemon zest
1 fennel bulb, cut into quarters and thinly sliced crosswise
$4^1/_2$ cups frozen shelled edamame, thawed
$^1/_2$ cup fresh parsley, finely chopped
1 teaspoon fennel seeds

Preheat oven to 400 degrees. Spray a baking sheet with nonstick cooking spray. Toss artichoke hearts with 3 tablespoons olive oil. Place on prepared pan. Sprinkle with salt and pepper to taste. Roast for 10 minutes. Let cool on baking sheet. Cut artichokes into quarters.

Whisk remaining $^1/_2$ cup olive oil, lemon juice, shallots and lemon zest in a large bowl. Stir in artichokes, sliced fennel, edamame, parsley and fennel seeds. Season with salt and pepper to taste; toss to coat well. (May be prepared in advance. Chill, covered, until ready to serve.) *Makes 8 servings.*

Note: May substitute fresh edamame in the shell for the shelled frozen edamame. Shell and blanch the fresh edamame before adding to the salad.

Green Bean, Watercress and Beet Salad

Parve

Salad

1¹/₂ pounds green
    beans, trimmed
  2 bunches watercress,
    trimmed
  1 (15-ounce) can
    sliced beets, drained
  ³/₄ cup walnuts or almonds,
    coarsely chopped
  ¹/₂ red onion, thinly sliced

Walnut Dijon Vinaigrette

  ¹/₄ cup walnut oil
  2 tablespoons Dijon mustard
  2 tablespoons wine vinegar
  1 tablespoon fresh
    parsley, chopped
    Salt and pepper to taste

For the salad, steam beans in a covered saucepan over boiling water for 4 to 5 minutes or until tender-crisp. Rinse under cold water; drain. Combine beans, watercress, beets, walnuts and onion in a large bowl. Pour dressing over salad and toss to coat

For the vinaigrette, whisk walnut oil, Dijon mustard, vinegar, parsley and salt and pepper to taste in a bowl. *Makes 8 to 10 servings.*

Avocado and Hearts of Palm Salad with Pesto Vinaigrette

Parve

Salad

  3 to 4 heads romaine hearts,
    cut into bite-size pieces
  4 Hass avocados, pitted,
    peeled and cut into
    small pieces
  1 (15-ounce) can hearts of
    palm, drained and sliced
  1 pint grape tomatoes,
    cut into halves
  1 small red onion, cut into
    halves and thinly sliced

Pesto Vinaigrette

  ¹/₂ cup fresh basil, chopped
  3 tablespoons fresh
    lemon juice
  2 garlic cloves, chopped
    Salt and pepper to taste
  ¹/₃ cup olive oil

For the salad, combine the romaine hearts, avocados, hearts of palm, tomatoes and red onion in a large bowl. Toss salad with vinaigrette just before serving.

For the vinaigrette, combine basil, lemon juice, garlic and salt and pepper to taste in a blender or food processor. Add oil gradually, processing constantly until smooth and emulsified. (May be prepared in advance and refrigerated.) *Makes 6 to 8 servings.*

Ripening and Slicing Avocados

Avocados ripen best after they have been picked. A ripe avocado yields to gentle pressure in the palm of your hand. To ripen avocados at home, place the fruit in a paper bag and let stand at room temperature for two to five days. Placing an apple in the bag will help the avocados ripen even more quickly. Store ripe avocados in the refrigerator for about one week.

To slice an avocado, slide a knife lengthwise around the entire fruit, cutting all the way down to the pit. Twist the halves with your hands to separate them. To remove the pit, carefully stick the knife blade into the center of the pit, then twist the knife slightly and it will lift out. Use a paring knife to slice or dice the avocado flesh without slicing through the peel. Scoop the flesh from the peel with a large spoon.

SPICY BEAN SALAD

Parve

You can substitute 1 or 2 (14-ounce) cans green beans, drained, for 1 or 2 cans of the kidney beans or chick-peas, if you prefer.

Juice of 6 lemons	2 (15-ounce) cans chick-
1/4 cup olive oil	peas, drained and rinsed
Cumin, red pepper, salt	2 bunches scallions, minced
and black pepper to taste	1 bunch flat-leaf parsley,
2 (15-ounce) cans red	finely chopped
kidney beans, drained	1 onion, finely chopped
and rinsed	1 head garlic, minced
1 (15-ounce) can cannellini	
beans, drained and rinsed	

Whisk lemon juice, olive oil, cumin, red pepper and salt and black pepper to taste in a large bowl until well blended. Add beans, chick-peas, scallions, parsley, onion and garlic and mix well. Marinate, covered, in the refrigerator for 8 to 12 hours. *Makes 10 to 12 servings.*

COUSCOUS SALAD
Substitute 1/2 cup couscous for the quinoa. Cook in 1/2 cup water for 2 to 3 minutes.

BLACK BEAN AND QUINOA SALAD

Parve

SALAD

1/2 cup (generous) water	1/2 cup loosely packed
Pinch of kosher salt	flat-leaf parsley
1/2 cup uncooked quinoa	Pepper to taste
1 (15-ounce) can black	
beans, rinsed and drained	LIME BALSAMIC VINAIGRETTE
1 red bell pepper, seeded	2 tablespoons olive oil
and finely chopped	2 tablespoons (about)
1/2 cup frozen corn, thawed	balsamic vinegar
	Juice of 1 lime
	1/4 to 1/2 teaspoon chili powder

For the salad, bring water to a boil in a small saucepan. Add salt. Sprinkle quinoa over water. Reduce heat to low. Simmer, covered, for 10 minutes or until water is absorbed. Stir with a fork to fluff grains. Combine quinoa, beans, bell pepper, corn, parsley and pepper to taste in a large bowl. Toss salad with vinaigrette. Season to taste. Serve at room temperature.

For the vinaigrette, whisk olive oil, vinegar, lime juice and chili powder in a bowl until well blended. *Makes 4 to 6 servings.*

MEXICAN SALAD

Parve

SALAD

1 (15-ounce) can black beans, rinsed, drained
1 (15-ounce) can yellow and white corn, drained
2 ripe Hass avocados, cut into cubes
2 tomatoes, diced
1 jicama, peeled and chopped (optional)
1/2 red onion, chopped (optional)
1 head green romaine lettuce
1 head red romaine lettuce or red leaf lettuce

SALSA LIME DRESSING

3/4 to 1 cup salsa
Juice of 1 lime
1 teaspoon chili powder

For the salad, combine beans, corn, avocados, tomatoes, jicama and onion in a bowl. Alternate green and red lettuce leaves on a serving platter or individual plates. Spoon salad in center and sprinkle Tortilla Slices (see sidebar) on top.

For the dressing, combine salsa, lime juice and chili powder in a bowl. Pour over salad and toss gently to coat. *Makes 12 servings.*

TORTILLA SLICES

For tortilla slices, stack six 8-inch corn tortillas and cut into quarters. Cut each quarter into 1/4-inch slices. Heat 3 to 4 tablespoons vegetable oil in a skillet. Add tortilla slices and fry until crisp and golden. Remove with a slotted spoon; drain on paper towels. Sprinkle with salt to taste. Let cool. (May be prepared in advance and stored in an airtight container.)

CHOPPED GREEK SALAD

Dairy

SALAD

3 cups cherry tomatoes, cut into halves
1 English cucumber, chopped
1 1/2 green bell peppers, chopped
1 red onion, chopped
1 1/2 cups kalamata olives, cut into halves
6 to 8 ounces ZURIEL feta cheese, crumbled

LEMON OREGANO DRESSING

6 tablespoons olive oil
2 tablespoons lemon juice
2 tablespoons chopped fresh oregano

For the salad, combine tomatoes, cucumber, bell peppers, onion and olives in a large bowl. Add dressing, tossing to coat.

For the dressing, whisk olive oil, lemon juice and oregano in a small bowl and mix well. Sprinkle cheese over the top. *Makes 8 servings.*

AUTUMN SALAD WITH WALNUT VINAIGRETTE

Parve

*T**his very attractive salad combines a colorful variety of greens with the crunch of apples and the sweetness of grapes.***

SALAD

- 8 cups mixed greens (such as romaine, watercress, arugula, frisée)
- 1 red apple, unpeeled and thinly sliced
- 1 green apple, unpeeled and thinly sliced
- 1 cup red grapes, cut into halves
- 1 cup green grapes, cut into halves
- 2 ribs celery, chopped
- 1/2 cup thinly sliced red onion

WALNUT VINAIGRETTE

- 1/2 cup walnuts
  Juice of 1/2 orange
- 2 tablespoons GREY POUPON Dijon Mustard
- 1 1/2 tablespoons red wine vinegar
- 1 tablespoon brown sugar
- 1 garlic clove, minced
  Salt and pepper to taste
- 1/2 cup olive oil

For salad, combine greens, apples, grapes, celery and onion in a large bowl. Toss salad with vinaigrette.

For vinaigrette, combine walnuts, orange juice, Dijon mustard, vinegar, brown sugar, garlic and salt and pepper to taste in a food processor. Add oil gradually, processing constantly until well blended. (May be prepared in advance and refrigerated.)
Makes 8 servings.

Mediterranean Chicken Salad

Meat

A great way to use leftover roast chicken!

SALAD

- 1/2 cup uncooked orzo
- 3 cups diced roasted chicken
- 1 cup cherry tomatoes, cut into halves
- 1 (6-ounce) jar marinated artichoke hearts, drained
- 1/2 cup kalamata olives, pitted and coarsely chopped
- 1 1/2 tablespoons capers, drained

FRESH TARRAGON VINAIGRETTE

- 6 tablespoons olive oil
- 2 tablespoons plus 2 teaspoons tarragon vinegar
- 1 tablespoon lemon juice
- 1 tablespoon Dijon mustard
- 1 tablespoon chopped fresh tarragon
- Salt and pepper to taste

For the salad, cook orzo according to the package directions. Rinse under cold water; drain. Combine orzo, chicken, tomatoes, artichoke hearts, olives and capers in a large bowl. Toss salad with vinaigrette until well coated.

For the vinaigrette, whisk olive oil, vinegar, lemon juice, Dijon mustard and tarragon in a bowl until well mixed. Season with salt and pepper to taste. (May be prepared in advance and refrigerated.) *Makes 4 to 6 servings.*

Roasted Corn Salad

Parve

- 4 cups fresh corn kernels (5 to 6 ears)
- 2 red bell peppers, seeded and finely chopped
- 1/2 cup fresh cilantro, chopped
- 5 scallions, thinly sliced
- 1 1/2 tablespoons honey

- 3 tablespoons apple cider vinegar
- 1 1/2 tablespoons olive oil
- 2 teaspoons Dijon mustard
- 3/4 teaspoon salt

Preheat oven to 425 degrees. Spray a baking sheet with nonstick cooking spray. Spread corn kernels on prepared pan. Roast for about 20 minutes or until light brown, stirring occasionally. Cool completely.

Combine bell peppers, cilantro, scallions, honey, vinegar, olive oil, Dijon mustard and salt in a large bowl. Stir in corn. Refrigerate, covered, until chilled. *Makes 8 servings.*

DRYING HERBS
Dried herbs have a shelf life of six months if stored in a cool, dark place. Those stored near an oven can lose their flavor in as quickly as a week. Discard herbs after storing for one year as they will have lost all their flavor. Fresh herbs can be air dried in small bunches in brown paper bags; it will take several weeks for them to become completely dry. Don't dry fresh herbs in the sun as they will lose their oils and fragrance. Fresh herbs can also be dried in a microwave oven. Arrange the herbs in a single layer between three or four sheets of paper towels. Microwave on High for two minutes or until dry.

RASPBERRY VINAIGRETTE
Parve

Whisk 2 tablespoons raspberry vinegar, 1 tablespoon balsamic vinegar, 1 tablespoon soy sauce, 3/4 tablespoon Dijon mustard, 1 1/2 teaspoons grated fresh ginger, 1 minced garlic clove 1/2 teaspoon salt and 1/4 teaspoon chili powder in a bowl. Add 1/3 cup extra-virgin olive oil gradually, whisking constantly until emulsified. **Makes about 2/3 cup.**

CREAMY SWEET AND SOUR DRESSING
Parve

"This is the easiest and best salad dressing. I never have any left over."

Whisk 1 cup mayonnaise, 1/4 cup sugar, 1/4 cup water, 1/4 cup vinegar, garlic powder to taste and pepper to taste in a bowl. **Makes 1 3/4 cups.**

CANTONESE CHICKEN SALAD
Meat

E asily made when you have leftover cooked chicken. Otherwise, poach or fry a chicken breast.

SALAD
- 2 cups cooked chicken breast strips
- 8 ounces carrots, shredded (about 1 cup)
- 8 ounces snow peas, cut into bite-size pieces
- 1 red bell pepper, cut into julienne strips
- 1/2 cup slivered almonds, toasted
- 1/4 cup fresh cilantro, chopped
- 4 scallions, thinly sliced
  Fresh spinach leaves

SESAME SOY DRESSING
- 3 tablespoons dark brown sugar
- 3 tablespoons rice vinegar
- 3 tablespoons sesame oil
- 2 tablespoons teriyaki sauce
- 1 tablespoon dry mustard

For the salad, combine chicken, carrots, snow peas, bell pepper, almonds, cilantro and scallions in a large bowl. Set aside. Pour dressing over salad and toss until coated. Serve on a bed of spinach leaves.

For the dressing, whisk dark brown sugar, vinegar, sesame oil, teriyaki sauce and dry mustard in a small bowl until smooth.
Makes 4 servings.

CHICKEN SALAD WITH ROASTED GARLIC MAYONNAISE

Meat

The roasted garlic mayonnaise adds nice flavor to traditional chicken salad, and the radicchio adds rich color.

2 heads garlic	1 cup mayonnaise
2 pounds chicken cutlets CARMEL CHARDONNAY® and or water for poaching	1 (15-ounce) can hearts of palm, drained and sliced
2 (6-ounce) jars marinated artichoke hearts	2 tablespoons capers, drained
	1 small head radicchio

Preheat oven to 375 degrees. Wrap each head garlic separately in foil. Roast for 45 minutes to 1 hour or until soft when gently squeezed. Let stand until slightly cooled.

Meanwhile, place chicken cutlets in a large skillet or saucepan. Add enough wine or water (or a combination of both) to cover. Bring to a boil over medium heat. Reduce heat to low. Simmer for about 12 minutes or until chicken is just cooked through. Remove with a slotted spoon. Cool to room temperature. Slice chicken into bite-size pieces.

Remove garlic from foil; squeeze cloves from skins into a large bowl. Drain artichokes, reserving marinade from one jar. Chop artichokes into small pieces. Add artichokes, reserved marinade and mayonnaise to garlic and mix well. Add chicken, hearts of palm and capers and toss until well coated.

Line serving platter with radicchio leaves; spoon salad in center. Shred any remaining radicchio leaves to garnish top of salad. (May be prepared ahead and refrigerated.) *Makes 6 servings.*

CREAMY MUSTARD VINAIGRETTE
Parve

Whisk 3 tablespoons white wine vinegar, 1 egg yolk, at room temperature, 3/4 teaspoon kosher salt, 1/2 teaspoon Dijon mustard, 1/2 teaspoon minced fresh garlic and 1/4 teaspoon freshly ground pepper in a small bowl. Add 1/2 cup olive oil gradually, whisking constantly until emulsified. *Makes about 3/4 cup.*

HONEY MUSTARD VINAIGRETTE
Parve

Whisk 3/4 cup olive oil, 3/4 cup apple cider vinegar, 1/4 cup honey, 2 tablespoons Dijon mustard and 1 teaspoon dry mustard in a bowl and mix well. Chill, covered, until ready to serve. *Makes about 13/4 cups.*

SIMPLY DELICIOUS BEET SALAD

Parve

Remove and discard stems and roots of 2 bunches beets. Place beets in a large pot with enough salted water to cover. Bring to a boil. Reduce heat to low. Simmer for 50 minutes to 1 hour or until tender; drain. Let cool to room temperature.

Peel beets and cut into bite-size pieces; place in a large bowl. Whisk 3 tablespoons extra-virgin olive oil, 2 tablespoons apple cider vinegar, 1 tablespoon dark brown sugar, 1 teaspoon kosher salt and 1/2 teaspoon freshly ground pepper in a small bowl. Pour over beets; toss to coat. *Makes 6 servings.*

DELI MEAT SALAD

Meat

There was a toss up over which dressing was preferred in this recipe, so we've included them both and leave you to be the judge.

SALAD

- 4 romaine hearts, cut into bite-size pieces
- 3 Hass avocados, pitted, peeled and cut into small pieces
- 8 ounces thinly sliced deli smoked turkey, cut into small pieces
- 8 ounces thinly sliced deli pastrami, cut into small pieces
- 1 (15-ounce) can hearts of palm, drained and sliced
- 1 cup cherry or grape tomatoes, cut into halves
- 1/2 red onion, thinly sliced
- 1/2 (7-ounce) bag terra root vegetable chips (optional), lightly crushed

TANGY DRESSING

- 1/4 cup sugar
- 1/4 cup honey
- 1/4 cup vegetable oil
- 1/4 cup wine vinegar
- 1 tablespoon Dijon Mustard
- 1 to 2 garlic cloves, minced

FIESTA DRESSING

- 1 cup salsa
- 1/2 cup mayonnaise
- 3 tablespoons Worcestershire sauce

For the salad, combine romaine, avocados, turkey, pastrami, hearts of palm, tomatoes and onion in a large bowl. Toss with preferred dressing. Sprinkle with vegetable chips.

For either dressing, combine all ingredients in a bowl and mix well. (Dressing may be prepared in advance.) *Makes 6 servings.*

GREEK TORTELLINI SALAD

Dairy

SALAD

1 (9-ounce) package plain or tri-color refrigerator cheese tortellini, cooked and drained

2 red and/or green bell peppers, cut into thin strips (2 cups)

1 small red onion, thinly sliced

1/4 cup sliced black olives

1/2 cup crumbled ZURIEL feta cheese

MINT VINAIGRETTE

1/2 cup rice vinegar or white wine vinegar

1/2 cup olive oil or vegetable oil

3 tablespoons snipped fresh mint, or 2 teaspoons dried mint

3 tablespoons lemon juice

2 tablespoons dry sherry

1 1/2 teaspoons seasoned salt

1 teaspoon garlic powder

1 teaspoon pepper

1/8 to 1/4 teaspoon crushed red pepper

For the salad, combine pasta, bell peppers, onion and olives in a large bowl. Pour the dressing over pasta mixture and toss to coat. Chill, covered, for 4 hours or up to one day. Stir in cheese just before serving. Serve with a slotted spoon.

For the dressing, combine vinegar, olive oil, mint, lemon juice, sherry, seasoned salt, garlic powder, pepper and red pepper in a jar. Cover and shake to blend. *Makes 6 to 8 servings.*

PLATING IDEAS

When serving a beet salad, dress up the plate by slicing peeled oranges into rounds and placing them in an overlapping circle around the edge of the plate. Mound the beets in the center of the orange slices and garnish with a chiffonade of fresh mint.

EMERALD GOODNESS

You can use many different types of lettuce and other salad-worthy greens to make attractive and tasty salads in a variety of textures and colors.

SWEET LETTUCES
Bibb
Boston
iceberg
red and green leaf
romaine

PEPPERY GREENS
arugula
watercress

BITTER CHICORIES
endive
frisée
radicchio

ARUGULA
A member of the cabbage family, arugula is a crisp green with a slightly peppery flavor.

BELGIAN ENDIVE
Recognized by its cylinder-shaped heads of tightly packed, yellowish-tipped white leaves, Belgian endive has a slightly bitter flavor and makes an attractive garnish.

BIBB LETTUCE
This butterhead lettuce has a slightly buttery flavor and crisper texture than Boston lettuce. It is deeply colored with a whitish green hue toward the center of the leaves.

BOSTON LETTUCE
This butterhead lettuce has a subtle, sweet taste and soft, tender green leaves. The heads are tightly packed with dark outer leaves and light inner leaves.

RADICCHIO
A variety of red chicory, radicchio has a somewhat bitter, acidic flavor that complements the sweeter flavor of other greens. It adds texture and a lovely color to salads.

FREEZING HERBS

The next time you have leftover packaged fresh herbs, don't discard them—freeze them. Place in sealable plastic bags marked with the names of the herbs and freeze them whole. If the herb requires chopping later, it will be easier to chop while frozen. Otherwise, simply thaw and use as needed.

STORING SALAD GREENS

Remove ties or rubber bands from fresh, unwashed greens and discard any wilted leaves. Refrigerate in a perforated plastic bag for up to three or four days. Delicate greens, such as arugula, will keep only one or two days in the refrigerator.

Store washed salad greens in a paper towel-lined salad spinner, layering the greens with additional paper towels. Refrigerate for one to two days. For longer storage, loosely roll the washed greens in paper towels and place in a sealable plastic bag. Refrigerate for up to one week.

SALAD TIP

If washed salad greens begin to wilt and go limp, place them in the freezer for exactly two minutes (no longer, to prevent freezing) and they will be revived.

*A succulent array of salad vegetables. Clockwise from top left: romaine lettuce,
Boston lettuce, red-leaf lettuce, radicchio, flat-leaf parsley, Belgian endive.*

Place 1 tablespoon Dijon mustard in a bowl. Whisk in 3 tablespoons vinegar, 4 teaspoons sugar, $1/2$ teaspoon salt, $1/2$ teaspoon freshly ground pepper and minced fresh parsley or chives to taste. Add $1/2$ cup good-quality olive oil gradually, whisking constantly until thickened. Adjust seasoning to taste. Vinaigrette is best when made just before serving. If made in advance, whisk again before serving. *Makes 1 cup.*

SLAW IT DOWN

This salad has a real kick. If you're not a garlic lover, reduce the amount of garlic in the dressing to suit your taste.

MUSHROOM SALAD

Parve

SALAD	SWEET & SOUR RED DRESSING
2 to 3 tablespoons olive oil	$1/3$ cup olive oil
3 to 4 large portobello mushrooms	$1/4$ cup sugar
	$1/4$ cup lemon juice
4 to 5 cups mesclun	$1/4$ cup ketchup
1 pint grape tomatoes	1 garlic clove, minced
$3/4$ cup honey cashews	$1/2$ teaspoon salt
	$1/4$ teaspoon dry mustard
	$1/4$ teaspoon paprika

For the salad, heat olive oil in a skillet and sauté mushrooms until tender. Remove from heat; set aside to cool. Cut into slices. Combine mushrooms and dressing in a large bowl, turning to coat. Marinate, covered, in the refrigerator for at least 1 hour or up to 12 hours. Place mesclun and tomatoes in a serving bowl. Add mushrooms with dressing; top with cashews.

For the dressing, whisk olive oil, sugar, lemon juice, ketchup, garlic, salt, dry mustard and paprika in a large bowl. *Makes 6 to 8 servings.*

VEGGIE SLAW

Parve

SALAD	GARLIC HERB DRESSING
1 head red cabbage, shredded, or 2 (12-ounce) bags shredded red cabbage	$1/2$ cup olive oil
	$1/3$ cup red wine vinegar or apple cider vinegar
1 pound carrots, shredded	$1/4$ cup fresh dill weed, chopped
1 red onion, finely chopped	3 tablespoons fresh parsley, chopped
1 each orange, yellow and red bell peppers, chopped	2 tablespoons lemon juice
	1 tablespoon mustard
1 Hass avocado, peeled, pitted and cut into small pieces	2 to 3 garlic cloves
	2 teaspoons salt
	$1/2$ teaspoon pepper

For the salad, combine cabbage, carrots, onion and bell peppers in a bowl; set aside. Toss salad with dressing and avocado and mix well.

For the dressing, combine all the ingredients in a food processor and process until well mixed. *Makes 12 to 14 servings.*

SALAD NIÇOISE

. . . .

Parve

SALAD

- 2 pounds string beans, trimmed
- 5 red potatoes, cooked until tender and sliced
- 2 (6-ounce) cans solid white tuna, drained well
- 1 pint grape tomatoes, cut into halves
- 4 ribs celery, chopped
- 1 large red onion, diced
- $1/3$ cup finely chopped scallions
- $1/4$ cup green olives, pitted and cut into halves
- $1/4$ cup black olives, pitted and cut into halves
- 3 tablespoons capers, drained
- 4 hard-cooked eggs, peeled and cut into wedges

FRESH DILL DRESSING

- 6 tablespoons vegetable oil
- 6 tablespoons olive oil
- 6 tablespoons red wine vinegar
- 2 tablespoons chopped fresh dill weed
- 2 teaspoons GREY POUPON Dijon Mustard
- 2 garlic cloves, minced
- $1^1/2$ teaspoons salt
- 1 teaspoon dried thyme
- 1 teaspoon dried basil
- 1 teaspoon pepper

For the salad, fill a large saucepan $3/4$ full with water. Bring to a boil. Add beans. Blanch for 3 minutes. Drain and rinse under cold water to stop the cooking process; drain. Combine beans, potatoes, tuna, tomatoes, celery, onion, scallions, olives and capers in a bowl. Pour dressing over salad and toss to coat well. Spoon into a serving bowl or onto a platter. Top with egg wedges.

For the dressing, whisk the oils, vinegar, dill weed, Dijon mustard, garlic, salt, thyme, basil and pepper in a bowl and mix well. *Makes 8 servings.*

LEMONADE VINAIGRETTE

Parve

Whisk 1/4 cup olive oil, 3 tablespoons frozen lemonade concentrate, 2 tablespoons balsamic vinegar and 1/4 teaspoon Dijon mustard in a bowl until well mixed. *Makes about 1/2 cup.*

CITRUS VINAIGRETTE

Parve

Whisk 1¹/2 tablespoons fresh orange juice, 1¹/2 tablespoons fresh grapefruit juice, 2 teaspoons extra-virgin olive oil, 1 teaspoon grated lemon zest, 1 teaspoon fresh lemon juice, 1 teaspoon honey, 1/4 teaspoon salt and 1/4 teaspoon pepper in a bowl until well mixed. (May be prepared up to a day ahead.) *Makes 1/4 cup.*

CRUNCHY NUTTY SALAD

Parve

" I *often toast a lot of nuts at one time and store them in an airtight container to use as needed."*

SALAD

1/2	cup slivered almonds
1	tablespoon vegetable oil
2	tablespoons sesame seeds
1	(16-ounce) package coleslaw mix
1	(10-ounce) package fresh baby spinach, cleaned
8	scallions, thinly sliced
2	(3-ounce) packages Chinese soup noodles, crumbled

RICE VINAIGRETTE

3/4	cup vegetable oil
6	tablespoons rice vinegar
1/4	cup sugar
2	teaspoons salt
1	teaspoon pepper

For the salad, preheat oven to 350 degrees. Toss almonds with oil. Place on a baking sheet. Bake for 5 to 6 minutes or until brown, adding sesame seeds during last 2 minutes. Watch carefully to prevent burning. Let stand until cool. Combine coleslaw mix, spinach and scallions in a bowl and toss well. Discard flavor packets from noodles. Toss salad with dressing, noodles, almonds and sesame seeds just before serving.

For the dressing, whisk oil, vinegar, sugar, salt and pepper in a bowl. *Makes 8 to 10 servings.*

PEAR, ARUGULA AND ENDIVE SALAD WITH SPICED WALNUTS

Parve

SALAD

- 12 cups arugula, torn into pieces
- 4 heads Belgian endive, trimmed and leaves separated
- 2 firm, ripe pears, cut into halves, cored and thinly sliced

SPICED WALNUTS

- 1 cup walnuts
- 2 tablespoons light corn syrup
- 1 tablespoon sugar
- 1/2 teaspoon salt
- 1/4 teaspoon pepper
- Pinch of cayenne pepper

PARSLEY DIJON DRESSING

- 2 tablespoons red wine vinegar
- 2 tablespoons fresh lemon juice
- 1 tablespoon fresh parsley, chopped
- 1 tablespoon Dijon mustard
- 6 tablespoons walnut oil
- 6 tablespoons olive oil
- Salt and pepper to taste

For the salad, toss arugula in a large bowl with enough dressing to coat. Arrange endive leaves around the edge of a platter. Place arugula in the center and top with pears and spiced walnuts or middle eastern spiced nuts (see sidebar).

For the spiced walnuts, preheat oven to 325 degrees. Spray baking sheet with nonstick cooking spray. Combine walnuts, corn syrup, sugar, salt, pepper and cayenne pepper in a bowl and toss to coat. Spread on the prepared pan. Bake about 15 minutes or until walnuts are deep brown and sugar mixture is bubbling, stirring occasionally to break up clumps. Cool completely on pan. (May be prepared ahead and stored in an airtight container.)

For the dressing, whisk vinegar, lemon juice, parsley and Dijon mustard in a bowl and mix well. Add oils gradually, whisking until well blended. Season with salt and pepper to taste. (May be prepared ahead and refrigerated.) *Makes 6 servings.*

MIDDLE EASTERN SPICED NUTS
Parve

Once you try seasoned and flavored nuts on salads, you'll be hooked. Try this additional flavored nut for this or any salad. Melt 1/4 cup (1/2 stick) margarine in a saucepan over medium heat. Add 1 teaspoon ground cinnamon, 1/2 teaspoon cumin and a pinch of salt. Cook for 1 minute. Stir in 1/2 cup blanched almonds, 1/2 cup pecans and 2 tablespoons pine nuts. Cook until nuts are toasted, stirring occasionally. Remove from heat. Let cool. (May be prepared in advance and stored in an airtight container.) *Makes about 1 cup.*

Strawberry Brie Salad with Poppy Seed Dressing

Dairy

"*My dear friend loves to bake and cook and try new recipes. The best thing about her is that she loves to share her recipes. She told me that when I made this salad, there would not be a lettuce leaf left in the bowl—and she was right! I can never miss with a recipe from her.*"

SALAD
- 1 1/2 cups sliced almonds
- 1/4 cup sugar
- 4 heads romaine hearts, washed and torn
- 1 (7- to 8-ounce) wheel Brie cheese, cut into 1/2-inch pieces
- 2 pints strawberries, sliced

POPPY SEED DRESSING
- 1/2 cup vegetable oil
- 1/3 cup sugar
- 1/4 cup apple cider vinegar
- 1/4 cup balsamic vinegar
- 1/4 cup chopped red onion
- 1 teaspoon dry mustard
- 1 1/2 teaspoons poppy seeds

For the salad, combine almonds and sugar in a saucepan. Cook over medium heat for 10 minutes or until sugar melts and almonds turn brown, stirring constantly. Cook for 2 to 3 minutes longer. Spread almonds on a sheet of foil. Let stand until cool. Combine romaine, cheese, strawberries and almonds in a bowl. Add dressing and toss to coat.

For the dressing, combine oil, sugar, apple cider vinegar, balsamic vinegar, onion and dry mustard in a food processor and process until well mixed. Stir in poppy seeds. (May be prepared one day in advance and refrigerated.) *Makes 6 to 8 servings.*

Note: The Brie cheese may be omitted to make this a parve recipe.

STORING FRESH STRAWBERRIES

To keep strawberries fresh, place the unwashed berries on a paper plate layered with a single paper towel. Refrigerate until ready to use. Wash and hull the berries just before serving.

VERY WILD BASMATI SALAD

Parve

This was a favorite at the salad testing for its combination of flavors. This colorful salad also displays beautifully. It would be a great addition to any summertime picnic or barbecue.

SALAD

- 4 cups water
- 1/2 cup uncooked wild rice
- 1 1/2 cups uncooked brown basmati rice
- 2 to 3 carrots, diced
- 1 (10-ounce) package frozen peas, thawed
- 1 (10-ounce) package frozen white shoepeg corn, thawed
- 1/2 red bell pepper, seeded and diced
- 1/2 cup chopped pecans or slivered almonds

BASIL DRESSING

- 1/4 cup olive oil
- 1/4 cup fresh basil, chopped
- 2 tablespoons plum vinegar
  Salt and pepper to taste

For the salad, combine water and wild rice in a saucepan. Bring to a boil. Boil for 5 minutes. Stir in basmati rice; return to a boil. Reduce heat to low. Cook, covered, for 1 hour or until liquid is absorbed. Meanwhile, blanch carrots, peas and corn in boiling water; drain well. Combine rice, blanched vegetables, bell pepper and pecans in a bowl. Add the dressing and toss to coat. Refrigerate, covered, until chilled.

For the dressing, whisk olive oil, basil, vinegar and salt and pepper to taste in a bowl and mix well. *Makes 12 servings.*

VEGETABLE OIL FACTS

Vegetable oils include those made from plant sources, such as nuts, ·ds, and vegetables. ⸱ are generally low ın saturated (bad) fat and high in mono- and polyunsaturated (good) fats, which can help lower blood cholesterol levels.

With the exception of walnut, olive and sunflower oils, most vegetable oils have high smoke points, which makes them a good choice for frying and sautéing.

Most vegetable oils will keep for several months in a cool, dark place in tightly sealed containers. Refrigerate them for longer storage. Nut oils will go rancid quickly once opened, so they should always be refrigerated.

Canola Oil: With the lowest amount of saturated fat (6%), this mild-tasting all-purpose oil also contains omega-3 fatty acids, which may help lower blood cholesterol. ➤

ASIAN SALAD

Parve

Add strips of grilled chicken or salmon to salad to create an appetizer or entrée.

SALAD

- 1 pound snow peas, cut into bite-size pieces
- 1 (15-ounce) can baby corn on the cob, drained
- 1 (10-ounce) bag fresh spinach
- 10 ounces fresh mushrooms, cut into cubes
- 1 red bell pepper, cut into thin strips
- 4 to 5 scallions, sliced
- 1/3 cup toasted almonds
  Chinese soup noodles (optional)

TAMARI VINAIGRETTE

- 1/4 cup vegetable oil
- 2 tablespoons sugar
- 2 tablespoons rice vinegar
- 1 tablespoon hoisin sauce
- 2 teaspoons toasted sesame oil
- 1 teaspoon tamari sauce
- 1/2 teaspoon dry mustard

For the salad, combine snow peas, corn, spinach, mushrooms, bell pepper, scallions, almonds and noodles in a large bowl. Add vinaigrette and toss just before serving

For the vinaigrette, whisk vegetable oil, sugar, vinegar, hoisin sauce, sesame oil, tamari sauce and dry mustard in a bowl and mix well. (May be prepared in advance and refrigerated.). *Makes 6 servings.*

Mixed Vegetable Salad with Basil Vinaigrette

Parve or Dairy

This salad calls for a lot of ingredients and chopping, but the results are definitely worth the work!

SALAD
- 1 large head red leaf lettuce, torn into bite-size pieces, about 6 cups
- 2 tomatoes, cut into wedges
- 1½ cups shredded carrots
- 1½ cups canned beets, drained and cut into matchstick-size strips
- 1 cup drained canned chick-peas
- 1 cup fresh alfalfa or bean sprouts
- ½ cup shredded red cabbage
- 1 cup crumbled ZURIEL feta cheese (optional)
- 3 tablespoons slivered almonds, toasted
- 3 tablespoons unsalted sunflower seeds, toasted

BASIL BALSAMIC VINAIGRETTE
- 1 cup fresh basil leaves
- 1½ tablespoons balsamic vinegar
- 1 tablespoon red wine vinegar
- 1 tablespoon honey
- 3 garlic cloves
- 1½ teaspoons GREY POUPON Dijon Mustard
- 6 tablespoons olive oil
- Salt and pepper to taste

For the salad, combine lettuce, tomatoes, carrots, beets, chick-peas, alfalfa sprouts and cabbage in a bowl. Add vinaigrette and toss to coat. Sprinkle cheese, almonds and sunflower seeds over salad just before serving.

For the vinaigrette, combine basil, balsamic vinegar, red wine, honey, garlic and Dijon mustard in a food processor and process until well mixed. Add olive oil gradually, processing constantly until well mixed. Season with salt and pepper to taste. *Makes 6 servings.*

Photograph for this recipe is on page 143.

Peanut Oil: This oil is especially good for stir-frying. It also adds a peanut flavor to sauces and dressings.

Walnut Oil: Nutty-t— walnut oil can — used in baked goods, such as yeast breads, as well as dressings. It is not recommended for sautéing.

Sunflower Oil: Pale yellow in color and delicately flavored, this oil from sunflower seeds has a low smoke point and is best used for baking and salad dressings.

Corn Oil: Odorless and tasteless, corn oil is used for baking and frying. It's very high in polyunsaturated fats and is also used in making margarine.

Olive Oil: Olive oil is a favorite among chefs for sautéing meats and chicken. Olive trees are grown in warm climates and areas with sandy soil, particularly in Italy, southern France, Spain, Greece, and Israel. To yield the finest quality oil, trees must be at least 35 years old.

VINEGAR FACTS

Ranging in color and flavor, the following vinegars are the ones you're most likely to use.

Balsamic Vinegar:
Prized for its sweetness, this dark brown vinegar actually starts out as white grape juice that is cooked and aged for several years in wooden barrels. Due to its intense flavor, balsamic vinegar should be used in moderation. It's particularly delicious in vinaigrettes and drizzled over strawberries.

Distilled Vinegar:
With its sharp taste, distilled vinegar is ideal for acidity without flavor. Traditionally used for preserving fruits and vegetables and for pickling, this vinegar also has the ability to clean coffeepots a lesser known fact.

White Wine Vinegar:
Similar to other wine vinegars, white wine vinegar is pleasantly sharp. Its light color makes it a great choice for light-colored foods, ➤

SUMMERTIME COUSCOUS SALAD

Parve

SALAD

- 1³/₄ cups water
- ¹/₂ teaspoon salt
- 1¹/₃ cups uncooked couscous
- 2 (15-ounce) cans chick-peas, drained and rinsed
- 1 pound Kirby cucumbers, cut into small chunks
- 1 pint grape tomatoes, cut into quarters
- ¹/₂ cup jarred roasted red peppers, chopped
- ¹/₂ cup finely chopped fresh mint
- 5 scallions, chopped
- 2 tablespoons capers, drained

LEMON CUMIN DRESSING

- ¹/₂ cup fresh lemon juice (about 2 large lemons)
- 2 tablespoons olive oil
- 1³/₄ teaspoons paprika
- 1¹/₂ teaspoons cumin
- Salt and pepper to taste

For the salad, bring water and salt to a boil in a saucepan. Remove from heat; stir in couscous. Let stand, covered, for 10 minutes or until water is absorbed; fluff with a fork. Meanwhile, combine chick-peas, cucumbers, tomatoes, roasted peppers, mint, scallions and capers in a bowl. Add the couscous and dressing and toss well. Chill, covered, for up to 2 days before serving.

For the dressing, whisk lemon juice, olive oil, paprika, cumin and salt and pepper to taste in a bowl. *Makes 12 servings.*

TURKEY CAESAR SALAD

Meat

This salad is a real crowd pleaser for both young and old. It's a great answer to a meat salad with the flavors of a traditional Caesar salad.

SALAD

- 3 to 4 heads romaine hearts, cut into small pieces
- 1 pound deli-smoked turkey breast, cut into 1-inch cubes
- Croutons

GARLIC CAESAR DRESSING

- 2/3 cup vegetable oil
- 6 tablespoons mayonnaise
- 2 tablespoons Dijon mustard
- 2 tablespoons apple cider vinegar
- 2 teaspoons Worcestershire sauce
- 6 garlic cloves, minced
- 1 teaspoon salt
- 1 teaspoon pepper
- 1 teaspoon fresh lemon juice

For the salad, place lettuce, turkey and croutons in a bowl. Add dressing and toss just before serving.

For the dressing, whisk oil, mayonnaise, Dijon mustard, vinegar, Worcestershire sauce, garlic, salt, pepper and lemon juice in a bowl and mix well. (May be prepared in advance and refrigerated.)

Makes 4 to 6 servings.

---

such as creamy salad dressings and vinaigrettes used in rice salads and German potato salad.

Red Wine Vinegar: Made from fermented red wine, this vinegar has a rich red color. Since wine vinegars are usually higher in acidity than fruit vinegars, they are frequently used in marinades and salad dressings and as last-minute additions to stews and sauces.

Rice Vinegar: Used extensively in Asian cooking as well as in salad dressings and marinades, rice vinegar is made from fermented rice wine and has a subtle, sweet flavor. The mildest rice vinegars are colorless. Some varieties are seasoned, so check the label to make sure you purchase the type you need.

Apple Cider Vinegar: Mild-tasting and slightly sweet, this fruit vinegar is made from fermented apple cider. It gives coleslaw and sauerkraut their familiar tang. Cider vinegar may be substituted for lemon juice to enhance the flavor of sweet and savory apple dishes.

Poultry

SAMPLER

FAMILY FRIENDLY

Beer Can-Roasted Chicken 80 • Baja Burritos 81

Oven-Glazed Chicken 82 • Crumb-Coated Chicken 83

Herb-Crusted Chicken Potpie 84

Chicken Ruby 86 • Lacquered Chicken 87

Roasted Chicken with Garlic Confit 87 • Saucy Chicken Cutlets 90

Hawaiian Schnitzel (sidebar) 90 • Grilled Luau Chicken 91

Honey-Ginger Chicken 91

Rolled Chicken Filled with Pastrami 93

Linguini with Chicken, Leeks and Tomatoes 99

Tangy Turkey Breast 103 • Turkey Burgers 103

Apricot-Glazed Turkey 104

QUICK AND EASY

Beer Can-Roasted Chicken 80 • Oven-Glazed Chicken 82

Crumb-Coated Chicken 83 • Chicken Kabobs 86

Lacquered Chicken 87 • Roasted Chicken with Garlic Confit 87

Honey-Ginger Chicken 91 • Rosemary Chicken 94

Tangy Turkey Breast 103

SOPHISTICATED

Grecian Chicken 82 • Balsamic Chicken 83

Chicken Ruby 86 • Roasted Chicken with Garlic Confit 87

Lemon-Pistachio Chicken Sliced over Greens 90

Chicken Monterey 92 • Georgian Pomegranate Chicken 95

Shiitake Ginger Chicken 96

Sun-Dried Tomato and Artichoke Chicken 97

Duck à l'Orange 100 • Tarragon-Stuffed Cornish Hens 101

GOOD GRILLED, TOO!

Beer Can-Roasted Chicken may also be grilled. Omit the marinade and season the chicken with this dry rub. Combine 1/4 cup packed brown sugar, 1/4 cup paprika, 2 tablespoons salt and 1 tablespoon pepper in a bowl. Position chicken with the beer can following roasting directions. Grill chicken, covered, until cooked through.

BEER CAN-ROASTED CHICKEN

Meat

"When my friend recently had a baby, I made this chicken for her family for Shabbat dinner. When she called to thank me, she said, 'I know you need an honest review for the cookbook, so here it is: It was outstanding! The chicken was so moist and delicious we picked it clean! A real winner!'"

1	cup lemon juice	1	teaspoon oregano
1/2	cup vegetable oil	1/2	teaspoon pepper
1/4	cup BARON HERZOG CHENIN BLANC®	1	(3- to 4-pound) roasting chicken
2	garlic cloves, minced	1	(12-ounce) can beer
1	teaspoon kosher salt		

Combine lemon juice, oil, wine, garlic, salt, oregano and pepper in a large sealable plastic bag. Add chicken; seal bag. Turn bag over several times to coat chicken evenly. Marinate in refrigerator for 2 to 4 hours, or as long as 12 hours, turning bag occasionally.

Preheat oven to 350 degrees. Discard 1/3 of beer from can. Remove chicken from marinade and reserve. Place beer can in the center cavity of the chicken and stand upright in roasting pan. Roast chicken for 1 1/2 to 2 hours or until chicken is cooked through, basting frequently with marinade. *Makes 5 to 6 servings.*

Note: May add vegetables to the roasting pan. Toss with vegetable oil and seasonings and place in bottom of pan around chicken.

Baja Burritos

Meat

FILLING

2 to 3 tablespoons
vegetable oil

1 to 1½ pounds chicken
cutlets (about 4)

1 red bell pepper, seeded
and diced

1 yellow bell pepper, seeded
and diced

1 onion, chopped

2 to 4 garlic cloves,
minced

1 (15-ounce) can black
beans, drained
Juice of 1 lemon

1 envelope taco
seasoning mix

1 teaspoon cayenne pepper

AVOCADO SPREAD

3 ripe Hass avocados, pitted,
peeled and cut into chunks

1 small red onion,
finely diced

¼ cup olive oil
Juice of 1 lime

1 tablespoon white vinegar

2 garlic cloves, minced
Salt and pepper to taste

TOPPING

1 red onion, diced

1 ripe Hass avocado, pitted,
peeled and diced

2 plum tomatoes, diced

1 (8-count) package burrito-
size flour tortillas

For the filling, heat oil in a large skillet and cook chicken for about 4 minutes on each side or until cooked through. Let stand until cool. Cut into bite-size strips; set aside. Sauté bell peppers, onion and garlic in remaining oil in the same skillet for 3 to 5 minutes or until tender. Remove from the heat. Stir in chicken, beans, lemon juice, seasoning mix and cayenne pepper; set aside.

For the avocado spread, combine avocados, onion, olive oil, lime juice, vinegar, garlic and salt and pepper to taste in a bowl and mash until smooth; set aside.

For the topping, combine onion, avocado and tomatoes in a bowl.

For each burrito, spread tortilla with avocado spread. Spoon chicken filling and topping down center. Fold bottom of tortilla over filling; fold in two sides, leaving top open. Repeat to form eight burritos. *Makes 8 servings.*

**RASHI MOSCATO
D'ASTI
(WHITE, ITALY)**

Delightfully fresh,
semisweet, with
outstanding floral,
melon, pear, and
tangerine aromas and
flavors that pair well
with lightly flavored
chicken dishes.

OVEN-GLAZED CHICKEN

Meat

1	(3- to 3 1/2-pound) chicken, cut up Garlic powder, onion powder, paprika, salt and pepper to taste	2	onions, chopped
		1 1/4	cups apricot jam
		1/4	cup vinegar
		2	tablespoons soy sauce
2	tablespoons vegetable oil	1	tablespoon each ginger and mustard

Preheat oven to 325 degrees. Place chicken in a roasting pan; sprinkle with garlic powder, onion powder, paprika, salt and pepper. Turn chicken skin side down in the pan; set aside.

Heat oil in a large skillet over medium-high heat and sauté onions for about 15 minutes or until golden brown. Add jam, vinegar, soy sauce, ginger and mustard. Simmer for 5 minutes. Pour over chicken. Bake for 1 hour. Turn chicken skin side up. Bake for 15 minutes or until chicken is cooked through, basting frequently with the pan juices. *Makes 4 to 5 servings.*

GRECIAN CHICKEN

Meat

3	pounds boneless chicken breasts	1	(10-ounce) package frozen artichoke hearts
1	cup all-purpose flour	1	(8-ounce) can tomato sauce
2	to 3 eggs, beaten		
2	cups seasoned bread crumbs	1/2	cup CARMEL VINEYARDS SAUVIGNON BLANC®
3	tablespoons vegetable oil	1	(14-ounce) can MANISCHEWITZ® Chicken Broth
3	pounds leeks, white parts only, sliced		Salt and pepper to taste
1	(14-ounce) can Israeli green olives, sliced		

Preheat oven to 350 degrees. Dredge chicken in flour; dip in eggs, then coat in bread crumbs. Cook in small amount of oil in a skillet until light brown. Arrange in a 9×13-inch baking dish; set aside.

Heat 3 tablespoons oil in a skillet and sauté leeks for about 5 minutes. Add olives, artichokes, tomato sauce, wine, broth and salt and pepper to taste. Simmer for 5 minutes. Let cool slightly. Pour over chicken; cover dish tightly with foil. Bake for 45 minutes or until chicken is cooked through. *Makes 6 servings.*

CRUMB-COATED CHICKEN

Meat

1   (12-ounce) package
   round crackers
1   cup olive oil

1 1/2   teaspoons thyme
1   (3-pound) chicken, cut up
   Honey to taste

Preheat oven to 350 degrees. Crush crackers in a food processor, then spread on a plate. Combine olive oil and 1 teaspoon of the thyme and pour onto another plate. Dip chicken in oil mixture; roll in crackers to coat. Place in a roasting pan; sprinkle with remaining 1/2 teaspoon thyme. Bake, covered, for 1 hour. Drizzle honey over chicken. Continue baking for 15 minutes or until chicken is cooked through. *Makes 4 to 5 servings.*

BALSAMIC CHICKEN

Meat

1   (3-pound) chicken, cut up
2   garlic cloves, crushed
   Salt and pepper to taste
3/4   cup BARON HERZOG
   CABERNET SAUVIGNON®
3   tablespoons red
   wine vinegar
2   tablespoons vegetable oil

1   tablespoon margarine
8   to 10 shallots, peeled and
   cut into halves
3   tablespoons balsamic
   vinegar
1   to 2 tablespoons
   fresh thyme

Rub chicken with garlic and place in a nonmetallic roasting pan. Season with salt and pepper to taste. Combine wine and red wine vinegar in a bowl and pour over chicken. Cover and marinate in refrigerator for 8 to 12 hours.

Preheat oven to 350 degrees. Heat oil and margarine in a skillet over medium-high heat and cook shallots for 5 to 7 minutes or until softened. Add balsamic vinegar and thyme to shallots and mix well. Pour over chicken. Bake, covered, for 45 minutes. Uncover; continue baking for 45 minutes or until chicken is cooked through, basting frequently. *Makes 4 to 5 servings.*

**FREEZING
LEFTOVER WINE**
How many times have you been left with a small amount of wine in the bottle? Pour the unfinished wine by tablespoonfuls into ice cube trays and freeze. When frozen, remove with a knife and store in a sealable plastic bag. Now when you need wine for a sauce, add the frozen wine and you won't need to open a new bottle.

HERB-CRUSTED CHICKEN POTPIE

Meat

“*When you think of chicken potpie, memories of home are usually evoked. We received a recipe with a delicious blend of flavors and a beautiful crust. Close your eyes for your first bite and you will be right back home! Don't be scared by this recipe's length—it's really very easy to make and can be baked as one large family-style potpie or in individual ramekins. The tarragon might not suit children's tastes, so omit it if you like.*”

CRUST

2	cups flour	Dash of salt
1	cup (2 sticks) margarine	1 to 2 tablespoons ice water

For the crust, combine flour, margarine and salt in a food processor and pulse until crumbly. Add ice water and pulse 3 to 4 times. Dough should feel uniformly moist and clump together when pressed. You may need to add additional water. Turn dough out onto large sheet of plastic wrap; shape into large disk. Chill, wrapped in plastic wrap, for 1 hour or up to 2 days.

FILLING

- 5 tablespoons margarine, divided
- 1 cup chopped carrots
- 1 cup chopped celery
- 1 cup chopped leeks
- 1 tablespoon fresh tarragon (optional)
- 1/4 cup flour
- 2 1/2 cups MANISCHEWITZ® Chicken Broth
- 1 cup nondairy creamer or soy milk
- 3 cups leftover roasted or soup chicken, cut into 1/2-inch chunks
- 1 cup frozen baby peas
  Salt and pepper to taste

ASSEMBLY

- 2 to 3 tablespoons fresh herbs (such as dill weed, flat-leaf parsley, bay leaves, chives, rosemary, sage)
- 1 egg yolk
- 1 tablespoon water

ALL ABOUT PARSLEY

The two most popular types of parsley are flat-leaf, or Italian, parsley and curly-leaf parsley. Flat-leaf parsley has a stronger flavor than curly leaf. Parsley freezes well and can be added frozen to soups and stews. When using fresh parsley, add it during the last few minutes of cooking time to preserve its color and flavor.

Fried parsley can be a tasty side dish or garnish. Heat a small amount of vegetable oil in a skillet until very hot. Add flat-leaf or curly-leaf parsley a bit at a time. When the parsley turns bright green, remove and drain on paper towels. Sprinkle with grated Parmesan cheese and serve immediately.

For the filling, heat 2 tablespoons of margarine in a large skillet over medium-high heat and sauté carrots, celery, leeks and tarragon until tender. Remove to a bowl. Melt remaining 3 tablespoons margarine in same skillet over medium heat. Whisk in flour until well blended. Add 2 cups of the broth. Cook for about 1 minute or until well blended, whisking constantly. Add nondairy creamer. Cook for 3 to 5 minutes or until thickened, whisking constantly. (If sauce is too thick, thin with additional broth.) Add sautéed vegetables, chicken, peas and salt and pepper to taste; set aside.

To assemble, preheat oven to 350 degrees. Roll half the dough to an 11-inch circle between two sheets of floured waxed or parchment paper, turning and flouring often. Fit bottom crust into a deep 9-inch pie dish. Pour filling into pie shell. Repeat rolling with second piece of dough. When dough is the desired size, remove top layer of paper and scatter some herbs on dough. Replace top sheet of paper and, using the rolling pin, press them in. Flip over the dough between the sheets, remove the paper and cover the filled pie. Trim the overhang and, using the tines of a fork, seal the edges all around. Poke a knife in a few locations evenly around the top to create vent holes. Combine egg yolk and 1 tablespoon water; brush over top. Bake for 45 minutes or until golden brown. *Makes 6 servings.*

Note: If making individual potpies in ramekins, omit bottom crust. This recipe may be doubled and the baked potpies frozen.

CHICKEN RUBY

Meat

8	chicken breasts	$1/4$	cup chopped onion
$1/2$	cup all-purpose flour	1	teaspoon grated
1	teaspoon salt		orange zest
6	tablespoons margarine	$1/4$	teaspoon ground ginger
2	cups fresh cranberries	$1/4$	teaspoon ground
1	cup sugar		cinnamon
1	cup orange juice		

Preheat oven to 350 degrees. Dredge chicken in mixture of flour and salt to coat. Heat margarine in a large skillet and brown chicken, turning once.

Meanwhile, combine cranberries, sugar, orange juice, onion, orange zest, ginger and cinnamon in a saucepan. Bring to a boil.

Place chicken in a large baking dish. Pour cranberry mixture over chicken. Bake, covered, for 45 minutes to 1 hour or until chicken is cooked through. Serve with seasoned rice or noodles. *Makes 8 servings.*

CHICKEN KABOBS

Meat

	Juice of 5 lemons		Salt and pepper to taste
$1/2$	cup diced onion plus	2	pounds chicken breasts,
	2 onions, cut into chunks		cut into cubes
$1/2$	cup olive oil	3	portobello mushrooms,
8	garlic cloves, crushed		cut into chunks
$2^1/2$	teaspoons zahtar	1	bell pepper, cut into chunks
	seasoning		

Combine lemon juice, diced onion, olive oil, garlic, zahtar seasoning and salt and pepper to taste in a large glass dish. Add chicken, mushrooms, onion chunks and bell pepper. Marinate, covered, in the refrigerator for at least 3 hours. (Marinade should cover all ingredients.)

Alternately, thread chicken and vegetables on skewers; discard marinade. Grill or broil kabobs for 5 to 7 minutes on each side or until chicken is cooked through. Serve on a bed of rice. *Makes 6 to 8 servings.*

COOKING WITH GARLIC

A common ingredient in a wide range of dishes, from salad dressings to stir-fries, garlic is even easier to work with than you may think.

What to look for
Each bulb, or head, of garlic contains a cluster of cloves that are connected at the root but separated by papery skins. Look for firm heads covered with dry, unblemished skins. Avoid bulbs with soft spots or green shoots protruding from the top, a sign of age. ➤

LACQUERED CHICKEN

Meat

1 (3¹/₂- to 4-pound) chicken, cut up	Paprika
3 small onions, cut into eighths	1 cup orange juice
8 garlic cloves, crushed	1 cup WEINSTOCK CABERNET SAUVIGNON®
Salt and pepper to taste	¹/₄ cup honey
	¹/₄ cup soy sauce

Preheat oven to 400 degrees. Place chicken and onions in a roasting pan. Rub garlic over chicken; season with salt and pepper to taste. Sprinkle with paprika to coat. Combine orange juice, wine, honey and soy sauce in a bowl. Spoon over chicken. Bake for 1¹/₂ hours or until skin is crisp and dark brown and chicken is cooked through, basting frequently. *Makes 6 servings.*

ROASTED CHICKEN WITH GARLIC CONFIT

Meat

The high oven temperature used in this chicken recipe makes it different from usual roasting methods. It's perfect if you don't have a lot of time and produces wonderful, crunchy results.

1 (3-pound) chicken, cut up
Salt and pepper to taste
³/₄ cup olive oil, plus more to taste
12 garlic cloves, peeled (about 1 head)

Position oven rack in the upper third of the oven. Preheat oven to 500 degrees. Sprinkle chicken with salt and pepper to taste. Drizzle with olive oil to taste. Roast for 25 minutes.

Meanwhile, cook garlic in ³/₄ cup olive oil in a 1¹/₂-quart heavy saucepan over low heat for about 15 minutes or until garlic is very tender but not golden. Strain garlic, reserving oil. Mash garlic in a bowl with 1 tablespoon strained oil. Spread over chicken. Continue baking for 10 minutes or until chicken is cooked through. *Makes 6 servings.*

Note: Use reserved oil for salads or over steamed vegetables. Store oil in refrigerator.

How to store
Unpeeled garlic will keep for up to three weeks when stored in an open container in a cool, dry place; do not refrigerate.

Prepping and cooking
Garlic that's crushed, chopped, or minced gives dishes a sharper flavor than whole or sliced cloves. Use a garlic press to release the maximum amount of oil from garlic for use in sauces, stews, and marinades. Cooking mellows all cuts.

Getting the most from garlic
Sauté garlic over low heat to bring out its piquant flavor. Draw out its sweetness by boiling it in liquid over low heat. Roast garlic for that delicious, caramelized taste. If you want only the suggestion of garlic in cream sauce, rub the pan or a wooden mixing spoon with a cut clove instead of adding it to the sauce.

Easy Everyday Entertaining Ideas

Everyone can make a table look a little more
special with these easy floral arrangements.

Fruit and Flowers

Fill a bowl, basket, or vase with a single type of fruit, such as apples, pears, lemons, limes, peaches, plums, or grapes. Dress up the arrangement with flowers if desired. Take about a dozen flowers and cut the stems very short. Tie two or three flowers together, forming small clusters, and insert them randomly into the open spaces between the fruit. See page 21.

Fluted Glasses Filled with Flowers

Take four to five large or small drinking glasses with fluted sides and cluster four or five flowers in each. Trim the flower stems shorter than the glasses so only the tops of the flowers are showing. See page 50.

Floral Dessert Display

A nice, simple way to dress up your dessert table is to place one large flower in the center of a bundt or tube cake. This is an easy yet beautiful presentation.

Floral Napkin Rings

Tie a ribbon around each napkin, selecting a color that complements your tablecloth. Insert a flower in the center of the bow, choosing a flower that coordinates with the napkin and ribbon colors. Try highlighting a flower from your centerpiece. See page 137.

Sand Pails Filled with Flowers

Take a few colored sand pails and fill them with your favorite summertime flower. These are great centerpieces for a summer table. Scatter some sand and shells around the pails to create a beach feeling. See page 123.

Stacked Table with Flowers

It's easy to set up a professional-looking buffet table. Arrange several different size boxes on a table and drape them with the same or coordinating fabrics. Place a large, pretty bottle or jug filled with several long-stemmed flowers behind, beside, or on each box. The contrast of varying heights, flowers and fabrics will be stunning! Save all your tall bottles. See page 283.

Gourds and Nuts

For a fall centerpiece, arrange a grouping of gourds, squash, and eggplant and accent it with burgundy and chocolate dahlias. Use an autumn-colored cloth and spread a variety of unshelled nuts around the table. Accent the table with tall, fat candles in fall colors. See page 89.

A feast for the eye as well as the appetite. Clockwise from center:
Apricot Glazed Turkey 104 • Leek and Mushroom Stuffing 214
Crunchy Top Pumpkin Bread 207 • Fall Starburst 200 • Traditional Chestnut Stuffing 215
Sweet Potato Purée with Almond Streusel 197

**BARON HERZOG
ROSÉ OF CABERNET
SAUVIGNON
(ROSÉ, CALIFORNIA)**
Bright, fresh, and fruity,
with a soft feel and
excellent balance that
matches nicely with
tangy poultry dishes.

HAWAIIAN SCHNITZEL

Meat

Coat chicken cutlets
with egg and bread
crumbs and brown in oil
as directed in Saucy
Chicken Cutlets. Place in
a 9×13-inch roasting
pan. Omit remaining
ingredients. Combine
1 (20-ounce) can
undrained crushed
pineapple, 3/4 cup
ketchup, 1/4 cup packed
brown sugar, 1/4 cup red
wine and 1/2 green bell
pepper, chopped. Pour
over cooked cutlets and
warm before serving.

LEMON-PISTACHIO CHICKEN SLICED OVER GREENS

Meat

3/4 cup cornflakes	4 (4-ounce) boneless skinless
2 tablespoons pistachios,	chicken breasts
toasted and chopped	1 tablespoon honey
1 teaspoon grated	Salad greens
lemon zest	Lemon juice and olive oil
1/2 teaspoon salt	to taste
1/2 teaspoon pepper	

Combine cornflakes, pistachios, lemon zest, salt and pepper in a food processor and process into crumbs; set aside.

Pound chicken into 1/4-inch thickness. Brush with honey and dredge in crumb mixture. Spray a skillet with nonstick cooking spray. Add chicken. Sauté over medium-high heat for 5 minutes per side or until chicken is cooked through. Cut into strips. Serve chicken over salad greens tossed with equal parts of lemon juice and olive oil. *Makes 4 servings.*

SAUCY CHICKEN CUTLETS

Meat

6 chicken cutlets	2 onions, sliced
3 eggs, beaten	1 (12-ounce) jar apricot
2 cups bread crumbs	preserves
Vegetable oil	1 cup ketchup
1 pound mushrooms, sliced	3 tablespoons dark
1 red bell pepper, sliced	brown sugar
1 yellow bell pepper, sliced	

Preheat oven to 350 degrees. Dip chicken in eggs then coat in bread crumbs. Fry in small amount of oil in a skillet over medium-high heat for about 3 minutes per side. Remove to a 9×13-inch roasting pan. Sauté mushrooms, bell peppers and onions in same skillet until tender, adding more oil if needed. Arrange over chicken. Combine preserves, ketchup and brown sugar in a small saucepan. Bring to a boil. Pour over chicken and vegetables. Bake, covered, for 45 minutes or until chicken is cooked through. *Makes 6 servings.*

GRILLED LUAU CHICKEN

Meat

This dish was a unanimous favorite at the poultry testing. It's simple to prepare, yet delicious and elegant.

Marinade (your favorite store-bought variety)	$^1/_2$ cup olive oil
	$^1/_4$ cup red wine vinegar
2 pounds boneless skinless chicken breasts	2 scallions, chopped
	2 tablespoons sugar
1 pound asparagus spears	2 garlic cloves, crushed
2 heads Boston lettuce	1 teaspoon soy sauce
1 (6-ounce) can mandarin oranges, drained	2 tablespoons pine nuts

Marinate chicken. Grill for 3 to 5 minutes per side or until cooked through. Cut into 1-inch strips; set aside. Steam asparagus; drain. Cut into 3-inch pieces. Layer lettuce leaves, asparagus, oranges and chicken on a platter. Just before serving, combine oil, vinegar, scallions, sugar, garlic and soy sauce in a bowl. Pour over chicken. Sprinkle with pine nuts and serve at room temperature.
Makes 6 to 8 servings.

HONEY-GINGER CHICKEN

Meat

12 scallions, white and green parts, coarsely chopped	$^3/_4$ cup low-sodium soy sauce
	$^3/_4$ cup honey
1 (6-inch) piece fresh ginger, peeled and chopped (about 1 cup)	$^1/_4$ teaspoon five-spice powder
	Freshly ground pepper to taste
12 garlic cloves, minced	2 (3-pound) chickens, cut up

Preheat oven to 350 degrees. Combine scallions, ginger, garlic and 6 tablespoons of soy sauce in a food processor and process for 2 minutes. Add remaining 6 tablespoons of soy sauce, honey, five-spice powder and freshly ground pepper to taste and process until well mixed. Combine chicken and honey mixture in a large bowl and toss to coat. Place chicken skin side down in a large baking dish ($1^1/_2$ to 2 inches deep). Spoon honey mixture over chicken. Bake for 45 minutes. Turn chicken over and baste with honey mixture. Continue baking for 45 minutes or until chicken is cooked through. Serve hot or cold with rice and a platter of steamed green vegetables, such as snow peas, broccoli or spinach. *Makes 12 servings.*

BARBECUE MARINADE FOR CHICKEN
Parve

Combine 1 garlic clove, $^1/_4$ cup chopped onion, 3 tablespoons sugar, $^1/_4$ cup ketchup, 5 tablespoons vinegar, 2 tablespoons Worcestershire sauce, $^1/_2$ teaspoon salt and $^1/_2$ teaspoon pepper in a saucepan. Cook over low heat for 5 minutes. Marinate chicken in the mixture for 1 to 3 hours. *Makes about $1^1/_4$ cups.*

STICKY SOLUTION
Coat measuring cups or spoons with nonstick cooking spray, and honey will easily slide out instead of staying behind. This also works with other sticky ingredients, such as syrup, molasses and peanut butter.

PIQUANT MARINADE

Parve

Process 2 peeled garlic cloves in a food processor fitted with a steel blade for about 8 seconds. Add $1/2$ cup vegetable oil, $1/2$ cup dry red wine, $1/4$ cup soy sauce, 2 tablespoons ketchup, 1 tablespoon curry powder, 1 teaspoon pepper, $1/4$ teaspoon ginger and chili powder to taste and process until blended. Marinate chicken or meat for at least 12 hours or up to 24 hours in the refrigerator, turning once or twice to marinate evenly. *Makes about 1$1/2$ cups.*

HONEY MUSTARD MARINADE

Parve

Combine 1 cup honey, $1/2$ cup brown mustard and 1 teaspoon ginger (optional) in a bowl and mix well. Pour over chicken and marinate. *Makes 1$1/2$ cups.*

CHICKEN MONTEREY

Meat

$3/4$	cup all-purpose flour	1	pound mushrooms, sliced
2	teaspoons salt	2	cups MANISCHEWITZ®
$3/4$	teaspoon tarragon		Chicken Broth
1	(3-pound) chicken, cut up	3	to 4 tablespoons CARMEL
6	tablespoons margarine, divided		777® Orange Brandy

Preheat oven to 325 degrees. Combine $1/2$ cup of flour, salt and tarragon in a bowl. Coat chicken in flour mixture. Melt 2 tablespoons of margarine in a large skillet over medium-high heat and sauté chicken until brown on both sides. Remove to a roasting pan; set aside.

Sauté mushrooms in the same skillet until tender; spoon over chicken. Melt remaining 4 tablespoons margarine in same skillet. Whisk in remaining $1/4$ cup flour and broth. Cook until smooth and thickened, whisking constantly. Stir in liqueur. Pour over chicken. Bake, covered, for 1 hour or until chicken is cooked through. *Makes 4 to 5 servings.*

MUSHROOM-STUFFED CHICKEN BREASTS

Meat

2	tablespoons plus $1/3$ cup vegetable oil		Salt and pepper to taste
		2	egg whites, beaten
4	ounces fresh mushrooms, chopped	$1/4$	teaspoon rosemary
		$1/4$	teaspoon sage
$1/4$	teaspoon salt Several tablespoons plus $1/4$ cup bread crumbs	2	teaspoons chopped fresh parsley
6	boneless skinless chicken breasts	$1/2$	cup BARON HERZOG CHENIN BLANC® dry white wine

Preheat oven to 350. Heat 2 tablespoons oil in a skillet and sauté the mushrooms until tender. Stir in $1/4$ teaspoon salt and enough bread crumbs to absorb the oil.

Season chicken on both sides with salt and pepper. Spoon 1 to 2 tablespoons filling on each chicken breast. Roll to enclose filling and secure with wooden picks. Dip each roll into egg whites then coat with remaining $1/4$ cup bread crumbs. Arrange in a greased shallow baking pan. Combine remaining oil, rosemary, sage and parsley in a small bowl. Pour over chicken. Bake, uncovered, for 25 minutes. Pour wine over chicken and bake for 15 minutes longer, basting occasionally. *Makes 4 servings.*

ROLLED CHICKEN FILLED WITH PASTRAMI

Meat

1 cup seasoned bread crumbs
1 cup crushed cornflakes
1 teaspoon onion powder
1 teaspoon garlic powder
1 teaspoon salt
1/2 cup mayonnaise
1/4 cup white horseradish sauce
1/4 cup Dijon mustard
2 pounds chicken cutlets, pounded thin
8 ounces thinly sliced deli pastrami
Duck sauce

Preheat oven to 350 degrees. Combine bread crumbs, cornflake crumbs, onion powder, garlic powder and salt on a plate; set aside.

Combine mayonnaise, horseradish sauce and Dijon mustard in a bowl. Spread a thin coating on 1 side of each cutlet; top with 2 to 3 pastrami slices. Roll up cutlets and secure with wooden picks. Spread tops of roll-ups with mayonnaise mixture; roll in crumb mixture to coat. Place rolls seam side down in a 9×13-inch baking dish. Bake for 30 to 40 minutes or until chicken is cooked through. *Makes 6 to 8 servings.*

Note: For a sweeter flavor, pour duck sauce over chicken rolls to cover and follow cooking directions above. Another variation is to fry the chicken rolls first. Brown them on all sides and then bake for an additional 10 minutes at 350 degrees.

SLIGHTLY THAI MARINADE
Parve

Combine 3 tablespoons soy sauce, 2 tablespoons minced garlic, 1 tablespoon each minced fresh ginger, chopped cilantro, lime juice, vegetable oil and 1 to 2 teaspoons chili flakes in a bowl and mix well. *Makes 1/2 cup.*

CHINESE MARINADE
Parve

Process 4 scallions and 2 garlic cloves in a food processor until minced. Add 2 tablespoons soy sauce, 2 tablespoons dry sherry or wine, 2 tablespoons honey, 1 tablespoon ketchup, 1 tablespoon chili sauce and salt and pepper to taste and process until blended. Makes enough marinade for 3 pounds of chicken or meat. Broil or grill marinated chicken or meat, brushing often with reserved marinade. *Makes about 1/2 cup.*

ROSEMARY CHICKEN

Meat

1   (3-pound) chicken, cut up
1/2   cup packed dark brown sugar plus
      additional for browning (optional)
1/4   cup honey
1/4   cup warm water
2   tablespoons vegetable oil
1   teaspoon salt
1   teaspoon pepper
1   teaspoon grated orange zest
1/2   teaspoon garlic powder
1/2   teaspoon onion powder
3   sprigs of fresh rosemary plus fresh rosemary sprigs for garnish
2   plum tomatoes, cut into rounds for garnish

Preheat oven to 375 degrees. Arrange chicken in a 9×13-inch baking dish. Combine 1/2 cup brown sugar, honey, water, oil, salt, pepper, orange zest, garlic powder and onion powder in a bowl and mix well. Pour over chicken. Top with 3 rosemary sprigs.

Bake, covered, for 35 minutes. Uncover chicken. Continue baking for 40 minutes or until golden brown and chicken is cooked through. (If chicken has not browned well after 25 minutes, sprinkle with additional brown sugar during last 10 to 15 minutes of baking.) Remove and discard rosemary sprigs. Garnish with tomatoes and fresh rosemary sprigs. *Makes 6 servings.*

Georgian Pomegranate Chicken

. . . .

Meat

2   cups diced white onions (about 2 medium)
2   cups diced red onions (about 2 medium)
1¹/2 cups chopped fresh cilantro, divided
10 garlic cloves, sliced or pressed
1   teaspoon sweet paprika
1   teaspoon cayenne pepper
1   teaspoon black pepper
3   tablespoons tamarind paste or prune butter
1   cup pomegranate juice
2   tablespoons tomato paste
1¹/2 teaspoons salt
2   (3-pound) chickens, cut up and skin removed
    Seeds of ¹/2 pomegranate for garnish

Combine onions, 1 cup of cilantro, garlic, paprika, cayenne pepper and black pepper in a Dutch oven. Stir in tamarind paste, pomegranate juice, tomato paste and salt. Add chicken and ladle sauce over top.

Cook, covered, over medium-high heat for 10 minutes. Reduce heat to low. Cook for 1 hour and 20 minutes or until chicken is cooked through. Remove chicken and sauce to a serving platter. Garnish with remaining ¹/2 cup cilantro and pomegranate seeds. Serve hot. *Makes 8 to 10 servings.*

Lemon Wine Marinade
Parve

Combine 1¹/2 cups vegetable oil, ³/4 cup soy sauce, 2 tablespoons Worcestershire sauce, 2 tablespoons dry mustard, 1 cup dry red wine, 2 teaspoons parsley flakes, ¹/3 cup lemon juice and salt and pepper to taste. Use to marinate meat for a few hours or overnight. *Makes 3³/4 cups.*

Cutlet Marinade
Parve

Combine 1 cup teriyaki sauce and 1 tablespoon chili powder in bowl. Marinate chicken cutlets in the mixture and grill to desired degree of doneness. *Makes about 1 cup.*

Shiitake Ginger Chicken

Meat

1 (3-pound) chicken, cut up
2 to 3 tablespoons vegetable oil
1 tablespoon minced shallot
1 tablespoon minced fresh ginger
3 garlic cloves, minced
4 ounces shiitake mushrooms, sliced
1/2 cup dry sherry
2 tablespoons dark soy sauce
1/2 teaspoon five-spice powder
   Salt and freshly ground pepper to taste
2 tablespoons finely chopped scallions
1 tablespoon chopped fresh cilantro

Preheat oven to 350 degrees. Place chicken in a baking dish. Bake for 45 minutes to 1 hour or until light brown.

Meanwhile, heat oil in a large skillet over medium-low heat and cook shallot, ginger and garlic for about 1 minute. Add mushrooms. Increase heat to medium-high. Sauté until the mushrooms begin to brown. Stir in sherry, soy sauce and five-spice powder. Pour over chicken. Continue baking for 30 to 45 minutes or until juices run clear and chicken is cooked through, basting with pan juices. Season with salt and freshly ground pepper to taste.

Remove chicken to a warm serving platter. Stir scallions and cilantro in pan juices; pour over chicken. Serve immediately.
Makes 4 to 6 servings.

GINGER AT THE READY

Cut unpeeled fresh ginger into 1-inch pieces and place in zip-top freezer bags. Store in the freezer for one month or longer.

SUN-DRIED TOMATO AND ARTICHOKE CHICKEN

Meat

Serve this dish as an entrée or slice the chicken into strips and serve over mixed greens as an appetizer.

2 to 3 pounds chicken cutlets	2 garlic cloves, minced
1 cup TEAL LAKE SAN GIOVESE® red wine	1 teaspoon basil
3/4 cup packed dark brown sugar	1 medium to large onion, sliced
1/2 cup plus 1 tablespoon olive oil, divided	2 (14-ounce) cans artichoke hearts, drained and cut into halves
1/4 cup fresh parsley	1 (7-ounce) jar oil-packed sun-dried tomatoes
1/4 cup balsamic vinegar	
3 bay leaves, crushed	

Preheat oven to 375 degrees. Place chicken in a large rectangular baking pan; set aside.

Combine wine, brown sugar, 1/2 cup olive oil, parsley, vinegar, bay leaves, garlic and basil in a bowl. Pour over chicken. Bake, covered, for 45 minutes.

Heat remaining 1 tablespoon olive oil in a skillet and sauté onion until translucent. Add artichokes and sun-dried tomatoes. Spoon over chicken. Continue baking, covered, for 15 minutes or until chicken is cooked through.
Makes 6 to 10 servings.

Note: Dry-packed sun-dried tomatoes, reconstituted in boiling water and drained, may be substituted for oil-packed tomatoes.

TOMATO TIP

Whole peeled tomatoes
are perfect in soups,
stews, and meat sauces.
Crushed tomatoes make
a great base for tomato
sauce. Add a little
garlic, pepper, and
oregano for a quick
pasta sauce.

BACKSBERG
CHARDONNAY
(SOUTH AFRICA)

Off-dry, medium-bodied
wine with lively apple,
pear, and melon flavors
that pair well with
medium-flavored
poultry dishes.

TOMATO AND WINE-INFUSED CHICKEN

Meat

$^1/_2$ cup all-purpose flour	1 large onion, chopped
Salt, pepper and garlic powder to taste	8 ounces mushrooms, sliced
1 (3-pound) chicken, cut up	1 cup tomato sauce
3 to 4 tablespoons vegetable oil	$^1/_2$ cup HAMASREK CHARDONNAY®

Combine flour, salt, pepper and garlic powder. Remove and discard skin from chicken, if desired. Dredge chicken in flour mixture to coat.

This recipe may be prepared on top of the stove or in the oven:

Stove-Top Method: Heat oil in a skillet. Add coated chicken. Cook on both sides until brown. Remove from pan; set aside. Sauté onion and mushrooms in same skillet for about 5 minutes or until tender. Stir in tomato sauce and wine. Return chicken to pan; spoon sauce over chicken. Cook, covered, over medium-low heat for about 45 minutes or until chicken is cooked through.

Oven Method: Preheat oven to 350 degrees. Place coated chicken in a lightly greased roasting pan. Bake for 45 minutes. Heat oil in a skillet and sauté onions and mushrooms for about 5 minutes or until tender. Stir in tomato sauce and wine. Cook until heated through. Pour over chicken. Continue baking, covered, for 45 minutes to 1 hour or until chicken is cooked through. *Makes 6 servings.*

Linguini with Chicken, Leeks and Tomatoes

Meat

This dish is also terrific as an appetizer.

1	pound boneless skinless chicken breasts	1	(28-ounce) can whole tomatoes, undrained and chopped
1	teaspoon salt	2	cups (or more) MANISCHEWITZ® Chicken Broth
1	teaspoon garlic powder		
1	teaspoon paprika		
1	teaspoon pepper	1	tablespoon chopped fresh basil, or 1 teaspoon dried basil
1/2	teaspoon cumin (optional)		
1 1/2	tablespoons margarine		
3 to 4	leeks, washed and cut into 1-inch slices	8	ounces uncooked linguini, broken into 2-inch pieces
6	garlic cloves, minced		

Pound chicken to 1/4 inch thick between sheets of plastic wrap. Combine salt, garlic powder, paprika, pepper and cumin; sprinkle over both sides of chicken. Melt margarine in a skillet over medium-high heat. Add chicken. Cook for 2 to 3 minutes per side or until light brown. Remove from the skillet. Slice chicken into thin strips; set aside.

Add leeks and garlic to the same skillet. Sauté over medium-high heat for about 3 minutes or until tender. Add undrained tomatoes, broth and basil. Bring to a boil. Add linguini and chicken. Cook, covered, over medium-low heat for about 15 minutes or until pasta is al dente. (If liquid is absorbed before pasta is tender, add more broth.) *Makes 4 servings.*

Scrubbing Leeks

Leeks need to be washed carefully to remove the grit and sand trapped between their layers. To loosen the dirt, slice leeks lengthwise into halves and soak for 15 minutes in enough cold water to cover. Remove from water; rinse, pat dry, and chop.

DUCK À L'ORANGE

Meat

This is a timeless classic to be enjoyed by all.

**BARKAN CLASSIC
PETITE SYRAH
(ISRAEL)**

Lively blackberry and smokey character; firm, with a bright, clean feel that's best with full-flavored poultry entrées.

1 (5-pound) duckling	3/4 cup ALTOONA HILLS CHARDONNAY® dry white wine
1 orange, cut into quarters	
1 tablespoon garlic powder	2 tablespoons orange marmalade
1 tablespoon ginger	
1 tablespoon paprika	2 teaspoons duck pan juices
Salt and pepper to taste	
1 (6-ounce) can frozen orange juice concentrate	

Preheat oven to 400 degrees. Rinse duck and pat dry. Trim any extra fat from duck. Prick all over through the skin with a fork. Place orange quarters in cavity. Combine garlic powder, ginger, paprika and salt and pepper to taste in a small bowl. Rub over entire surface. Place breast side down in a roasting pan. Roast for 1¼ hours, pricking skin with fork every 15 to 20 minutes to release fat.

Meanwhile, melt orange juice concentrate in a saucepan. Stir in wine, marmalade and pan juices. Simmer until smooth. Turn duck breast side up. Pour sauce over duck. Continue roasting for 35 to 45 minutes or until duck tests done, basting frequently.

Makes 4 servings.

TARRAGON-STUFFED CORNISH HENS

Meat

2   to 3 tablespoons
    vegetable oil
1/2 cup minced onion
2   (6-ounce) packages long
    grain and wild rice mix
3   cups MANISCHEWITZ®
    Chicken Broth or bouillon
1   cup water
2   (2- to 2¹/₂ -pound)
    Cornish game hens

1   garlic clove, cut into halves
1/2 cup (1 stick) margarine
1   tablespoon tarragon
1   tablespoon fresh
    parsley, minced
1   cup BARON HERZOG
    CHENIN BLANC® (optional)

Heat oil in a skillet and sauté onion. Add both packages of rice mix. Sauté for 1 minute. Bring broth and water to a boil in a saucepan. Add rice mixture. Reduce heat to low. Simmer, covered, until rice is tender and liquid is absorbed.

Preheat oven to 350 degrees. Rub skin of each hen with garlic. Stuff cavities with rice mixture. Place hens in a baking dish. Melt margarine in a small saucepan. Add tarragon and parsley and mix well. Brush over hens and pour wine into the roasting pan. Roast for 1¹/₂ to 2 hours or until hens test done, basting every 15 minutes with tarragon mixture. *Makes 4 to 6 servings.*

SQUASH AND APPLE-STUFFED TURKEY BREAST

Meat

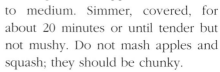

5 tablespoons olive oil, divided

2 small leeks, washed and thinly sliced (3/4 cup)

1 small onion, finely chopped (1/2 cup)

2 garlic cloves, minced (2 teaspoons)

1 pound butternut squash, peeled and cut into 1/2-inch cubes (2 cups)

2 Granny Smith apples, peeled, cored and cut into 1/2-inch cubes (2 cups)

1 (5-pound) skin-on turkey breast, butterflied (see Note below)

2 teaspoons kosher salt

1/4 teaspoon pepper

1 cup MANISCHEWITZ® Chicken Broth

1/2 cup HERZOG LATE HARVEST CHENIN BLANC®

Preheat oven to 350 degrees. Heat 3 tablespoons of olive oil in a large skillet over medium-high heat and sauté leeks, onion and garlic for about 4 minutes or until tender. Add squash and apples. Reduce heat

to medium. Simmer, covered, for about 20 minutes or until tender but not mushy. Do not mash apples and squash; they should be chunky.

Stuff turkey breast with squash mixture. Seal pocket with metal skewers or wooden picks. Rub turkey with salt and pepper and brush skin with the remaining 2 tablespoons olive oil. Place in a roasting pan. Pour broth and wine over turkey. Roast for 1 1/2 to 2 hours or until a meat thermometer inserted into the thickest part registers 170 degrees and juices run clear, basting frequently. Remove from pan; let stand for 10 minutes. Remove skewers or wooden picks before slicing. *Makes 12 servings.*

Note: Ask your butcher to cut the turkey breast for stuffing. If you are making a roulade, ask the butcher to double butterfly the breast to make a large, thin rectangle.

TANGY TURKEY BREAST

Meat

*S*imple and delicious are the best ways to describe this turkey. It will be a real crowd pleaser.

³/4 cup ketchup	1 (4- to 6-pound)
¹/2 cup duck sauce	turkey breast
¹/2 cup garlic sauce	

Combine ketchup, duck sauce and garlic sauce in a bowl and mix well. Place turkey breast side down in a large glass baking dish. Cover with sauce mixture. Marinate, covered, in the refrigerator for 8 to 12 hours.

Preheat oven to 325 degrees. Bring turkey to room temperature. Roast for 20 minutes per pound or until a meat thermometer registers 180 degrees and juices run clear, deducting 15 minutes from the total cooking time. Turn turkey over after about 1 hour and baste frequently. (May be prepared ahead, sliced and chilled. Reheat in sauce when ready to serve.) *Makes 10 to 12 servings.*

TURKEY BURGERS

Meat

1 pound ground turkey breast	¹/4 cup finely chopped mushrooms
1 onion, chopped and sautéed until golden brown	1 egg, lightly beaten
	2 tablespoons onion flakes
¹/4 cup finely shredded carrots	2 tablespoons soy sauce
	Lettuce, red onion slices and tomato slices
¹/4 cup finely shredded zucchini	

Combine turkey, onion, carrots, zucchini, mushrooms, egg, onion flakes and soy sauce in a large bowl with your hands and mix well. Chill, covered, for 1 to 4 hours.

Form turkey mixture into four 3-inch-diameter patties. Grill patties for 4 to 5 minutes per side or until just cooked through. (Patties may also be cooked in a hot skillet sprayed with nonstick cooking spray over medium-high heat.) Serve in buns topped with lettuce, red onion slices and tomato slices. *Makes 4 servings.*

Photograph for this recipe is on page 123.

ROASTING RACKS

A roasting rack, either flat or V-shaped, keeps poultry from sitting in its own juices during roasting. This prevents the bird from becoming soggy on the bottom and possibly falling apart when removed from the pan. If you don't have a roasting rack, shape foil into a ring that the bird can sit on top of, like a nest.

A perfectly roasted chicken should have golden brown skin and juicy meat. Serve on a large platter for an attractive presentation.

APRICOT-GLAZED TURKEY

Meat

APRICOT GLAZE
- 1 cup apricot nectar
- 1 cup apricot preserves
- 1 tablespoon honey
- 1 teaspoon ginger

HERB RUB
- 1/2 cup (1 stick) unsalted margarine, softened
- 3 tablespoons each of chopped fresh thyme and sage, or 1 tablespoon each dried thyme and sage
- 1 teaspoon pepper
- 1/2 teaspoon salt

ONION MIXTURE
- 2 tablespoons unsalted margarine
- 3 large onions, thinly sliced (about 2 pounds)
- 6 large shallots, thinly sliced (about 6 ounces)

TURKEY
- 1 (15- to 18-pound) turkey
  Salt and pepper to taste
- 1 can MANISCHEWITZ® Chicken Broth

For the glaze, combine nectar, preserves, honey and ginger in a small heavy saucepan. Bring to a boil. Reduce heat to medium-low. Simmer for about 15 minutes or until thickened and reduced to 1 1/4 cups; set aside.

For the rub, combine margarine, thyme and sage, pepper and salt in a small bowl; set aside.

For the onion mixture, heat margarine in a large heavy skillet over medium heat and sauté onions and shallots for about 20 minutes or until light brown. (Apricot glaze, herb rub and onion mixture may be prepared one day ahead. Chill, covered, in separate containers. Soften herb rub before using.)

For the turkey, position rack in the lower third of the oven. Preheat oven to 325 degrees. Pat turkey dry with paper towels. Season cavity with salt and pepper. Place in a large roasting pan. Slide hand under breast skin to loosen. Spread half the herb rub under skin and over breast. If stuffing turkey, spoon stuffing into cavity. Spread remaining rub over outside of turkey. Tie legs loosely together. Place turkey breast side down in pan. Roast for 1 1/2 hours, basting occasionally with pan drippings. Add onion mixture, broth and if desired, additional thyme and sage to pan. Pour glaze over the turkey. Continue roasting for about 1 hour or until a meat thermometer inserted into the thickest part of thigh registers 180 degrees and the juices run clear, brushing occasionally with glaze and adding more broth to pan if liquid evaporates. Place turkey on a platter or carving board; tent with foil. Let stand 20 to 30 minutes before carving. Reserve pan drippings for gravy, if desired. *Makes 10 to 12 servings.*

TURKEY PREPARATION

Preparing a Turkey for Roasting

The neck and giblets are usually in the turkey's neck cavity. Remove them and either store in the refrigerator for another use or discard. Wash the whole turkey, inside and out, with cold water. Drain and pat dry with paper towels. Season the turkey with your favorite herbs and spices. Tuck the wings under the shoulders and tie the legs together with kitchen twine, if desired.

- Never brine kosher turkeys or the meat will be soggy.

If you enjoy stuffing cooked inside the turkey, here is what you need to know:

- A stuffed turkey takes longer to roast than a bird that is not stuffed.
- Prepare the stuffing just before placing it inside the turkey.
- Stuff the turkey just before roasting it. Do not stuff a turkey the night before roasting.
- Loosely place the stuffing inside the bird's cavity—do not pack it in tightly.
- The center of the stuffing must be cooked to 165 degrees.

Testing a Turkey

When the innermost part of the thigh reaches 180 degrees, the turkey is done. Place the turkey on a cutting board that allows juices to drain. Let stand for at least 20 minutes before carving.

Carving a Turkey

Breast Meat: Choose from one of the following methods, according to how you want the slices to look:

- For short, thick slices, remove each breast half in one piece. Place skin side up on a cutting board and slice crosswise.
- For long, thin slices, slice parallel to the breastbone from the wing end to the leg end.

Wings: Separate the wings from the shoulders and carve at the joint. Serve wings in one piece.

Legs and Thighs: Pull the legs until you hear the thighs separate from the rest of the turkey. Secure the turkey with a fork and remove the entire leg/thigh sections. Slice the thigh meat off the bone and then slice the meat off the drumsticks, cutting parallel to the bone.

STORING LEFTOVER TURKEY
Refrigerate sliced turkey in an airtight plastic container or sealable plastic bag for up to three days. Refrigerate within two hours of carving. Cooked turkey can be frozen for up to six months. To freeze, tightly wrap the turkey in plastic wrap, then wrap again in heavy-duty foil. A turkey carcass can be refrigerated for up to three days or frozen for up to six months. Store the carcass in a large sealable plastic bag.

MEATS

SAMPLER

FAMILY FRIENDLY
Top-of-the-Rib au Café 108 • Dutch Oven Brisket 109
London Broil 113 • Teriyaki Steak 115 • Succulent Spareribs 117
Sweet-and-Sour Meatballs 117 • Jay's Burgers 119
Slow-Cooking Country-Style Stew 120
Baked Veal Chops with Rice 121
Crusty Meat Loaf 124 • Bistro-Style Pasta Napolitana 124
Quick Lamb Chops 125 • Lamb Stew 129

QUICK AND EASY
London Broil 113 • Teriyaki Steak 115 • Citrus-Glazed Spareribs 116
Succulent Spareribs 117 • Sweet-and-Sour Meatballs 117
Jay's Burgers 119 • Baked Veal Chops with Rice 121
Bistro-Style Pasta Napolitana 124 • Quick Lamb Chops 125

SOPHISTICATED
Pepper-Crusted Roast 111
Cranberry California Roast with Portobello Mushrooms 112
Fillet Split with Port Glaze 113 • Herbed Standing Rib Roast 114
Firecracker Rib-Eye Steaks 116 • Citrus-Glazed Spareribs 116
Rack of Lamb 125 • Cajun Veal Roast with Mango Purée 126
Pan-Seared Veal Chops with Mustard Sage Sauce 127
Stuffed Breast of Veal 128

FREEZES WELL
Top-of-the-Rib au Café 108 • Dutch Oven Brisket 109
Sweet and Savory Brisket with Mushrooms and Caramelized Onions 110
Cranberry California Roast with Portobello Mushrooms 112
Sweet-and-Sour Meatballs 117
Crusty Meat Loaf 124 • Lamb Stew 129

TOP-OF-THE-RIB AU CAFÉ

· ·

Meat

T his is a quick and easy recipe. The beauty of it is that it is so simple to prepare and yet the flavor is memorable.

1/2 teaspoon MAXWELL HOUSE® instant coffee granules	1/2 cup honey
	1/3 cup Worcestershire sauce
	1 tablespoon soy sauce
1/2 cup boiling water	1 garlic clove, minced
1/2 cup ketchup	1 (3- to 4-pound) beef top of
1/2 cup chili sauce	the rib

Preheat oven to 325 degrees. Dissolve coffee granules in boiling water in a heatproof bowl. Stir in ketchup, chili sauce, honey, Worcestershire sauce, soy sauce and garlic. Pour coffee mixture over beef in a baking pan.

Roast, covered, for 2 1/2 to 3 hours. Remove from oven and let stand. Place beef on a serving platter and slice against the grain, reserving the pan drippings. Pour reserved pan drippings into a gravy boat and serve with the beef. *Makes 10 to 12 servings.*

Note: When using coffee in a recipe, try an individual coffee bag rather than instant coffee or brewing a pot. This dish freezes well.

THE FROST FACTOR

As a rule, the fresher food is when you freeze it, the better it will taste when defrosted and eaten. Freezing preserves freshness and essentially puts your food into hibernation. Make sure that your container is airtight and moisture proof. Label all foods and date them prior to freezing them.

Freezing meat The less fatty the meat, the longer it will last
Breads and baked goods The lower the moisture level, the better they will freeze. Always make sure that the baked goods are completely cool prior to freezing them to avoid moisture.
Freezing fruit Fruit should be frozen in a plastic container or plastic bag after it has been sliced and seeded. Fruit will taste just as luscious after freezing, but may be a little softer.

How long can you freeze it?

Vegetables—8 to 10 months	*Chicken or turkey, uncooked*— 9 months
Fruit—6 to 12 months	
Steaks, uncooked—6 to 12 months	*Chicken or turkey, cooked*— 4 to 6 months
Butter—6 to 9 months	*Baked goods*—3 months
Fish, uncooked—6 months	*Soups or stews, cooked*— 2 to 3 months
Roasts, uncooked—4 to 12 months	
Ground meat—3 to 4 months	*Ice cream or sorbet*—2 to 3 months

DUTCH OVEN BRISKET

Meat

The flavor is enhanced if prepared two days in advance.

> 2   tablespoons olive oil
> 6   onions, chopped
> 4   garlic cloves, minced
> 1   (6-pound) beef brisket
>   Salt and pepper to taste
> 1¹/₂ cups BARON ROTHSCHILD HAUT MEDOC®
> 1   cup ketchup
> 1   (10-ounce) can tomato soup
> 2   tablespoons lemon juice
> 2   tablespoons brown sugar
> 1¹/₂ teaspoons GREY POUPON Dijon Mustard
> 1   teaspoon soy sauce

Heat olive oil in a large Dutch oven and sauté onions and garlic for 20 minutes or until onions are golden brown. Remove onion mixture to a bowl using a slotted spoon, reserving pan drippings. Season brisket with salt and pepper and brown on all sides in reserved pan drippings. Simmer, covered, over low heat for 1¹/₂ hours.

Combine wine, ketchup, soup, lemon juice, brown sugar, Dijon mustard and soy sauce in a bowl and mix well. Pour wine mixture and onion mixture over brisket and bring to a boil. Reduce heat to low and simmer, covered, for 1 hour longer or until brisket is tender. Freeze for future use if desired. *Makes 24 servings.*

SUCCESSFUL BRAISING

Pan: Flameproof baking dish with good lid, or heavy saucepan.
Temperature: Must be even.
Meat: Uniform size and shape with no fat.
Flavor: Salt and delicate herbs, such as cilantro, basil, and parsley, should be added at the end. Robust herbs, such as thyme, rosemary, and bay leaves, should be added at the beginning.

Watch the amount of liquid in the pan. Start by bringing the liquid to a boil, then simmer. Some recipes call for searing meats and vegetables before braising to retain flavor and juices. This can be done by sautéing in a skillet so that all sides are brown. Often, braised foods taste best when prepared one day in advance. Chill overnight and skim off all fat before reheating.

For even heating bring to a boil on the stovetop, and then bake in a preheated 325-degree oven for 30 minutes.

SWEET AND SAVORY BRISKET WITH MUSHROOMS AND CARAMELIZED ONIONS

Meat

There are some surprising ingredients that give this dish a wonderfully rich flavor. You may prepare up to two days in advance.

1/2 cup olive oil, divided
1 3/4 pounds onions, cut into halves and sliced
2 pounds mushrooms, trimmed and sliced
1 (5-pound) beef brisket
Salt and pepper to taste
1 3/4 cups MANISCHEWITZ® Chicken Broth

2 tablespoons Worcestershire sauce
1/4 cup ketchup
2 tablespoons dark brown sugar
1 tablespoon all-purpose flour
2 teaspoons MAXWELL HOUSE® instant coffee granules
1/2 teaspoon thyme

Preheat oven to 325 degrees. Heat 1/4 cup of olive oil in a large skillet. Add onions and cook over low heat for 25 minutes or until golden brown, stirring frequently. Remove onions to a bowl using a slotted spoon, reserving pan drippings. Heat 2 tablespoons olive oil and reserved pan drippings in the skillet and sauté mushrooms for 20 minutes or until brown and juices have evaporated. Remove mushrooms to a bowl with onions using a slotted spoon, reserving pan drippings.

Season brisket with salt and pepper. Heat remaining 2 tablespoons olive oil with reserved pan drippings and add brisket fat side down. Cook for 6 minutes on each side or until brown. Remove to a platter.

Spread 1/2 of mushroom mixture in a large roasting pan. Top with brisket fat side up and remaining mushroom mixture. Whisk broth, Worcestershire sauce, ketchup, brown sugar, flour, coffee granules and thyme in a bowl until blended and pour over brisket.

Bake, covered, for 2 hours. Remove cover and spoon pan juices over the brisket and vegetables. Cook, covered, for 45 to 60 minutes longer or until tender. Let stand until cool. Remove brisket to an ovenproof platter and slice against the grain. Spoon gravy and vegetables over brisket. Reheat or cover and chill for future use.
Makes 20 servings.

Pepper-Crusted Roast

Meat

1 (4- to 5-pound) silver tip roast
   Vegetable oil
   Salt to taste
1/2 cup (1 stick) unsalted margarine, softened
2 tablespoons cracked or coarsely ground pepper
4 large garlic cloves, minced
1/2 teaspoon salt
1 red onion, cut into wedges
2 cups beef broth
1 cup BARON HERZOG CABERNET SAUVIGNON®

Position oven rack in bottom third of oven. Preheat oven to 350 degrees. Arrange roast fat side up in a roasting pan. Brush with oil and sprinkle lightly with salt to taste. Combine margarine, pepper, garlic and 1/2 teaspoon salt in a small bowl and spread over top and sides of roast. You may prepare in advance up to this point and store, covered, in the refrigerator. Arrange onion wedges around roast and pour a mixture of broth and wine around roast.

Bake for 2 hours or until a meat thermometer inserted in the thickest portion of roast registers 130 degrees, basting every 20 minutes with pan juices and adding boiling water as needed. Remove roast to a platter and cover loosely with foil. Let stand for 30 minutes. Slice and serve with roasted onion. *Makes 8 to 10 servings.*

PEPPER
When it comes to pepper, it's all a matter of taste. White pepper is milder than black pepper but heavily aromatic. Pepper burns off in the cooking process and its heat is reduced, especially when combined with oils.

CRANBERRY CALIFORNIA ROAST WITH PORTOBELLO MUSHROOMS

Meat

1 cup dry red wine
1 cup MANISCHEWITZ® Chicken Broth
1 cup jellied cranberry sauce
1/4 cup all-purpose flour
1 large onion, sliced
4 garlic cloves, chopped
1 1/2 tablespoons chopped fresh rosemary
1 (4-pound) California roast
Salt and pepper to taste
12 ounces portobello mushrooms, stems and gills removed and caps thinly sliced
1 cup (about 6 ounces) dried cranberries

Preheat oven to 300 degrees. Whisk wine, broth, cranberry sauce and flour in a bowl until blended and pour into a roasting pan. Add onion, garlic and rosemary. Season roast with salt and pepper and arrange fat side up in a roasting pan. Spoon some of wine mixture over top.

Roast, covered with heavy-duty foil, for 2 1/2 hours, basting with pan juices every hour. Add mushrooms and cranberries to roasting pan and roast, covered, for 30 to 45 minutes longer or until roast is tender. Cool at room temperature for 1 hour. Thinly slice roast across the grain and arrange on a serving platter. Spoon sauce over slices. You may prepare up to two days in advance and store, covered, in the refrigerator.
Makes 8 to 10 servings.

FILLET SPLIT WITH PORT GLAZE

Meat

1/2 cup KEDEM® port	1 to 2 pounds minute
1/4 cup balsamic vinegar	steak, split
1 1/2 teaspoons olive oil	Salt and freshly ground
1/2 teaspoon Dijon mustard	pepper to taste

Mix wine, vinegar, olive oil and Dijon mustard in a small saucepan and bring to a boil over high heat, stirring occasionally. Reduce heat to medium-high and boil for 15 minutes or until the liquid is reduced to 2 tablespoons and of a glaze consistency. You may prepare in advance and store, covered, in the refrigerator.

Preheat broiler and line the rack of a broiler pan with foil. Place the steak on the foil and broil 6 inches from heat source for 5 minutes per side for rare. Sprinkle both sides lightly with salt and freshly ground pepper and wrap steak in foil. Let stand for 2 to 3 minutes, depending on the desired degree of doneness. Remove steak to a platter and slice diagonally across the grain. Drizzle with the glaze. *Makes 4 to 6 servings.*

WINE SUBSTITUTES
If you cannot find kosher port, combine one-half cup dry red wine and one-half cup Málaga or sweet red wine in a saucepan and cook over medium heat until reduced by one-half.

LONDON BROIL

Meat

1 (2- to 2 1/2-pound) London broil	1 1/2 tablespoons Worcestershire sauce
4 large garlic cloves, minced	1 tablespoon soy sauce
1/4 cup balsamic vinegar	1 teaspoon oregano
1/4 cup lemon juice	1 teaspoon basil
3 tablespoons GREY POUPON Dijon Mustard	1 teaspoon thyme
2 tablespoons olive oil	1/2 teaspoon red pepper flakes

Place beef in a large sealable plastic bag. Mix garlic, vinegar, lemon juice, Dijon mustard, olive oil, Worcestershire sauce, soy sauce, oregano, basil, thyme and red pepper flakes in a bowl and pour over beef. Seal tightly and turn to coat. Marinate in the refrigerator for 2 to 10 hours, turning once or twice.

Preheat broiler. Drain beef, reserving marinade. Arrange beef in a heavy broiling pan and broil for 7 minutes per side or until desired degree of doneness, basting frequently with reserved marinade. *Makes 4 to 6 servings.*

GREAT PLATE
Marinate and then grill the meat as directed. Then try this pretty presentation.

Arrange your cooked vegetables onto a platter in an attractive pattern, such as a flower, or in alternating colors. Drizzle vegetables with balsamic syrup in big round circles just before serving.

HERBED STANDING RIB ROAST

Meat

This recipe is for special occasions. Although the roast is expensive, it will be worth it once you enjoy the flavor.

1 tablespoon black peppercorns	1 teaspoon chopped fresh rosemary
2 bay leaves, crushed	3 garlic cloves, finely minced
1 tablespoon kosher salt	1 tablespoon olive oil
1 teaspoon chopped fresh thyme	1 (7- to 8-pound) standing rib roast

Grind peppercorns, bay leaves and salt in an electric coffee or spice grinder until it reaches a powdery consistency. Combine peppercorn mixture with thyme, rosemary and garlic in a bowl. Mash the mixture with the back of a spoon until a smooth paste forms; a mortar and pestle is ideal for this step. Stir in olive oil. Rub paste mixture over the surface of roast. Place roast in a roasting pan and chill, covered, for 8 to 24 hours.

Let roast stand at room temperature for 1 hour. Preheat oven to 450 degrees. Arrange roasting pan on middle oven rack and roast for 20 minutes. Reduce oven temperature to 350 degrees and roast for 1 1/2 to 1 3/4 hours longer or until a meat thermometer inserted in center registers 110 degrees. Remove roast to a large serving platter and let stand for 25 minutes. The roast will continue to cook, reaching about 130 degrees for medium-rare.

Makes 8 to 10 servings.

Note: If you do not have a coffee grinder or mortar and pestle, wrap the spices in plastic wrap or place in a sealable plastic bag and pulverize with a meat mallet or hammer.

TERIYAKI STEAK

. . . .

Meat

2	garlic cloves
$1/4$	cup soy sauce
$1/4$	cup pineapple juice
1	tablespoon lemon juice or vinegar
1	tablespoon ketchup
2	tablespoons vegetable oil
2	to 3 tablespoons dark brown sugar
$1/4$	tablespoon paprika
$1/2$	teaspoon ground ginger
	Chopped scallions to taste
1	(2-pound) beef fillet steak

Process garlic in a food processor fitted with a steel blade until minced. Add soy sauce, pineapple juice, lemon juice, ketchup, oil, dark brown sugar, paprika, ginger and scallions and process for 3 to 4 seconds longer. Pour soy sauce mixture over fillet in a shallow dish, turning to coat.

Marinate, covered, in refrigerator for 1 to 10 hours, turning occasionally. Preheat grill or broiler. Drain beef, reserving marinade. Grill over hot coals or broil for 10 minutes, basting with reserved marinade. Turn and grill for 7 minutes longer, basting with remaining reserved marinade. Slice fillet across grain and serve immediately. *Makes 4 servings.*

COOKING WITH KOSHER SALT

What's special about kosher salt? Its coarse, rough grains do not penetrate food, making it perfect for coating the rims of cocktail glasses or for sprinkling on mild foods such as pretzels. Table salt is treated with anti-clumping agents so that it can be absorbed by food.

THAT'S A THINKING CAP!

Many meat recipes recommend that you marinate for an hour or overnight. Place the meat in a large bowl and prepare according to the recipe. A clean unused shower cap, like the ones that are part of the complimentary toiletry kit in hotel rooms, makes a perfect bowl cover.

**BARON HERZOG
ZINFANDEL (RED,
CALIFORNIA)**

A spicy, smoky wine
with plum and pepper
notes and vibrant food-
friendly acidity that
works especially well
with smoked and spicy
meat entrées.

FIRECRACKER RIB-EYE STEAKS

Meat

Begin marinating the steaks one day in advance.

STEAK	RUB
1/2 cup vegetable oil	1 tablespoon paprika
1 onion, thinly sliced	1 1/2 teaspoons cayenne pepper
1 tablespoon garlic powder	1 to 1 1/2 teaspoons salt
1 tablespoon pepper	1/2 teaspoon black pepper
3 (16-ounce) rib-eye steaks	1/2 teaspoon white pepper

For the steaks, mix oil, onion, garlic powder and 1 tablespoon pepper in a 9×13-inch dish. Add steaks and turn to coat. Place the sliced onion over steaks. Marinate, covered, in refrigerator for 8 to 10 hours. Preheat grill to medium-high or preheat broiler. Remove steaks from marinade. Sprinkle both sides of each steak with 1 teaspoon of the rub. Grill or broil for 8 minutes per side for medium-rare. Cut each steak into halves and serve immediately.

For the rub, mix paprika, cayenne pepper, salt, black pepper and white pepper in a bowl. *Makes 6 servings.*

CITRUS-GLAZED SPARERIBS

Meat

3 to 4 pounds beef spareribs	1 cup orange juice
1 cup soy sauce	1 tablespoon minced garlic
1 cup orange marmalade	1 teaspoon ground ginger

Arrange spareribs in a shallow dish. Whisk soy sauce, marmalade, orange juice, garlic and ginger in a bowl and pour over ribs, turning to coat. Marinate, covered, in the refrigerator for 8 to 10 hours, turning occasionally.

Preheat oven to 350 degrees. Remove ribs and marinade to a large roasting pan. Roast for 1 1/2 hours or until spareribs are golden brown and tender, turning halfway through roasting process and basting frequently with marinade. Serve warm or at room temperature. *Makes 4 to 6 servings.*

SUCCULENT SPARERIBS

Meat

3 to 4 pounds beef spareribs	$^1/_2$ cup water
1 (12-ounce) jar chili sauce	1 teaspoon GREY POUPON
1 cup packed dark brown sugar	Dijon Mustard
$^1/_2$ cup ketchup	1 teaspoon lemon juice

Arrange spareribs in an ovenproof roasting dish. Mix chili sauce, brown sugar, ketchup, water, Dijon mustard and lemon juice in a bowl and pour over ribs. Marinate, covered, in the refrigerator for 1 hour or longer, turning occasionally.

Preheat oven to 400 degrees. Roast for 1 to 1$^1/_2$ hours or until ribs are cooked through, basting with marinade occasionally.
Makes 4 to 6 servings.

SWEET-AND-SOUR MEATBALLS

Meat

"This is one of those recipes that is an old staple in everyone's recipe files. We received about seven versions of this recipe, and this is the one that tested the best. We hope this will now become one that holds a special place in your family's recipe files."

2 pounds ground beef	3 (8-ounce) cans tomato
$^1/_2$ cup plain bread crumbs	sauce
2 eggs, lightly beaten	1 (15-ounce) can jellied or
Garlic powder to taste	whole cranberry sauce
Salt and pepper to taste	$^1/_4$ cup lemon juice
3 tablespoons vegetable oil	$^1/_4$ cup packed dark brown
1 onion, chopped (optional)	sugar

Combine ground beef, bread crumbs, eggs, garlic powder and salt and pepper to taste in a bowl and mix well. Heat oil in a skillet over low heat and sauté onion until tender. Stir in tomato sauce, cranberry sauce, lemon juice and brown sugar and cook until cranberry sauce and brown sugar dissolve, stirring occasionally.

Roll beef mixture into desired size meatballs and add to sauce. Cook, covered, for 45 to 60 minutes or until meatballs are cooked through, stirring occasionally. *Makes 6 to 8 servings.*

STAINPROOF YOUR STORAGE CUPS
When storing unused tomato sauce in a plastic container, first spray the container with nonstick cooking spray. This will prevent any discoloration and stains.

WATERCRESS AND HERB SALAD

Parve

Prepare Watercress and Herb Salad by tossing 2 cups packed small watercress sprigs, 2 teaspoons chopped fresh tarragon, 2 teaspoons chopped fresh chives and 2 teaspoons chopped fresh basil in a large salad bowl. Drizzle with a mixture of 2 tablespoons extra-virgin olive oil and 1 tablespoon red wine vinegar. Season to taste with salt and pepper. *Makes 2 servings.*

SAUTÉED SKIRT STEAK WITH CARAMELIZED SHALLOTS

Meat

This steak makes an impressive presentation when served with *Watercress and Herb Salad (sidebar) and roasted potatoes.*

1 tablespoon olive oil	Roasted potatoes (see Note)
1 (10-ounce) skirt steak	Watercress and Herb
Salt and pepper to taste	Salad (sidebar)
3 large shallots, thinly sliced	
1 tablespoon chopped fresh thyme	

Preheat oven to 450 degrees. Heat olive oil in a large ovenproof skillet over high heat. Sprinkle steak with salt and pepper and brown for 1¹/₂ minutes per side. Remove steak to a platter using a slotted spoon, reserving pan drippings.

Sauté shallots in pan drippings for 5 minutes. Add thyme and sauté for 2 minutes longer or until shallots are brown. Return steak and any accumulated juices to skillet. Spoon shallots over steak and place in oven. Arrange roasted potatoes in baking dish and heat in oven.

Roast steak for 5 minutes for medium-rare or until desired degree of doneness. To serve, arrange steak and shallots and any pan juices in the center of a serving platter. Place potatoes on one side of steak and salad on opposite side. Serve immediately. *Makes 2 servings.*

Note: Follow your favorite recipe for roasted potatoes.

JAY'S BURGERS

Meat

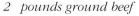

" These burgers were the talk of the town and it was very difficult to
procure the recipe. But we got it. Enjoy!"

2 pounds ground beef	3 eggs, lightly beaten
1 onion, finely chopped	2 tablespoons Dijon mustard
1 cup (about) seasoned bread crumbs	1 teaspoon salt
1/2 cup barbecue sauce	1/2 teaspoon garlic powder
4 to 6 garlic cloves, finely chopped	1/2 teaspoon pepper
	Barbecue sauce to taste

Preheat grill on high. Place ground beef in a bowl. Add onion, bread crumbs, 1/2 cup barbecue sauce, garlic, eggs, Dijon mustard, salt, garlic powder and pepper and knead ground beef until combined. Add additional bread crumbs if needed for desired consistency.

Decrease grill heat to medium. Divide ground beef mixture into six to eight equal portions. Shape each portion into a ball. Arrange the balls on grill rack and flatten with a metal spatula. Spread the patties generously with barbecue sauce and immediately turn. Spread remaining side generously with barbecue sauce. Grill for 10 to 12 minutes and turn. Grill for 8 to 10 minutes longer or until a meat thermometer registers 160 degrees. Serve with a mixture of sautéed onions, mushrooms and garlic. *Makes 6 to 8 burgers.*

Photograph for this recipe is on page 123.

CLEAN HANDS GRILL-GREASING

Here is an innovative way to grease a grill. Cut an unpeeled onion into halves and dip one onion half into vegetable oil. Pierce the oil-coated onion half with a long grill fork and rub the grill rack. This not only greases the grill rack, but it adds a layer of flavor to the grilling process as well.

SLOW-COOKING
COUNTRY-STYLE STEW
. . . .
Meat

This is a nice alternative to cholent on Shabbat. It is also great if you need to prepare dinner in advance. You set it up in the morning and when you come home dinner is ready.

1 cup all-purpose flour	6 potatoes, peeled and cut into chunks
1 teaspoon salt	
1/2 teaspoon pepper	4 ounces pastrami, thinly sliced and chopped
5 pounds beef stew meat, cut into 1-inch pieces	3 bay leaves
3 to 4 tablespoons vegetable oil	1/2 teaspoon thyme
	4 cups boiling water
5 large carrots, peeled and cut into 1-inch slices	1 tablespoon beef bouillon powder
2 large onions, chopped	1 1/2 cups SASLOVE CABERNET SAUVIGNON® red wine
5 garlic cloves, chopped	
8 ounces mushrooms, trimmed and sliced	1 tablespoon hoisin sauce
	1 tablespoon tomato paste

Mix flour, salt and pepper in a large bowl. Add beef in batches and toss to coat. Heat oil in a large skillet over medium-high heat and brown beef in batches. Remove beef with a slotted spoon to a slow cooker, reserving pan drippings. Add carrots, onions and garlic to reserved pan drippings and sauté for 10 minutes or until vegetables are tender. Remove carrot mixture to the slow cooker using a slotted spoon. Add mushrooms, potatoes, pastrami, bay leaves and thyme to beef mixture.

Mix boiling water and bouillon powder in heatproof bowl until dissolved. Mix in wine, hoisin sauce and tomato paste and pour into the slow cooker, adding additional water if needed to cover beef. Cook on High for 1 hour. Reduce heat to Low and cook for 8 hours to overnight. Remove slow cooker ceramic bowl and let stand for 15 minutes or until stew thickens. Remove and discard bay leaves; stir the stew and ladle into individual bowls. *Makes 8 to 10 servings.*

BAKED VEAL CHOPS WITH RICE

Meat

"This was my brother's favorite dinner at home. He enjoyed it so much that he always requested it for his special birthday dinner. Now this recipe has become a favorite in all of our homes."

1 cup uncooked rice	1 large onion, thinly sliced
4 veal chops	2 cups MANISCHEWITZ®
Salt and pepper to taste	Chicken Broth
2 tablespoons vegetable oil	

Preheat oven to 350 degrees. Grease a 9×13-inch baking dish and spread rice over the bottom. Season veal chops with salt and pepper. Heat oil and sauté veal in a skillet for 6 minutes per side. Remove veal chops to prepared baking dish using a slotted spoon, reserving pan drippings.

Sauté onion in reserved pan drippings until golden brown and spoon onion over veal chops. Pour broth over top and cover tightly. Bake for 1 hour or until all the liquid is absorbed. *Makes 4 servings.*

Note: For variety, add a sliced tomato, 10-ounce package of frozen peas or vegetable of choice.

TEAL LAKE SHIRAZ (RED, AUSTRALIA)
Light and distinctive for its spicy cherry and anise flavors, which echo nicely on a soft finish that's ideal with lightly seasoned meat dishes.

Marinade Savvy

Great Steak Marinade

1 cup soy sauce
1/2 cup water
1/4 cup packed dark brown sugar
1/4 cup single-malt scotch
2 teaspoons each ground ginger, garlic salt and Worcestershire sauce
2 garlic cloves, minced

Whisk together and pour over meat. Marinate in the refrigerator for 4 to 6 hours. *Makes about 2 cups.*

Wonderfully Flavorful Marinade

1/2 cup olive oil
1/4 cup Dijon mustard
2 tablespoons lemon juice
1 tablespoon soy sauce
2 garlic cloves, minced
1 teaspoon oregano

Whisk together and pour over meat. Marinate in the refrigerator for 6 to 10 hours. Drain and bring meat to room temperature before grilling. *Makes 1 cup.*

Meat Marinade

1/4 cup dark brown sugar
1/4 cup soy sauce
1/4 cup balsamic vinegar

Whisk together, pour over desired meat and marinate in the refrigerator. *Makes 3/4 cup.*

Give steak and other grillables the royal treatment with marinades, rubs, and sauces!

Overnight marinades with an acidic base, such as lemon or orange, flavor meats throughout. Not enough time to marinate overnight? Rub or baste your meat to give it a burst of flavor on the outside. Oil-based marinades will help keep lean meats from becoming too dry and will add a crispness to their surface.

Sweet Marinade

1/4 cup soy sauce
1/4 cup lemon-lime soda or ginger ale
3 tablespoons honey
3 tablespoons duck sauce
2 teaspoons vinegar

Whisk together and pour over desired meat. Marinate in the refrigerator. *Makes 3/4 cup.*

Honey Soy Soak

1/3 cup honey
1/3 cup soy sauce
1 1/2 teaspoons garlic powder
1 drop of lemon juice

Whisk together, pour over desired meat and marinate in the refrigerator. *Makes 2/3 cup.*

Chimichurri Sauce

1 cup fresh Italian parsley
1 cup fresh cilantro
2/3 cup olive oil
3 tablespoons white wine vinegar
2 tablespoons chopped fresh oregano
2 garlic cloves
1/2 teaspoon crushed red pepper
Salt and pepper to taste

Process the first 7 ingredients in a food processor until almost smooth and season to taste with salt and pepper. *Makes 1 1/4 cups.*

Cajun Rub

6 tablespoons sweet paprika
1/4 cup garlic powder
1/4 cup salt
3 tablespoons onion powder
2 tablespoons cayenne pepper
2 tablespoons black pepper

Mix the ingredients in a jar with a tight-fitting lid and seal tightly. Shake to mix. Rub on chicken or beef. *Makes 1 1/4 cups.*

COME AND GET IT

Get the family outdoors for a burger—you have so many choices!
Pictured on platter: Salmon Burgers 144 • Tuna Steak Burgers 151. In basket:
Jay's Burgers 119 • Veggie Burgers 181 • Turkey Burgers 103. Citrus Water 145

CHATEAU LEOVILLE
POYFERRE
(RED, FRANCE)
Intensely rich aromas of
licorice and chocolate,
full bodied and
accompanied by a
subtle oak flavor and
silky, smooth texture
that's perfect with
steaks and other hearty
meat dishes.

CRUSTY MEAT LOAF

Meat

The texture and flavor of this meat loaf is a refreshing adaptation to the meat loaf you remember.

1 cup beef broth, divided	1 egg, lightly beaten
1/2 cup old-fashioned oats	2 tablespoons coarse grain
1 1/2 pounds chopped beef	Dijon mustard
1/2 cup minced onion	1/2 teaspoon salt
3 tablespoons chopped	1/2 teaspoon freshly
fresh dill weed	ground pepper

Preheat oven to 450 degrees. Grease two 3×6-inch loaf pans. Mix 1/2 cup of broth and oats in a bowl and let stand for 5 minutes. Stir in the next seven ingredients. Divide beef mixture into 2 equal portions and shape each portion into a loaf in prepared loaf pans.

Bake for 25 minutes or until brown and a meat thermometer registers 160 degrees. Remove loaves to a platter using large spatula, reserving pan juices. Combine remaining 1/2 cup broth and reserved juices in saucepan and bring to a boil over high heat. Boil for 2 to 4 minutes or until reduced by half. Drizzle over loaves and serve immediately. *Makes 6 servings.*

BISTRO-STYLE PASTA NAPOLITANA

Meat

This is a family favorite, a great weeknight all-in-one dinner.

4 to 5 tablespoons	3 (8-ounce) cans tomato
vegetable oil	sauce
2 pounds chopped beef	2 cups water
1 large onion, chopped	Garlic powder to taste
16 ounces uncooked rotini,	Salt and pepper to taste
macaroni or small shells	

Heat oil in a skillet over medium-high heat and sauté beef and onion until beef is brown and onion is translucent, breaking meat into small pieces. Stir in pasta, tomato sauce, water, garlic powder and salt and pepper to taste. Simmer, covered, until pasta is tender and most of liquid is absorbed, about 30 to 40 minutes, stirring occasionally. *Makes 8 servings.*

RACK OF LAMB

Meat

This recipe is outrageous! You will want to eat this alone in the kitchen so that you can pick up the bones and make sure you get every morsel of meat!

2 racks of lamb with 5 to 6 bones each (about 4 to 5 pounds)
1/2 cup light olive oil
7 large garlic cloves, crushed

Juice of 1/2 lemon
1 tablespoon chopped fresh rosemary
2 teaspoons kosher salt
1/2 teaspoon red pepper flakes

Arrange lamb in a baking dish. Mix olive oil, garlic, lemon juice, rosemary, salt and red pepper flakes in a bowl and pour over lamb, turning to coat. Marinate, covered with plastic wrap, in the refrigerator for 8 to 10 hours. Preheat oven to 400 degrees. Bring lamb to room temperature and remove cover. Roast for 15 minutes. Reduce oven temperature to 325 degrees and roast for 45 minutes longer or until lamb is desired degree of doneness. *Makes 4 servings.*

QUICK LAMB CHOPS

Meat

3 tablespoons extra-virgin olive oil
5 garlic cloves
2 1/2 teaspoons chopped fresh rosemary

2 1/4 teaspoons salt
1 teaspoon freshly ground pepper
6 shoulder or baby lamb chops

Combine olive oil, garlic, rosemary, salt and pepper in a food processor and process until garlic is finely chopped. Coat lamb chops with garlic mixture and arrange in a single layer on a baking sheet. Chill, covered, for up to 8 hours.

Preheat broiler. Broil 4 to 5 inches from heat source for 4 to 5 minutes per side for medium-rare or to desired degree of doneness. Serve immediately. *Makes 3 to 4 servings for shoulder lamb chops and 2 servings for baby lamb chops.*

CAJUN VEAL ROAST WITH MANGO PURÉE

Meat

A wonderful dish with spicy flavors that enhance the veal. The mango purée and mango garnish add a nice color and are the perfect complement.

1 teaspoon salt	1 (3- to 4-pound) shoulder
1 teaspoon dried	veal roast
minced onion	2¹/₂ teaspoons beef
1 teaspoon garlic powder	bouillon powder
1 teaspoon basil	2¹/₂ cups boiling water
³/₄ teaspoon white pepper	2 large mangos, peeled,
³/₄ teaspoon black pepper	1 chopped, 1 sliced
¹/₂ teaspoon cayenne pepper	2 tablespoons olive oil
¹/₂ teaspoon marjoram	

Preheat oven to 325 degrees. Mix salt, onion, garlic powder, basil, white pepper, black pepper, cayenne pepper and marjoram in a bowl. Make vertical slits 1 inch wide, 1 inch deep and ³/₄ inch apart down the center of the top of the roast. Open the slits and spoon in enough spice mixture to fill the entire opening. Reserve 1 teaspoon of remaining spice mixture and set aside. Rub remaining mixture over surface of roast. Let stand at room temperature for 30 minutes so the flavors can penetrate veal and rub will adhere.

Dissolve bouillon powder in boiling water in a heatproof bowl. Combine 2 cups of bouillon broth and chopped mango in a saucepan. Bring to a boil and reduce heat. Cook for 20 minutes or until thickened, stirring occasionally. Stir in 1 teaspoon reserved spice mixture. Purée with an immersion blender or in a food processor. You may prepare purée in advance and store, covered, in the refrigerator.

Sear roast on all sides in olive oil in a large skillet. Remove roast to a roasting pan. Deglaze skillet with remaining ¹/₂ cup bouillon broth and pour mixture over veal. Roast, covered, for 1¹/₄ hours or until a meat thermometer registers 130 degrees. To serve, slice veal and alternate mango slices with veal on a serving platter. Top with mango purée. *Makes 10 to 12 servings.*

Pan-Seared Veal Chops with Mustard Sage Sauce

Meat

2   (1-inch-thick) veal chops
2   tablespoons minced fresh sage, or 2 teaspoons
     dried rubbed sage, dried rubbed sage to taste and fresh
     sage leaves for garnish, divided
     Pepper to taste
3   tablespoons vegetable oil
2¹/2   tablespoons chopped shallot
¹/3   cup beef broth
1   tablespoon Dijon mustard

Season veal chops with dried sage and pepper to taste. Heat oil in a skillet over medium-high heat and sauté veal for 5 minutes per side or until brown. Reduce heat to medium and cook for 1 minute longer per side for medium-rare or to desired degree of doneness. Remove veal to a platter using a slotted spoon and cover to keep warm, reserving pan drippings.

Sauté shallot in reserved pan drippings for 1 minute. Stir in broth, 1 tablespoon minced fresh sage and Dijon mustard. Bring to a boil and boil for 4 minutes or until thickened, stirring with wooden spoon to dislodge any browned bits on bottom of skillet. Stir in remaining 1 tablespoon minced sage and any accumulated juices from veal. Taste and adjust seasonings. Drizzle sauce over chops on two dinner plates. Garnish with fresh sage leaves. *Makes 2 servings.*

S'FORNO MONASTRELL (RED, SPAIN)
Intensely reddish-purple color, with ripe raspberry and dark cherry aromas, rich raspberry flavor, velvety smooth texture, and a long finish that's great with light- to medium-flavored meat dishes.

TIME AND TEMPERATURE GUIDE FOR ROASTING

Caveat:

Thin pieces of meat and those that include bones cook more quickly.

Lamb and Beef:

Sauté for five minutes or roast at 450 degrees for twenty minutes. Then roast at 325 degrees for fifteen minutes per pound for rare, twenty minutes per pound for medium, or twenty-five minutes per pound for well-done.

Preheat the oven and make sure it reaches roasting temperature before placing food in oven. Use a heavy gauge roasting pan. Baste or turn food every thirty minutes. To roast vegetables evenly, shake them midway through the roasting process.

STUFFED BREAST OF VEAL

. . . .

Meat

1/4 cup (1/2 stick) margarine	4 ounces pastrami, thinly sliced and chopped
1/2 cup chopped celery	1 tablespoon finely chopped fresh dill weed
1 onion, chopped	
2 garlic cloves, chopped	1 teaspoon salt
1/4 cup soy milk or nondairy creamer	1 teaspoon pepper
	1 (5 1/2-pound) veal breast with pocket
2 eggs	
2 cups cubed white bread or challah	2 tablespoons olive oil
	Salt and pepper to taste
8 ounces chicken livers, salted, broiled and chopped	1 cup MANISCHEWITZ® Chicken Broth

Preheat oven to 350 degrees. Heat margarine in a skillet over medium heat and sauté celery, onion and garlic for 4 to 5 minutes or until vegetables are tender. Whisk soy milk and eggs in a bowl until blended. Add celery mixture, bread, chicken livers, pastrami, dill weed, 1 teaspoon salt and 1 teaspoon pepper to egg mixture and let stand at room temperature for 10 minutes or until the liquid is absorbed.

Stuff bread mixture into veal pocket. Coat top of veal with olive oil and sprinkle with salt and pepper to taste. Arrange veal in a roasting pan and pour broth around veal. Roast, covered with foil, for 1 1/2 hours. Remove foil and baste with pan drippings. Roast, uncovered, for 1 hour longer or until a meat thermometer registers 190 degrees. Let stand, covered, for 20 to 30 minutes before slicing. *Makes 10 to 12 servings.*

LAMB STEW

. . . .

Meat

" I grew up in Manhattan on the fourteenth floor of a building. I could always smell the stew being cooked in our apartment by the time the elevator reached the sixth floor; I could not wait to get upstairs!"

2 tablespoons vegetable oil	1 (8-ounce) can tomato sauce
2½ to 3 pounds cubed lamb	1 cup water
3 onions, chopped	1½ teaspoons salt
2 garlic cloves, minced	½ teaspoon oregano
4 or 5 potatoes, cut into chunks (optional)	1 bay leaf
1½ cups sliced carrots (optional)	Pinch of thyme
	Pepper to taste
1 (28-ounce) can whole tomatoes in purée	Hot cooked noodles or rice

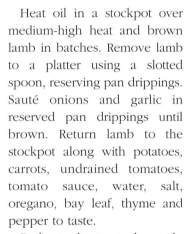

Heat oil in a stockpot over medium-high heat and brown lamb in batches. Remove lamb to a platter using a slotted spoon, reserving pan drippings. Sauté onions and garlic in reserved pan drippings until brown. Return lamb to the stockpot along with potatoes, carrots, undrained tomatoes, tomato sauce, water, salt, oregano, bay leaf, thyme and pepper to taste.

Reduce heat and cook, uncovered, for 1½ hours, stirring occasionally. Cook, covered, for 1 hour longer or until lamb is tender, stirring occasionally. Discard bay leaf and serve over hot cooked noodles or rice.

Makes 6 to 8 servings.

Note: You can substitute cubed beef or veal for the lamb.

FISH

SAMPLER

FAMILY FRIENDLY
Crispy Fried Fish 134 • Tangy Halibut 134 • Roasted Sea Bass 135
Cod Livornese 136 • Baked Salmon with Mustard and Tarragon 138
Pepper-Crusted Marinated Salmon 139
Salmon with Tomatoes and Shallots 139 • Salmon Burgers with Hoisin and Ginger 144
Tilapia Fillets with Pesto Butter 146 • Walnut-Crusted Trout Fillets 146
Trout with Hazelnuts, Lemon and Parsley Brown Butter 147
Tuna Steak Burgers with Ginger Mustard Spread 151

QUICK AND EASY
Roasted Sea Bass 135 • Cod Livornese 136
Oven-Roasted Whole Snapper with Black Olives 137
Baked Salmon with Mustard and Tarragon 138
Pepper-Crusted Marinated Salmon 139 • Salmon with Tomatoes and Shallots 139
Tilapia Fillets with Pesto Butter 146 • Walnut-Crusted Trout Fillets 146
Tuna Steak Burgers with Ginger Mustard Spread 151

SOPHISTICATED
Crunchy Sea Bass with Mango Salsa 132
Roasted Striped Bass with Scallion Cream Sauce 133
Red Snapper Algarve 135 • Oven-Roasted Whole Snapper with Black Olives 137
Carmela's Moroccan Fish 138 • Grilled Salmon Italiano 140
Rosemary Grilled Salmon and Vegetables with Balsamic Syrup 141
Zesty Slow-Roasted Salmon 144 • Sole with Orange Sauce 145
Rice-Stuffed Trout 148 • Seared Tuna Steaks with Wasabi Mayonnaise 149
Grilled Tuna with Herbed Aïoli 150

GREAT FOR THE GRILL
Rosemary Grilled Salmon and Vegetables with Balsamic Syrup 141
Salmon Burgers with Hoisin and Ginger 144
Seared Tuna Steaks with Wasabi Mayonnaise 149 • Grilled Tuna with Herbed Aïoli 150

CRUNCHY SEA BASS WITH MANGO SALSA

Parve

*T*he salsa recipe makes three cups of salsa, so you will have leftovers. Or reduce the measurements to make a smaller amount.

FISH

- 1   pound Chilean sea bass
  Salt and pepper to taste
- 1   tablespoon plus 1 teaspoon extra-virgin olive oil, divided
- 2   garlic cloves, minced
- 1/2   cup chopped macadamia nuts
- 1/4   cup seasoned bread crumbs
- 1/2   teaspoon black pepper
  Pinch of red pepper flakes

FRESH MANGO SALSA

- 2   cups diced peeled mango
- 1/3   cup diced red onion
- 2   tablespoons minced cilantro
- 1   tablespoon minced mint
- 1/2   teaspoon red pepper flakes
- 1   teaspoon minced peeled fresh ginger
- 2   tablespoons olive oil
  Salt and pepper to taste

For the fish, preheat oven to 350 degrees. Season fish with salt and pepper to taste. Heat 1 tablespoon olive oil over medium-low heat and sauté garlic. Add the fish and brown on both sides. Process the nuts, crumbs, 1 teaspoon olive oil, 1/2 teaspoon black pepper and red pepper flakes in a food processor until well mixed. Coat the fish with macadamia mixture. Bake for at least 25 minutes or until cooked through. Spoon the salsa over the hot fish.

For the salsa, combine all salsa ingredients. Season with salt and pepper to taste. (Salsa can be made in advance and refrigerated.) *Makes 2 servings.*

MANGO MANAGEMENT

To prepare a mango, remove a thin slice from one end to stand it easily on the work surface. Remove the skin in long thin strips with a paring knife. Cut down the sides of the flat pit to remove the fruit and trim around the pit. Slice or chop to use.

ROASTED STRIPED BASS WITH SCALLION CREAM SAUCE
. . . .
Dairy

FISH
6 (5-ounce) striped bass
   fillets with skin
   Salt and pepper to taste
1 1/2 tablespoons vegetable oil
1 lemon, cut into 6 wedges
   for garnish
1/4 cup chopped scallions
   for garnish

SCALLION CREAM SAUCE
2/3 cup BREAKSTONE'S
   Sour Cream
2 tablespoons water
4 teaspoons fresh
   lemon juice
1/4 teaspoon salt
1/2 cup sliced scallions
   Pepper to taste

For the fish, preheat oven to 450 degrees. Remove any bones from fish using tweezers. Pat fish dry with a paper towel. Score skin in several places with a thin, sharp knife to prevent fish from curling when cooking, but don't cut all the way through. Season with salt and pepper to taste. Heat oil in a 12-inch skillet over high heat. Sear fish skin side down in two batches until brown and crisp, about 3 to 4 minutes. (Fish will not be fully cooked.) Transfer fish, skin side up, to a greased shallow baking dish. Roast in the oven, uncovered, for 7 to 8 minutes or until fish is just cooked through. Spoon 3 tablespoons of the sauce on each plate or all of the sauce on a platter and top with the fish. Place a wedge of lemon on each fillet and sprinkle with 1/4 cup scallions.

For the sauce, blend sour cream, water, lemon juice, salt and scallions in a blender until mixture turns pale green. Season with pepper to taste. (Sauce can be made 1 to 2 days ahead of time and refrigerated.) *Makes 6 servings.*

Parve

*T*alk about classic! Who didn't grow up on fried fish? What's so nice about this recipe is that the cornmeal makes it really crunchy.

1 cup flour
  Salt, pepper, and garlic powder to taste
2 to 3 eggs
2 to 3 tablespoons water
1 cup seasoned bread crumbs
1 cup cornmeal
2 pounds fish fillets, such as flounder or sole
6 tablespoons vegetable oil

Pour flour on a plate and season with salt, pepper and garlic powder. Beat eggs and water in a flat-bottom bowl. Combine bread crumbs, cornmeal, salt, pepper and garlic powder on another plate. Coat each fish with flour mixture, dip into egg mixture to cover, then evenly coat with bread crumb mixture. Heat oil in a large skillet over high heat and fry the fish for 3 to 5 minutes on each side or until golden brown. *Makes 4 servings.*

TANGY HALIBUT

Parve

"*I* overheard two women discussing this recipe at the supermarket and commenting on how excellent it was. I wrote down the ingredients but didn't get the measurements. Fortunately, one of our most dedicated testers plugged away until she got it just right."

2 garlic cloves
2 shallots
1 1/2 tablespoons capers
1 (9-ounce) jar oil-pack sun-dried tomatoes, drained

1 (6-ounce) jar marinated artichoke hearts, undrained
4 pieces halibut
1 lemon, sliced for garnish

Preheat oven to 500 degrees. Combine garlic, shallots, capers, tomatoes and undrained artichokes in a food processor and process until well combined. Place the fish in a lightly greased roasting pan. Spoon the tomato mixture over the fish. Roast, uncovered, for 15 minutes or until opaque. Garnish with lemon slices. *Makes 4 servings.*

GREEN HERB MAYONNAISE

Try this fragrant herb mayonnaise for dressing up this fried fish.

Combine 1/2 cup chopped fresh dill weed, 1/2 cup chopped fresh parsley, 1/4 cup chopped fresh tarragon leaves, 1 tablespoon drained capers, 1 tablespoon Dijon mustard, 1 cup mayonnaise, 2 tablespoons fresh lemon juice, 1/4 cup water and salt and pepper to taste in a blender or food processor and purée. Refrigerate until ready to serve.

RED SNAPPER ALGARVE

Dairy

*S*triped bass works in place of snapper. Add small red potatoes and black olive bits to the baking dish along with the fish, if you like.

"C" BLANC DU CASTEL (WHITE, ISRAEL) Full-bodied, elegant Burgundy-style white, showing citrus, pineapple, green apple, toasted bread, and fig aromas that are ideal with full-flavored fish entrées.

- 8 (10-ounce) red snapper fillets
- Juice of 1 lemon
- 8 garlic cloves
- 1/2 cup olive oil, divided
- Salt and pepper to taste
- Flour for coating
- 1/2 cup (1 stick) butter, divided
- 12 Vidalia onions, thinly sliced
- 1 tablespoon kosher salt
- 2 teaspoons pepper
- 2 bay leaves

Combine fish, lemon juice, garlic, 1/4 cup of olive oil and salt and pepper to taste and marinate at room temperature for 1 hour. Preheat oven to 500 degrees. Remove fish from marinade, discarding marinade. Coat fish in flour, trying to keep garlic on fish. Heat remaining 1/4 cup olive oil and 3 tablespoons butter in a skillet. Sauté fish for 1 to 2 minutes per side. Fish should not cook through. Arrange fish in a large greased baking dish. Sauté onions with remaining 5 tablespoons butter, salt, pepper and bay leaves in a large skillet until brown and caramelized, stirring occasionally. Top fish with onions and bake for 10 minutes. Discard bay leaves and serve fish.
Makes 8 servings.

ROASTED SEA BASS

Parve

*Y*ou can flake the fish into pieces and serve over sesame noodles as an appetizer. (See recipe for Sesame Noodles, page 24.) This recipe also works well for salmon.

- 1/4 cup soy sauce
- 1 tablespoon sesame oil
- 3 tablespoons sugar
- 1/4 teaspoon crushed red pepper flakes
- 2 to 4 (6-ounce) pieces sea bass

Combine soy sauce, sesame oil, sugar and red pepper flakes in a sealable plastic bag. Add fish and marinate in the refrigerator for at least 20 minutes and up to 12 hours. Preheat oven to 450 degrees. Place the fish, with marinade, in a lightly oiled roasting pan. Bake for 12 to 15 minutes. *Makes 2 to 4 servings.*

COD LIVORNESE

Parve

2   teaspoons olive oil
1   onion, cut in half and thinly sliced
2   garlic cloves, crushed
$1/3$ cup TEAL LAKE CHARDONNAY® white wine
1   (14-ounce) can diced tomatoes, undrained
$1/4$ cup pitted kalamata olives
$1/4$ cup loosely packed fresh parsley leaves, chopped
2   tablespoons drained capers
$1/4$ teaspoon crushed red pepper flakes
4   (6-ounce) cod or scrod fillets
$1/4$ teaspoon salt
1   lemon, cut into wedges

Heat olive oil in a 12-inch nonstick skillet over medium-high heat
and sauté onion for 8 minutes or until light brown. Add garlic. Cook
for 30 seconds. Add wine and cook for 1 minute. Stir in tomatoes,
olives, parsley, capers and red pepper flakes; heat to boiling. Arrange
cod over tomato mixture and sprinkle with salt. Cover the skillet and
cook for 8 to 9 minutes or just until cod is opaque throughout.
Squeeze lemon over cod to serve. *Makes 4 servings.*

Photograph for this recipe is on page 143.

Oven-Roasted Whole Snapper with Black Olives

Parve

1/4   cup extra-virgin olive oil, divided
1/3   cup coarsely chopped pitted kalamata olives
1/3   cup finely chopped flat leaf parsley
        plus additional for garnish
   1   garlic clove, minced
   1   whole red snapper, at least 4 pounds
        Kosher salt and freshly ground pepper to taste
        Juice of 1 lemon plus the grated rind for garnish

Preheat oven to 375 degrees. Grease a large baking dish with 1 teaspoon of olive oil. Combine olives, parsley and garlic and stuff half the mixture inside the fish. Place fish in the baking dish and sprinkle with kosher salt and freshly ground pepper to taste. Combine remaining olive oil and lemon juice and pour over the fish and scatter remaining olive mixture over the top. Bake for 30 minutes, basting every 10 minutes with pan juices. To serve, garnish with parsley mixed with lemon rind. *Makes 4 servings.*

MUSTARD FACTS

This popular condiment comes in a variety of flavors and textures. When cooking with mustard or mixing in a dressing, make sure you are using the mustard called for in the recipe, or you will end up with food that has the wrong flavor.

Yellow

Made with ground white mustard seeds, this American-style mustard is very mild and gets its yellow color from turmeric.

Dijon

The most versatile, this French-style mustard is usually smooth, with a clean, sharp flavor. It is made with ground brown mustard seeds, white wine, unfermented grape juice (called must) and seasonings. Use it in dressings, on sandwiches, and in sauces for meats and vegetable dishes. ➤

CARMELA'S MOROCCAN FISH

Parve

" *Carmela serves this in her restaurant in Schunat Hatikva in Israel."*

2 tablespoons vegetable oil	2 to 3 garlic cloves, chopped
1 large onion, chopped	2 tablespoons chopped
1 teaspoon curry powder	fresh cilantro
4 to 6 fillets of any white fish	1 tomato, chopped
(such as sole, flounder or	1/2 (8-ounce) can tomato
tilapia)	sauce
1/4 teaspoon cayenne	Kosher salt to taste
pepper	

Heat oil in a large skillet. Add onion and fry until transulucent. Stir in curry powder. Arrange fish on top of onion mixture. Cook for 2 to 3 minutes and turn to coat other side with onion mixture. Add cayenne pepper, garlic, cilantro, tomato, tomato sauce and kosher salt to taste to the skillet. Pour in enough water to cover fish. Simmer, covered, for 10 to 15 minutes or until fish is cooked through and flakes easily when touched with a fork. *Makes 4 to 6 servings.*

BAKED SALMON WITH MUSTARD AND TARRAGON

Parve

4 salmon fillets	2 tablespoons Dijon mustard
Kosher salt and pepper	2 teaspoons dried tarragon
to taste	1/2 teaspoon white or red
1/2 cup mayonnaise	wine vinegar

Preheat oven to 350 degrees. Place salmon on a greased baking sheet or a foil-lined pan (for easy clean-up). Season with kosher salt and pepper to taste. Whisk together the remaining ingredients and spread over fish. Bake for 15 minutes, then broil for an additional 3 to 6 minutes or until brown. *Makes 4 servings.*

PEPPER-CRUSTED MARINATED SALMON

Parve

2 skinless salmon fillets,
    about 2 inches wide
1½ tablespoons soy sauce
1½ tablespoons lemon juice
1 garlic clove, minced

1 tablespoon olive oil
    Coarsely ground pepper
    to taste
    Lemon slices for garnish

Place fish in a sealable plastic bag. Add soy sauce, lemon juice, garlic and olive oil and shake to coat fillets. Refrigerate for at least 2 hours, turning at least once. Preheat broiler. Place fish on a foil-covered and greased baking sheet. Sprinkle with coarsely ground pepper to taste. Broil 6 inches from the heat source for 5 to 6 minutes. The fish should be barely pink on the inside. Garnish with lemon slices.
Makes 2 servings.

SALMON WITH TOMATOES AND SHALLOTS

Parve

"*At a recent dinner party, I served this salmon to a whole crowd with very diverse backgrounds and tastes. The challenge was that there were both young children and adults at the table. I was so relieved that it was enjoyed by all! I made it as one large salmon fillet and the preparation and clean-up were a breeze!*"

4 (4-ounce) salmon fillets or
    1½ to 2 pounds salmon
    fillet
2 teaspoons plus
    2 tablespoons olive oil,
    divided
    Salt and pepper to taste

5 plum tomatoes, chopped
2 shallots, chopped
2 tablespoons fresh lemon
    juice
1 teaspoon dried oregano
1 teaspoon dried thyme

Preheat oven to 400 degrees. Sprinkle salmon with 2 teaspoons olive oil and salt and pepper to taste. Place in a baking dish. Combine tomatoes, shallots, remaining 2 tablespoons olive oil, lemon juice, oregano, thyme and salt and pepper to taste in a bowl. Pour mixture evenly over salmon. Tightly cover the dish with foil. Bake for 25 minutes or until cooked through. The sliced salmon fillets can also be placed on individual squares of foil. Seal and bake packets. *Makes 4 servings.*

Grainy
A blend of whole and crushed mustard seeds gives mustards their course texture. Grainy mustards are usually mild, and they sometimes contain sugar. Use with cold cuts and corned beef, or for coating meat before cooking.

Powder
Finely ground mustard seed is the basic ingredient of prepared mustards. You can create your own mustard; just mix 2 parts mustard powder with 1 part water, wine, or vinegar to form a paste. Add seasonings if you wish. Mustard powder can also be used in sauces and in Asian cooking.

Spicy Brown
Most of these mustards are made German-style with ground brown and white mustard seeds, sugar, and seasonings. They range from mildly spicy to very hot; some are sweeter than others. Spicy brown mustard is often eaten on hot dogs.

GRILLED SALMON ITALIANO

. . . .

Parve

1/3 cup plus 1/4 cup olive oil, divided
2 tablespoons fresh rosemary, chopped
2 tablespoons fresh basil, chopped
2 tablespoons balsamic vinegar
8 garlic cloves, minced
6 salmon steaks, or salmon fillet
(2 to 4 pounds total)
2 garlic cloves, minced
20 green olives or kalamata olives, pitted and chopped
3 large tomatoes, seeded and chopped
1 bunch arugula, washed and chopped
1/2 onion, chopped
2 tablespoons capers, drained

Whisk together $^1/_3$ cup olive oil, rosemary, basil, vinegar and 8 garlic cloves. Arrange fish in a greased roasting pan. Pour oil mixture over fish and marinate in the refrigerator for 4 to 12 hours. In a separate bowl, whisk remaining $^1/_2$ cup olive oil and 2 cloves garlic together. Add olives, tomatoes, arugula, onion and capers and mix well.

Preheat broiler. Spoon tomato mixture over salmon and broil 6 inches from the heat source for 6 minutes or to desired doneness. *Makes 6 servings.*

BARON HERZOG CHENIN BLANC (WHITE, CALIFORNIA)
Focused and crisp, with intense passion fruit and citrus flavors that match zesty fish dishes.

Rosemary Grilled Salmon and Vegetables with Balsamic Syrup

Parve

"*This recipe might sound more extravagant and thus hard to prepare, but it is a simple preparation that has that rustic quality. This dish lends itself to patio dining, where you grill your fish on the outdoor barbecue. For those colder months, a cast-iron grill pan on the stove works nicely.*"

SALMON

- 2 tablespoons fresh rosemary leaves, minced
- 1 garlic clove, minced
- 1/4 cup pure olive oil
- Salt and pepper to taste
- 4 (7- to 8-ounce) skin-on salmon fillets

VEGETABLES

- Zucchini, cut diagonally into 1/4-inch rounds
- Eggplant, cut into 1/4-inch slices
- Red or Vidalia onions, cut into 1/4-inch rounds
- Endive, cut into halves
- Radicchio, not cored, cut into quarters
- Portobello mushrooms
- Asparagus
- Green beans

BALSAMIC SYRUP

- 1/2 cup balsamic vinegar
- 1/2 cup VALERO SYRAH® red or white wine
- 1 rosemary sprig
- 1 fresh bay leaf, or 2 dried bay leaves
- 1 teaspoon whole coriander seeds (optional)

For the salmon, combine rosemary, garlic and olive oil and pour into a shallow baking dish. Salt and pepper each fillet and place flesh side down into olive oil mixture. Marinate in the refrigerator for 30 minutes. Drain, reserving marinade.

For the vegetables, choose any combination of vegetables and toss in the marinating liquid drained from salmon. Grill vegetables, keeping a close eye on them so they don't char. Vegetables will be done at different times; remove them from grill once they are tender. Grill salmon, flesh side down first, for 3 to 4 minutes. Turn and grill 4 minutes longer and remove from the grill. (Fish continues to cook after it is removed from grill.) Serve salmon over a mound of vegetables. Drizzle with balsamic syrup or brush it over salmon.

For the balsamic syrup, combine balsamic vinegar, wine, rosemary sprig, bay leaf and coriander seeds in a nonreactive saucepan and cook over medium heat until reduced to 1/4 cup. Strain and cool. (May be made in advance.)
Makes 4 servings.

Breathe Life into Your Everyday Meals with a Glass of Wine

A simple and easy solution to enlivening the culinary experience that requires absolutely no cooking is wine. Wine was made to be paired with food, and when a fine wine is paired with the right dish, the naturally occurring flavor components of each complement one another to create a graceful symphony of mouth-watering flavors.

In general, white wines enhance the flavor of fish and poultry dishes, and red wines complement dark meats.

When preparing fish or poultry with lemon juice or other highly acidic ingredients, it's best to serve a wine with bright acidity as well, such as a Sauvignon Blanc or a Chenin Blanc. If spicy meat dishes are on the menu, a slightly spicy Zinfandel or Rioja variety would pair nicely. For desserts such as pastries and fruit, a naturally sweet Late Harvest Chenin Blanc or Late Harvest White Riesling would match well.

When in doubt, ask your local wine retailer for assistance in selecting the right wine for the dish you are preparing.

The best wine to cook with is the one you will be serving at the table. The real secret is to cook with a good wine, as the alcohol evaporates during the cooking process, leaving only the actual flavor of the wine.

Cooking with Wine

A fine wine with a rich body and aroma will ensure a distinct and delicate flavor. When used in cooking, the wine should accent and enhance the natural flavor of the food while adding its own inviting fragrance and taste.

CATCH-UP DINNER

A good meal for a quiet night to "catch up."
Cod Livornese 136 • Lemon Garlic Pasta 155
Mixed Vegetable Salad with Basil Vinaigrette 75

ZESTY SLOW-ROASTED SALMON

Parve

FISH

8 (5-ounce) skinless
    center-cut salmon fillets
    White pepper and salt
    to taste

TOPPING

1 tablespoon grated lime zest
3 tablespoons bread crumbs

6 tablespoons margarine,
    softened
2 tablespoons chopped
    fresh flat leaf parsley
1 tablespoon mustard seeds
1 tablespoon fresh lime juice
1 tablespoon Dijon mustard
1 teaspoon honey

For the fish, preheat oven to 225 degrees. Trim any dark flesh from fish and place skin side down in a large roasting pan. Season with white pepper and salt. Spread topping over salmon and roast, uncovered, in the middle of the oven for 25 to 30 minutes or until fish is cooked through.

For the topping, combine all ingredients in a bowl and mix well. *Makes 8 servings.*

SALMON BURGERS WITH HOISIN AND GINGER

Parve

MINIATURE BURGERS

For a terrific hors d'oeuvre, pat the mixture into patties small enough to serve as pick-up food. Watch closely as they cook— cooking time will be much shorter.

1 (1-pound) boneless
    skinless salmon fillet,
    cut into 1-inch pieces
1/4 cup fresh cilantro leaves
2 tablespoons hoisin sauce
    plus additional for
    spreading
2 tablespoons mayonnaise
    plus additional for
    spreading

1/4 cup chopped scallions
2 teaspoons minced peeled
    fresh ginger
1 garlic clove, minced
    Salt and pepper to taste
2 1/2 teaspoons oriental
    sesame oil
    Hamburger buns, toasted
    Lettuce

Blend salmon, cilantro, hoisin and mayonnaise in a food processor. Pour into a bowl and add scallions, ginger, garlic and salt and pepper to taste. Form into four 1/2-inch-thick patties and chill for 1 to 4 hours.

Heat sesame oil in a large nonstick skillet over medium heat and sauté salmon patties for 3 minutes per side or until cooked through. Serve on toasted hamburger buns spread with additional hoisin sauce and mayonnaise and topped with lettuce. *Makes 2 to 4 servings.*

Photograph for this recipe is on page 123.

SOLE WITH ORANGE SAUCE

. . . .

Dairy

If you're looking for a nice, refreshing fish, this fits the bill.

FISH

2	eggs
1	tablespoon water
3/4	cup all-purpose flour
1	teaspoon salt
1/8	teaspoon white pepper
1/4	teaspoon ground ginger
2	pounds sole fillets
3	tablespoons vegetable oil

ORANGE SAUCE

1	tablespoon orange zest
1	tablespoon lemon zest
1	cup orange juice
2	tablespoons dark brown sugar
1	tablespoon butter
2	tablespoons cornstarch
1/4	cup fresh lemon juice
1/8	teaspoon salt
	Lemon and orange slices for garnish

For the fish, preheat oven to 400 degrees. Beat eggs and water in a large bowl. Combine flour, salt, white pepper and ginger on a plate. Dip fish in egg mixture and coat with flour mixture. Heat oil in a large skillet and fry fish for 4 minutes per side. Drain on paper towels and place in a baking dish.

For the sauce, mix orange zest, lemon zest, orange juice, brown sugar and butter in a saucepan. Mix cornstarch with lemon juice in a separate bowl and add to orange mixture. Cook over medium heat for 3 minutes or until mixture thickens, stirring constantly. Add salt. Drizzle over hot fish and bake for 5 minutes. Garnish with lemon and orange slices to serve. *Makes 4 servings.*

SECTIONING CITRUS FRUIT

To section oranges and grapefruit, cut a slice from the top and bottom of the fruit. Place it on a work surface and cut away the peel and pith in strips, cutting from the top to the base in a curving motion. Hold over a bowl to catch the juice as you remove the sections from the membrane; discard the seeds.

CITRUS WATER

When a variety of sliced citrus is added to a glass pitcher of water, it's transformed into a beautiful presentation as well as delicious, flavored water.

FREEZING NUTS

Did you know that the oil in seeds and nuts can cause them to spoil if kept at room temperature? Avoid problems by storing them in your freezer. Place each type of nut or seed in its own plastic, airtight container or resealable plastic bag. Nuts keep for 6 to 8 months in the freezer, so be sure to write the storage date on the container.

TOASTING NUTS

If you want to enhance the flavor of nuts, try toasting them. Preheat the oven to 350 degrees. Place the shelled pecans, walnuts, almonds, or hazelnuts in a single layer on a cookie sheet. Bake the nuts for about 10 minutes, stirring periodically, until lightly browned and aromatic. Hazelnuts are done toasting when the skin begins to separate from the nut. Once the nuts are cool, they can be chopped.

TILAPIA FILLETS WITH PESTO BUTTER

Dairy

FISH

- 6 (4- to 5-ounce) tilapia fillets
- 1 tablespoon olive oil
  Salt to taste
- 1/2 teaspoon pepper
  Basil sprigs and lemon
  zest strips for garnish

PESTO BUTTER

- 1/2 cup (1 stick) butter, softened
- 1 cup fresh basil, packed
  and chopped
- 1/2 cup fresh parsley, packed
  and chopped
- 2 garlic cloves, minced
- 3 tablespoons grated
  Parmesan cheese
- 1 tablespoon olive oil
- 2 teaspoons lemon juice

For the fish, preheat oven to 400 degrees. Brush each side of fish with olive oil and season with salt and pepper. Arrange in a baking dish and top each with 1 to 2 tablespoons pesto butter, spreading evenly. Bake for about 8 minutes or until fish flakes easily. Garnish with basil sprigs and lemon zest strips. Serve immediately.

For the pesto butter, process all the ingredients in a blender until finely chopped and thoroughly blended. *Makes 6 servings.*

WALNUT-CRUSTED TROUT FILLETS

Dairy

- 1/2 cup all-purpose flour
- 3 tablespoons dried
  rubbed sage
- 1 tablespoon kosher salt
- 1 1/2 teaspoons pepper
- 2 eggs
- 2 cups (about 10 ounces)
  finely chopped walnuts

- 2 (9- to 10-ounce) trout,
  boned, heads removed,
  butterflied and halved
  (makes 4 fillets)
  Salt and pepper to taste
- 2 tablespoons butter, divided
- 2 tablespoons vegetable oil,
  divided
- 1 lemon, quartered lengthwise
  Chopped fresh parsley

Combine first four ingredients on a plate. Whisk eggs in a medium bowl. Spread walnuts over a large plate. Sprinkle trout fillets with salt and pepper to taste. Coat with flour mixture, then dip into eggs. Press both sides of trout in walnuts to coat. Melt 1 tablespoon butter with 1 tablespoon oil in each of 2 large heavy skillets. Sauté two trout in each skillet for 5 minutes per side or until light brown and cooked through. Squeeze lemon over each fillet, sprinkle with parsley and serve. *Makes 4 servings.*

TROUT WITH HAZELNUTS, LEMON AND PARSLEY BROWN BUTTER

. . . .

Dairy

3/4   cup seasoned bread crumbs
1/2   cup plus 3 tablespoons crushed toasted hazelnuts
  8   tablespoons chopped fresh Italian parsley
  4   boneless trout fillets
      Salt and pepper to taste
1/4   cup olive oil
1/2   cup (1 stick) butter
1/4   cup fresh lemon juice
  2   teaspoons grated lemon zest

Preheat oven to 350 degrees. Grease a large rimmed baking sheet. Combine bread crumbs, 1/2 cup hazelnuts and 2 tablespoons parsley in a medium bowl. Sprinkle trout with salt and pepper to taste. Coat both sides of the fillet with hazelnut mixture. Heat olive in a skillet and sauté fillets for 2 minutes on each side or until golden brown. Arrange flesh side up on a baking sheet. Roast for 5 minutes or until opaque in the center. Remove the fillets to a serving dish.

Heat butter in the same skillet over medium heat and allow to brown. Add remaining 3 tablespoons crushed hazelnuts, remaining 6 tablespoons chopped parsley, lemon juice and 1 teaspoon lemon zest and mix well. Season with salt and pepper to taste and pour over roasted fish. Sprinkle with remaining lemon zest.
Makes 4 servings.

RICE-STUFFED TROUT

Parve

I f you don't like fennel, you can substitute basil for it.

2   large red bell peppers, cut into $1/2$-inch-wide strips
1   large fennel bulb, thinly sliced and top stalks chopped to
    equal $1/4$ cup
1   tablespoon olive oil
    Kosher salt and pepper to taste
1   cup cooled cooked white rice (about $1/3$ cup uncooked)
2   tablespoons pine nuts
2   (12- to 16-ounce) whole boneless trout

Preheat oven to 400 degrees. Coat a large rimmed baking sheet with
nonstick cooking spray. Spread bell peppers and fennel bulb on the
sheet. Drizzle with olive oil. Sprinkle with kosher salt and pepper to
taste. Roast for about 30 minutes or until vegetables are brown, stirring
occasionally. Combine rice, pine nuts and $1/4$ cup chopped fennel tops
in a bowl and season with kosher salt and pepper.

Remove baking sheet from oven and push vegetables to the side of
the sheet. Place trout in center and sprinkle inside of trout with kosher
salt and pepper to taste. Spoon stuffing into trout cavity. Fold trout to
enclose stuffing. Roast trout for 20 minutes or until opaque. When
serving, cut each trout in half widthwise. Transfer one trout half and
some stuffing to each of four plates. Spoon vegetable topping over
fish. *Makes 4 servings.*

SEARED TUNA STEAKS WITH WASABI MAYONNAISE

Parve

- 1/2 cup mayonnaise
- 2 tablespoons minced scallions (green and white parts)
- 1 tablespoon wasabi paste, or to taste
- 2 tablespoons teriyaki sauce
- 1 tablespoon soy sauce
- 1 tablespoon unseasoned rice vinegar
- 4 (8-ounce) tuna steaks (preferably ahi), cut 1 1/2 inches thick
- 3 to 4 tablespoons vegetable oil

Whisk mayonnaise, scallions and wasabi paste in a small bowl until well mixed. Cover and refrigerate.

Whisk teriyaki sauce, soy sauce and rice vinegar in a small bowl until well blended. Place tuna in a sealable plastic bag with teriyaki mixture. Seal bag and turn to coat. Marinate at room temperature for 30 to 45 minutes, turning bag occasionally. Remove tuna from bag, discarding the marinade.

Heat oil in a large skillet over medium-high heat and sear tuna for 3 to 4 minutes on each side. Serve tuna with a dollop of the wasabi mayonnaise alongside. *Makes 4 servings.*

REMOULADE SAUCE

Dairy

This sauce can complement a variety of fish.

Combine 2 cups mayonnaise, 1 cup sour cream, 2 tablespoons capers, chopped, 2 teaspoons Dijon mustard, 1 tablespoon chopped parsley, 1 teaspoon crumbled tarragon, 1 teaspoon crumbled chervil, 1 teaspoon anchovy paste and the juice of 1 lemon in a small bowl and mix well. Refrigerate if not serving right away, and refrigerate leftover sauce for up to 3 days. *Makes 2¼ cups.*

GRILLED TUNA WITH HERBED AÏOLI

Parve

Kosher salt and pepper to taste
- ¼ cup olive oil
- 2 tablespoons red wine vinegar
- 2 tablespoons chopped fresh basil
- 2 teaspoons chopped fresh thyme
- 2 teaspoons dried tarragon
- 2 large garlic cloves, finely chopped
- 4 (7-ounce) tuna steaks, about 1 inch thick
- ⅓ cup mayonnaise

Sprinkle fish with kosher salt and pepper to taste.

Whisk olive oil, vinegar, basil, thyme, tarragon and garlic in a shallow dish. Set aside 1½ tablespoons of marinade for herb aïoli. Place fish in remaining marinade, turning to coat evenly. Marinate for at least 1 hour at room temperature or longer in the refrigerator, turning fish occasionally.

Whisk 1½ tablespoons of the marinade and mayonnaise together in a small bowl. Refrigerate the herbed aïoli until ready to use.

Oil grill rack. Preheat grill to medium heat. Grill fish for about 3 minutes per side for medium or to desired degree of doneness. Top fish with herbed aïoli and serve.

You can also prepare this fish in an oiled grill pan. *Makes 4 servings.*

Tuna Steak Burgers with Ginger Mustard Spread

. . . .

Parve

FISH

2	pounds (3/4-inch-thick) tuna steaks, cut into 6 pieces
3	to 4 tablespoons olive oil
	Salt and pepper to taste
	Buns, lettuce, sliced red onion and thinly sliced tomatoes

GINGER MUSTARD SPREAD

1/3	cup mayonnaise
1	teaspoon sesame oil
1 1/2	teaspoons grated peeled fresh ginger
1	tablespoon whole grain mustard
2	teaspoons fresh lemon juice
1	garlic clove, minced
	Salt and pepper to taste

For the fish, preheat the grill. Brush fish with olive oil. Grill on one side for 4 minutes or until golden brown. Turn and season with salt and pepper to taste. Grill for 3 to 4 more minutes or until golden brown outside but still pink in the center. Lightly brush the inside of buns with the spread. Oil the grill rack and grill the buns, cut side down, 4 inches from flame until light brown. Place fish on the bottom bun, adding more spread and top with bun. Serve immediately with lettuce, sliced red onion and thinly sliced tomatoes.

For the spread, whisk together mayonnaise, sesame oil, ginger, whole grain mustard, lemon juice, garlic and salt and pepper to taste. (Refrigerate until ready to use.) *Makes 6 servings.*

Photograph for this recipe is on page 123.

PASTA

SAMPLER

FAMILY FRIENDLY
Broccoli Alfredo 154
Three-Cheese Baked Penne with Broccoli 155
Lemon Garlic Pasta 155
Modern Mac and Cheese—Not Just for Kids 157
Thin Spaghetti with Garlic Herb Sauce 160
Mushroom Roll-Ups Florentine 164
Baked Ziti 165 • Stuffed Shells 165
Roasted Garlic and Cherry Tomatoes 166
Cheesy Fusilli Zucchini 167

SOPHISTICATED
Spring Garden Penne with Asparagus 154
Linguini with Garlicky Marsala Mushrooms 156
Spinach Linguini with Tuna, Artichokes and Mushrooms 158
Farfalle with Shiitakes, Sweet Potatoes and Peas 159
Mediterranean Pasta Shells 161
Spicy Tomato Olive Sauce à la Rigatoni 167

PREP TIME
Linguini with Garlicky Marsala Mushrooms 156
Farfalle with Shiitakes, Sweet Potatoes and Peas 159
Mediterranean Pasta Shells 161
Mushroom Roll-Ups Florentine 164

ALFASI MERLOT (RED, CHILE)

Well-balanced, with plum and mild oak notes, and a velvety smooth finish that's great with light pasta dishes.

SPRING GARDEN PENNE WITH ASPARAGUS

Parve

	Salt for water	6	tablespoons olive oil
1	pound penne	1	(2-ounce) can anchovy
2	to 3 pounds asparagus,		fillets, drained and cut
	trimmed and cut into		into quarters
	3/4-inch pieces		Salt and pepper to taste

Bring enough salted water to cover pasta and asparagus to a boil in a large saucepan. Add pasta to boiling water. Return water to a boil and add asparagus. Cook for 7 to 8 minutes or until pasta is al dente.

Heat olive oil in a large skillet over low heat. Add anchovies and mash with the back of a wooden spoon. Drain pasta and asparagus and add to skillet. Increase heat to medium and cook for 1 to 2 minutes, stirring. Season to taste with salt and pepper. *Makes 6 to 8 servings.*

BROCCOLI ALFREDO

Dairy

Love fettuccine Alfredo? Try our healthy version.

1	pound fettuccini	1	cup reserved cooking
	Salt for water		liquid
8	cups broccoli florets	1 1/2	teaspoons freshly ground
	(about 2 heads)		black pepper
1/4	cup (1/2 stick) butter	1/8	teaspoon cayenne pepper
1 1/3	cups grated Parmesan		Salt to taste
	cheese, divided		

Cook pasta in boiling salted water until al dente according to package directions. Add broccoli to pot for last 3 minutes of cooking. Drain in a colander, reserving 1 cup cooking liquid.

Heat butter in the pan and melt over medium heat. Add 1/2 cup of reserved liquid and 2/3 cup of Parmesan cheese. Return pasta and broccoli to pot. Sprinkle with black pepper, cayenne pepper and salt to taste. Toss to combine. Remove from heat and sprinkle with remaining cheese. If pasta seems sticky, add remaining reserved liquid as needed. Serve with additional Parmesan cheese.
Makes 6 to 8 servings.

Three-Cheese Baked Penne with Broccoli

Dairy

2 cups uncooked penne
  Salt for water
3 cups fresh broccoli florets,
  cut into 1-inch pieces
2 cups marinara sauce
1 cup (4 ounces) shredded
  mozzarella cheese, divided

1/2 cup ricotta cheese
1/2 cup fresh basil, chopped
2 to 3 tablespoons minced
  garlic
6 tablespoons grated
  Parmesan cheese, divided
  Salt and pepper to taste

Preheat oven to 400 degrees and grease a deep 9×13-inch baking dish. Cook pasta in boiling salted water until al dente according to package directions. Add broccoli and cook for an additional 3 minutes. Drain well.

Combine marinara sauce, 1/2 cup of mozzarella cheese, ricotta cheese, basil, garlic and 2 tablespoons of Parmesan cheese in a bowl and mix well. Add pasta and broccoli. Season with salt and pepper to taste and mix well. Pour mixture into the prepared baking dish. Top with remaining mozzarella cheese and Parmesan cheese. Bake, uncovered, for 30 minutes or until cheese is melted. *Makes 8 to 10 servings.*

BARTENURA PINOT GRIGIO (WHITE, ITALY)
Well-balanced, dry with pear and honeysuckle flavors and a fresh clean finish that's perfect with light pasta dishes.

Lemon Garlic Pasta

Parve or Dairy

1 pound capellini
  Salt for water
1/2 cup reserved cooking liquid
1/2 cup extra-virgin olive oil
4 large garlic cloves, minced
1/4 to 1/2 teaspoon red
  pepper flakes
  Finely grated zest of
  2 lemons

3 tablespoons fresh
  lemon juice
1/2 teaspoon salt
1/4 teaspoon freshly ground
  black pepper
1/2 cup fresh flat-leaf parsley,
  chopped
  Parmesan cheese
  (optional)

Cook pasta in boiling salted water until al dente according to package directions. Drain, reserving 1/2 cup cooking liquid. Heat olive oil in a skillet and sauté garlic and red pepper flakes until garlic is golden but not brown. Add lemon zest, lemon juice, salt, black pepper and reserved liquid. Mix well. Toss in pasta and parsley and mix well. Sprinkle with cheese and serve. *Makes 4 to 6 servings.*

Photograph for this recipe is on page 143.

LINGUINI WITH GARLICKY MARSALA MUSHROOMS

Dairy

5 tablespoons extra-virgin olive oil, divided
1 pound white mushrooms, sliced
1 pound shiitake mushrooms, sliced
Salt and freshly ground pepper to taste
2 large garlic cloves thinly sliced, plus 2 large garlic cloves minced, divided
1 shallot, thinly sliced

1½ teaspoons fresh rosemary, minced
½ cup KEDEM® marsala wine
3 tablespoons balsamic vinegar
6 kalamata olives, pitted and coarsely chopped
1 pound linguini
Salt for water
2 tablespoons butter
⅓ cup grated Parmesan cheese
2 tablespoons minced chives

Heat 2 tablespoons olive oil in a very large skillet over medium-high heat for 5 minutes, and sauté mushrooms, covered, stirring once. Season with salt and freshly ground pepper to taste. Uncover and cook over high heat about 3 minutes longer, until mushrooms are brown. Add sliced garlic, shallot and rosemary and cook 2 minutes longer or until mixture is fragrant. Add wine and vinegar and cook, stirring constantly, for 1 minute or until liquid is evaporated. Stir in minced garlic, olives and 3 tablespoons olive oil. Cover and remove from heat.

Cook pasta in boiling salted water until al dente according to package directions. Drain and return to pot. Stir in butter and mushroom mixture. Season with additional salt and pepper to taste. Stir in cheese. Spoon into a serving bowl and top with chives. Serve with additional Parmesan cheese, if desired.

Makes 4 to 6 servings.

MODERN MAC AND CHEESE—
NOT JUST FOR KIDS

. . . .

Dairy

1 pound macaroni	6 ounces shredded Cheddar
Salt for water	or American cheese
6 tablespoons butter, divided	1/2 teaspoon freshly ground
1/4 cup all-purpose flour	pepper
4 cups milk	4 small plum tomatoes, cut
12 ounces shredded	into slices (optional)
mozzarella cheese	1 to 11/2 cups bread crumbs

Preheat oven to 375 degrees. Grease a 3-quart baking dish. Cook pasta in boiling salted water until al dente according to package directions. Drain.

While water is boiling for pasta, begin sauce. Melt 1/4 cup butter in a medium saucepan over medium heat; stir in flour and cook for 1 to 2 minutes, stirring. Pour in milk and cook for 1 to 2 minutes longer or until thickened, stirring constantly. Remove from the heat and add cheeses and pepper, mixing well until cheeses are melted and smooth. Combine sauce with cooked pasta and mix until well blended.

Pour mixture into the prepared baking dish. Arrange sliced tomatoes on top. Melt 2 tablespoons butter and toss with bread crumbs. Sprinkle over tomatoes. Bake for 30 to 35 minutes or until sauce is bubbly and pasta is brown on top. *Makes 4 to 6 servings.*

Note: Although the tomatoes add a nice flavor, they can be omitted if your guests prefer.

**RASHI BARBERA
D'ALBA
(RED, ITALY)**
Brilliant ruby red hue,
complex aroma of roses
and violets, and a dry,
pleasantly ripe fruity
flavor highlight this full-
bodied wine that pairs
exceptionally well with
robust tomato sauce-
based pasta entrées.

TOMATO BASIL ANGEL HAIR PASTA

Parve

1	pound angel hair pasta	8	plum tomatoes, chopped
	Salt for water	3	tablespoons sliced basil
1/4	cup olive oil	1	tablespoon garlic salt
12	scallions	1	tablespoon onion powder
6	garlic cloves, minced	2	teaspoons garlic powder
1/4	cup olive oil		Salt and pepper to taste

Cook pasta in boiling salted water until al dente according to package directions. Drain and set aside. Heat the olive oil in a saucepan and cook scallions and garlic for about 5 minutes or until tender. Add tomatoes, cover pan and simmer 20 minutes or until sauce thickens, stirring occasionally. Stir in basil, garlic salt, onion powder and garlic powder. Simmer for 5 minutes. Season with salt and pepper to taste. (Sauce can be made in advance and refrigerated in a sealed container. Heat before using.) Pour hot sauce over pasta. Can also be served at room temperature. *Makes 4 to 6 servings.*

SPINACH LINGUINI WITH TUNA, ARTICHOKES AND MUSHROOMS

Parve or Dairy

1	pound spinach linguini	2	(6-ounce) cans solid white tuna, drained and flaked
	Salt for water		
2	tablespoons olive oil	1 1/2	teaspoons Italian seasoning
1	onion, chopped		
2	garlic cloves, chopped	3	tablespoons fresh basil, chopped
8	ounces mushrooms, thinly sliced		
		1	teaspoon kosher salt
2	(14-ounce) cans artichoke hearts, drained and diced	1/2	cup (2 ounces) grated Parmesan cheese
3	plum tomatoes, chopped		

Cook pasta in boiling salted water until al dente according to package directions. Drain. Heat olive oil in a large skillet over medium-high heat and sauté onion and garlic for about 7 minutes. Add mushrooms and sauté for an additional 3 minutes or until tender. Add artichokes, tomatoes, tuna, Italian seasoning, basil and salt and simmer for 10 minutes longer. Toss tuna mixture with hot pasta and top with cheese. *Makes 4 to 6 servings.*

FARFALLE WITH SHIITAKES, SWEET POTATOES AND PEAS

Parve

2¹/₂ cups bouillon

2 cups julienne-cut peeled sweet potatoes

2¹/₂ cups sugar snap peas (about 8 ounces), washed and trimmed

1 cup shiitake mushroom caps without stems (about 1 ounce), washed, dried and sliced

1 tablespoon margarine

3 cups thinly sliced onions

4 garlic cloves, minced

¹/₂ teaspoon salt

8 ounces farfalle
  Salt for water

¹/₄ cup fresh flat-leaf parsley, chopped

¹/₄ cup fresh chives, chopped

Bring bouillon to a boil in a saucepan and cook sweet potatoes for 1 minute. Add peas and cook, covered, for 2 minutes. Add mushrooms and cook, covered, for 1 additional minute. Drain through a colander, reserving liquid. Return liquid to saucepan and bring to a boil; cook for about 10 minutes or until liquid is reduced to ¹/₄ cup. Set aside.

Heat margarine in the same pot and cook onions and garlic until tender but not brown. Add vegetables, reserved liquid and salt. Bring to a boil and cook 1 minute longer, stirring constantly. Cook pasta in boiling salted water until al dente according to package directions. Drain. Add vegetable mixture to hot pasta along with parsley and chives, mixing well. Serve hot. *Makes 4 servings.*

Note: Can be made dairy or parve. This dish tastes great either way! Add ¹/₄ cup Parmesan cheese to pasta for dairy version. Do not make the pasta ahead of time, as it will be too cool when you add the remaining ingredients.

Thin Spaghetti with Garlic Herb Sauce

Dairy

1 *pound thin spaghetti*
   Salt for water
2 *tablespoons olive oil*
1 *bunch scallions, sliced*
2 *garlic cloves, thinly sliced*
3 *cups white mushrooms, sliced*
1 *(10-ounce) package frozen chopped spinach, thawed and drained*
1 *cup full-fat spreadable cheese with garlic and herbs*
1/2 *cup milk*
   Salt and freshly ground pepper to taste

Cook pasta in boiling salted water until al dente according to package directions. Drain and return to warm pan. While water is boiling, begin sauce. Heat olive oil in a skillet and sauté scallions and garlic until just softened but not brown. Add mushrooms and mix well. Cook for 15 to 20 minutes or until softened and liquid is absorbed.

Add spinach to mushroom mixture and cook for 1 to 2 minutes longer. Add cheese and allow to melt slightly. Stir in milk and heat slightly without boiling. Add more milk if mixture seems too thick. Pour over warm pasta. Season to taste with salt and freshly ground pepper. *Makes 4 to 6 servings.*

GOTTA HAVE ... TONGS

Anyone who ever wished for an extra pair of hands in the kitchen should try this multitalented, heatproof tool.

Why they are so great
Designed like giant tweezers, tongs can be used to hold and lift all kinds of food, hot or cold; they can also reach high-heat places, especially on the grill or in the oven.

What they are used for Tongs are ideal not only for turning meats as they cook, but for tossing and serving pasta and salads, lifting corn from boiling water, and removing baked potatoes from the oven.

Mediterranean Pasta Shells

Parve or Dairy

This requires a bit of preparation so you may not make it very often, but you will certainly enjoy it when you do.

2 red bell peppers	2 tablespoons fresh
2 yellow bell peppers	marjoram, chopped, or
3 tablespoons olive oil	2 teaspoons dried
1 large onion, chopped	marjoram
2 garlic cloves, minced	1/2 cup water
1/3 cup parsley, chopped	1 pound medium
2 pounds plum tomatoes,	pasta shells
chopped	Salt for water
1/2 cup kalamata olives, pitted	1/2 cup (2 ounces) grated
and chopped	Parmesan cheese
1/4 cup capers, drained	(optional)

Char bell peppers in a broiler until black on all sides. Place them in a brown paper bag and let stand 10 minutes. Peel, seed and chop bell peppers.

Heat olive oil in a skillet and sauté onion, garlic and half the parsley for about 3 minutes. Add bell peppers, tomatoes, olives, capers, marjoram and water. Cook, covered, over low heat for 15 minutes. (This portion of the dish can be prepared in advance and refrigerated. Reheat before serving.) Cook pasta in boiling salted water until al dente according to package directions. Serve sauce over hot pasta and top with remaining parsley and cheese. *Makes 4 to 6 servings.*

TOMATO BASICS
Chopping whole tomatoes To cut whole tomatoes, cut out core from the stem end, then place the tomato cored side down and slice to desired thickness. Stack the slices in twos and threes and cut into strips; then cut the strips into cubes.

Dicing whole tomatoes Cut a cored tomato into quarters, and with a paring knife, remove inner pulp and seeds. Cut each section into even strips and then into cubes.

Seeding tomatoes Cut a cored tomato in half and squeeze gently to remove liquid and seeds; scoop out any remaining seeds with a spoon. If using plum tomatoes, cut in half lengthwise, remove inner membrane with a paring knife, and then scoop out seeds.

PERFECT PASTA

For perfect pasta, boil 4 quarts water per 1 pound of pasta in a 6-quart or larger pot. Add 1½ teaspoons salt and pasta to the boiling water. Stir immediately. Cover the pot and return to a boil. Remove lid and stir often to prevent pasta from sticking together or to the pot. Since the cooking time on pasta boxes is often overstated, start testing the pasta for doneness 3 minutes before the time noted on the box. Cook until pasta is al dente, or slightly chewy.

Reserve ½ cup of the pasta water for your sauce. Drain pasta in a colander for about 30 seconds. Do not shake the colander, as shaking removes the starch that helps sauce adhere to pasta. Return pasta to empty pot or warm serving bowl. Top or toss with sauce, adding reserved liquid as needed, and serve immediately.

PESTO—PASTA'S PARTNER

Pesto is an uncooked sauce of fresh ingredients that are crushed, ground, or puréed together. Basil is the classic pesto, but other ingredients make great pesto, too.

CLASSIC BASIL PESTO

Dairy

2 cups fresh basil leaves
2 garlic cloves
2 tablespoons pine nuts
½ cup extra-virgin olive oil
½ cup (2 ounces) grated
  Parmesan cheese
  Salt and pepper to taste

Combine basil, garlic, pine nuts and olive oil in a food processor and process until finely chopped. Add cheese and mix until blended. *Makes enough for 1 pound pasta, about 4 servings.*

Note: All pestos can be made in advance and stored in the refrigerator. Adding a small amount of olive oil on top will prevent discoloration.

SPINACH AND WALNUT PESTO

Dairy

1 cup fresh stemmed
  spinach leaves
4 garlic cloves, crushed
3 tablespoons walnut pieces
6 tablespoons extra-virgin
  olive oil
½ cup (2 ounces) grated
  Parmesan cheese
  Salt and pepper to taste

Combine spinach, garlic, walnuts and olive oil in a food processor or blender. Process until finely chopped. Spoon into a bowl. Add Parmesan cheese and mix well. Season with salt and pepper to taste. *Makes 4 servings.*

RED PESTO

Dairy

2 ounces sun-dried
  tomatoes in oil, drained
¼ cup fresh basil leaves
2 tablespoons slivered
  almonds
2 garlic cloves, minced
2 tablespoons grated
  Parmesan cheese
  Salt and pepper to taste

Combine tomatoes, basil, almonds and garlic in a food process or blender and process until finely chopped. Spoon into a bowl. Add the Parmesan cheese and mix well. Season with salt and pepper to taste. *Makes 4 servings.*

Pestos are a quick sauce for pasta. From the top,
Classic Basil Pesto, Red Pesto, Spinach and Walnut Pesto.

MUSHROOM ROLL-UPS FLORENTINE

Dairy

*S*o good, it's sure to become a staple in your house! If you don't want to take the time to make the roll-ups, it also works as lasagna.

BÉCHAMEL SAUCE
2 tablespoons butter
2 tablespoons flour
1 cup milk

ROLL-UPS
2 cups ricotta cheese
8 ounces cream cheese
1/2 cup (2 ounces) plus
  additional grated
  Parmesan cheese
3 eggs

4 cups chopped portobello
  mushroom caps
1 cup chopped basil
  Salt and pepper to taste
  plus additional salt
  for water
1 pound lasagna noodles
4 cups tomato sauce
1 (10-ounce) package
  frozen leaf spinach,
  thawed and drained

For the sauce, melt butter in a saucepan and stir in flour. Cook for several minutes, stirring constantly. Add milk and cook until sauce is thickened; remove from the heat. Cover and set aside.

For the roll-ups, preheat oven to 400 degrees. Combine ricotta cheese, cream cheese 1/2 cup Parmesan cheese and eggs in a large bowl. Add mushrooms, basil and salt and pepper to taste. Mixture should be thick, not loose.

Cook pasta in boiling salted water until al dente according to package directions. Drain and pat dry. Place 2 to 3 tablespoons of filling on one end and roll to enclose. Spread tomato sauce in the bottom of a 9×13-inch baking dish. Spread spinach over sauce. Arrange roll-ups seam side down in the prepared dish. Top with Béchamel Sauce and additional Parmesan cheese. Bake uncovered for 30 to 40 minutes or until golden brown and bubbly. *Makes 8 to 10 servings.*

Note: If available, you can substitute kosher mascarpone.

BAKED ZITI

Dairy

1 pound ziti
  Salt for water
1 (15-ounce) container
  ricotta cheese or
  1 (16-ounce) container
  cottage cheese
1 (32-ounce) jar
  marinara sauce, divided

2 (8-ounce) packages
  shredded mozzarella
  cheese, divided
1 egg
1/4 cup milk
  Salt and pepper to taste
  Grated Parmesan cheese

Preheat oven to 350 degrees. Cook pasta in boiling salted water until al dente according to package directions. Drain. Combine with ricotta cheese, 3/4 of the marinara sauce, 1 1/2 packages of the mozzarella cheese, egg and milk in a large bowl. Season with salt and pepper to taste and mix well. Combine mixture with pasta and pour into a 9×13-inch baking dish coated with nonstick cooking spray. Top with remaining marinara sauce, mozzarella cheese and sprinkle with Parmesan cheese. Bake, uncovered, for 50 to 60 minutes.
Makes 10 to 12 servings.

STUFFED SHELLS

Dairy

1 package jumbo shells
  Salt for water
2 (10-ounce) packages
  frozen chopped spinach,
  thawed and drained
1 (15-ounce) container
  ricotta cheese, or
  16 ounces cottage cheese

1 (8-ounce) package
  shredded mozzarella
  cheese (about 2 cups)
8 ounces cream cheese,
  softened
1 to 2 teaspoons salt
  Pepper to taste
1 1/2 to 2 cups marinara sauce

Preheat oven to 350 degrees. Cook pasta in boiling salted water until al dente according to package directions. Drain and rinse in water. Combine spinach, ricotta cheese, mozzarella cheese, cream cheese, salt and pepper. Take a pasta shell and press both ends, opening up the center of the shell. Fill center of shell with about 1 tablespoon filling. Repeat until finished. Arrange in a greased baking dish. Spoon marinara sauce over shells. Bake for about 30 minutes or until bubbly.
Makes 4 to 6 servings.

NO-BAKE ZITI

Dairy

Cook 1 pound ziti or rigatoni pasta in boiling salted water until al dente according to package directions; drain and cool. Bring one 26-ounce jar marinara sauce to a simmer in a saucepan over medium heat. Add 1 cup part-skim ricotta cheese, 1/4 cup (1 ounce) grated Parmesan cheese, 2 tablespoons chopped fresh Italian parsley and 1/2 teaspoon freshly ground pepper. Pour over pasta and toss to combine.
Makes 4 to 6 servings.

ROASTED GARLIC AND CHERRY TOMATOES

Parve

2   pounds grape tomatoes,
    cut in half
16 garlic cloves, whole and
    peeled
$1/2$ cup extra-virgin olive oil
2   tablespoons balsamic
    vinegar
$1/4$ teaspoon red pepper flakes
$1/2$ teaspoon salt plus salt
    for water
$1/4$ teaspoon freshly ground
    black pepper
1   pound spaghetti or
    linguini
$1/2$ cup torn fresh basil leaves

Preheat oven to 400 degrees. Arrange tomatoes and garlic so that they fit closely in a baking dish. Drizzle with olive oil and balsamic vinegar. Sprinkle with red pepper flakes, salt and black pepper. Roast in the oven for about 35 minutes or until garlic is soft and golden brown and tomatoes are shriveled. Cook pasta in boiling salted water until al dente according to package directions; drain. Combine tomatoes and garlic with hot pasta and toss to coat. Top with torn basil leaves and serve immediately.

Tomatoes and garlic can be prepared in advance and stored in the refrigerator. Warm before serving. *Makes 4 to 6 servings.*

Note: Recipe is parve as written. If serving as dairy, top with Parmesan cheese.

CHEESY FUSILLI ZUCCHINI

Dairy

$^1/_4$ cup ($^1/_2$ stick) butter
5 zucchini, trimmed and
   cut into chunks
3 garlic cloves, minced
6 fresh basil leaves,
   finely chopped
$^1/_2$ teaspoon salt
$^1/_4$ teaspoon freshly
   ground pepper

1 pound fusilli
   Salt for water
$^1/_4$ cup reserved cooking
   liquid
4 ounces mascarpone or
   cream cheese
$^1/_2$ cup ricotta cheese
   Grated Parmesan cheese

Heat butter in a large nonstick skillet and sauté zucchini for 5 to 10 minutes or until golden brown, stirring frequently. Add garlic, basil, $^1/_2$ teaspoon salt and $^1/_4$ teaspoon pepper. Cook for an additional 5 minutes; set aside. Cook pasta in boiling salted water until al dente according to package directions. Drain, reserving $^1/_4$ cup cooking liquid. Add mascarpone and ricotta cheese to warm pasta and mix well. Add zucchini mixture and mix well. If pasta seems dry, add reserved cooking liquid until it reaches desired consistency. Top with grated Parmesan cheese. Serve immediately. *Makes 4 to 6 servings.*

SPICY TOMATO OLIVE SAUCE À LA RIGATONI

Parve

1 pound rigatoni
   Salt for water plus
   $^1/_2$ teaspoon salt
3 tablespoons olive oil
$1^1/_2$ cups pitted kalamata
   olives, cut into halves

2 garlic cloves, finely chopped
$^3/_4$ teaspoon crushed red
   pepper flakes
1 (14- to 15-ounce) can
   crushed tomatoes

Cook pasta in boiling salted water until al dente according to package directions. Drain. Heat olive oil in a saucepan over medium heat and cook olives, garlic and red pepper for 2 minutes or until garlic is golden brown. Stir in tomatoes and salt and simmer, breaking up tomatoes, for 10 to 15 minutes until sauce is slightly thickened. Toss with hot cooked pasta until well blended. *Makes 4 to 6 servings.*

Note: For dairy, serve with Parmesan on the side.

GREAT BIG TOMATO FACTS!
Did you know that canned tomatoes contain even more lycopene—a powerful antioxidant that may help prevent heart disease and certain cancers—than fresh tomatoes?

Unopened canned tomato products will keep on the shelf for up to a year. Once opened, store tomato products in the refrigerator in glass or plastic containers for up to a week.

Diced canned tomatoes—the closest to fresh—are great in pasta salads, quick-cook sauces, omelets, and guacamole, or on bruschetta.

Many canned tomato sauces are little more than thick tomato juice, sometimes flavored with garlic, onion, or other seasonings. These are good for chili.

Use tomato paste sparingly to thicken or enhance the flavor of soups and sauces.

Brunch and Dairy

SAMPLER

Family Friendly

Apple Soufflé Omelet 170 • Apricot Noodle Pudding 170

Mushroom Onion Torta 171 • Salmon Breakfast Bake 173

Classic Spinach Casserole 173 • Eggplant Rollitini 174

Zucchini, Tomato and Mozzarella Tart 175

Zucchini Frittata (sidebar) 176 • Vegetable Bundt Frittata 176

Cheese-Filled Portobello Mushrooms 177 • Polenta Lasagna 180

Chocolate French Toast with Raspberry Sauce 184

Make Your Own Pizza 185 • Pumpkin Apple Streusel Muffins 186

Very Berry Bread 187

Cranberry Orange Muffins with Cinnamon-Sugar Topping 187

Quick and Easy

Salmon Breakfast Bake 173 • Classic Spinach Casserole 173

Zucchini Frittata (sidebar) 176 • Cheese-Filled Portobello Mushrooms 177

Make Your Own Pizza 185 • Pumpkin Apple Streusel Muffins 186

Very Berry Bread 187

Sophisticated

Leek and Brie Tart 172 • Roasted Eggplant and Bell Pepper Terrine 178

Veggie Burgers 181 • Linguini, Basil and Mushroom Flan 181

Freezes Well

Apricot Noodle Pudding 170

Classic Spinach Casserole 173 • Eggplant Rollitini 174

Pumpkin Apple Streusel Muffins 186 • Very Berry Bread 187

Cranberry Orange Muffins with Cinnamon-Sugar Topping 187

If you like fluffy omelets, follow these simple steps. Beat 3 fresh eggs for about 30 seconds. Melt butter in a 7¹/₂- or 8-inch nonstick skillet with sloping sides. When the butter turns light brown, pour the eggs into the skillet and begin stirring. Continue to stir with one hand while shaking the skillet with the other hand, being sure to keep the skillet on the burner. As soon as the eggs begin to form small pieces (this takes about 30 seconds), spread the eggs over the bottom of the skillet and add the filling, such as cheese or vegetables. Remove the skillet from the heat and fold the top and bottom of the omelet to the center and slide onto a plate. For a firmer omelet, turn off the heat and allow the omelet to stand for 10 to 20 seconds before adding desired filling.

APPLE SOUFFLÉ OMELET

Dairy

3 tablespoons butter, divided
2 tablespoons light brown sugar
1 sweet apple, peeled and sliced
5 tablespoons light cream, divided

4 eggs, separated
1 tablespoon sugar
Confectioners' sugar to taste

Heat 2 tablespoons butter and brown sugar in a skillet and sauté apple until tender. Add 3 tablespoons cream and cook until heated through. Remove from the heat and cover to keep warm. Beat egg yolks, remaining 2 tablespoons cream and sugar with electric mixer until blended. Beat egg whites in a clean mixing bowl with an electric mixer until stiff peaks form and fold into the yolk mixture.

Preheat broiler. Heat 1 tablespoon butter in a large ovenproof skillet over a medium-high flame until melted. Add egg mixture, spreading evenly. Cook until golden brown on the bottom. Remove from the heat and place under the broiler until brown on top. Slide omelet onto a plate and spread with apple mixture. Fold over to enclose filling and dust with confectioners' sugar. Serve immediately. *Makes 2 servings.*

APRICOT NOODLE PUDDING

Dairy

1 pound wide egg noodles
8 ounces cream cheese, cubed
2 cups sour cream
1 cup (2 sticks) unsalted butter, melted

1 cup (scant) sugar
2 eggs
2 tablespoons vanilla extract
1 (6-ounce) jar apricot preserves
Ground cinnamon to taste

Grease a 9×13-inch baking pan. Cook noodles according to the package directions; rinse and drain. Combine cream cheese, sour cream, butter, sugar, eggs and vanilla in a bowl using an electric mixer and beat until blended. Add noodles, mixing well by hand. Spoon noodle mixture into the prepared pan and cover the top with preserves. Sprinkle with cinnamon.

Chill, covered, for 8 to 10 hours. Preheat oven to 350 degrees. Bring pudding to room temperature and bake for 1¹/₂ hours. *Makes 8 to 10 servings.*

MUSHROOM ONION TORTA

Dairy

he contributor of this recipe acknowledges that it is very rich. But on those occasions that you want something special, throw caution to the wind and look no further. This is great!

PASTRY
2¹/2 cups all-purpose flour
1 teaspoon baking powder
1 cup (2 sticks) butter, softened
8 ounces cream cheese, softened

ONION FILLING
3 tablespoons butter
4 onions, thinly sliced

8 ounces mushrooms, sliced
2 tablespoons soy sauce
¹/2 teaspoon salt
Paprika to taste
Pepper to taste

CHEDDAR TOPPING
¹/2 cup sour cream
2 eggs, lightly beaten
4 ounces Cheddar cheese, shredded

For the pastry, lightly grease a 9- or 10-inch springform pan. Mix flour and baking powder in a bowl. Add butter and cream cheese and mix until blended. Pat dough over bottom and up side of prepared pan.

For the filling, preheat oven to 350 degrees. Heat butter in a skillet over medium heat and sauté onions for 10 to 15 minutes or until golden brown. Add mushrooms and sauté for 3 to 5 minutes longer or just until mushrooms are tender. Stir in soy sauce, salt, paprika and pepper to taste. Spread over prepared pastry.

For the topping, mix sour cream and eggs in a bowl and spread over onion mixture. Sprinkle with cheese and bake for 30 to 40 minutes or until golden brown. *Makes 8 to 10 servings.*

LEEK AND BRIE TART

Duiry

Dairy

"I once again subjected my guests to an unknown dish during the holidays. I became even more uncomfortable when I found out that I had a guest from France who was knowledgeable about French cuisine ...and I was serving this Brie dish! To my good fortune, everybody unanimously approved and my French guest thoroughly enjoyed the results."

INDIVIDUAL TARTLETS

Instead of one large tart, individual tartlets can be made. Either use individual tartlet pans or make your own shells using two sheets of PEPPERIDGE FARM® Puff Pastry. Roll one sheet of pastry on a hard surface and cut into thirds. Cut each third into four equal portions creating twelve squares. Cut one-third of the remaining sheet into four squares, reserving the remaining pastry for the lips of the tartlets. Cut the reserved pastry into strips and attach as a frame around each square. Pinch the sides up, creating a lip on each square and making sure that the two parts are well sealed. Proceed as directed in the recipe.

1/2 (17.3 ounce) package (1 sheet) frozen PEPPERIDGE FARM® Puff Pastry, thawed
2 tablespoons butter
4 leeks, cleaned and thinly sliced, white part only
1/4 cup water
Salt to taste

2/3 cup heavy cream
7 ounces Brie cheese, rind removed and cheese cut into 1/2-inch pieces
1 egg, lightly beaten
Pinch of cayenne pepper
1/4 cup (1 ounce) grated Parmesan cheese

Grease a 10-inch tart pan with removable bottom. Roll puff pastry on a hard surface into a 15-inch round and press into prepared pan. Freeze for 10 minutes.

Preheat oven to 400 degrees. Heat butter in a medium saucepan over medium heat. Stir in leeks and water and cook for 15 minutes or until tender, stirring occasionally. Remove from heat, season to taste with salt and let stand until cool. Bring cream to a boil in a separate saucepan over medium heat. Reduce heat to low and add Brie cheese. Cook until blended, stirring frequently. Remove from heat and cool for 5 minutes. Whisk in egg and cayenne pepper. Sprinkle pastry with Parmesan cheese and spread with leek mixture. Pour warm cream mixture over the top and bake for 20 minutes or until golden brown.

Makes 8 to 10 servings.

SALMON BREAKFAST BAKE

Dairy

2 cups small broccoli florets	8 ounces cream cheese,
10 scallions, chopped	cut into $1/4$- to
8 ounces sliced smoked	$1/2$-inch cubes
salmon, cut into	2 cups milk
1-inch pieces	1 cup buttermilk baking mix
8 ounces mozzarella cheese,	2 eggs
shredded	$1/4$ teaspoon salt
	$1/4$ teaspoon freshly
	ground pepper

Preheat oven to 375 degrees. Coat a 9×13-inch baking dish with nonstick cooking spray. Layer broccoli, $1/2$ of scallions, salmon, mozzarella cheese, cream cheese and top with remaining scallions in the prepared dish. Process milk, baking mix, eggs, salt and pepper in a blender until smooth. Pour milk mixture over prepared layers and bake for 30 minutes or just until center is set. Let stand for 10 minutes before serving. *Makes 6 to 8 servings.*

CLASSIC SPINACH CASSEROLE

Dairy

Want to make your whole family happy for lunch or even dinner? This is a sure-fire classic hit that will be loved by one and all.

10 to 12 slices American	2 cups cottage cheese
cheese, torn into small	5 to 6 eggs, lightly beaten
pieces, or 8 ounces	6 tablespoons
shredded Cheddar cheese	all-purpose flour
2 (10-ounce) packages	Salt and pepper to taste
frozen chopped spinach,	
thawed and drained	

Preheat oven to 350 degrees. Grease a 9×13-inch baking dish. Reserve a small amount of American cheese for topping. Combine remaining American cheese, spinach, cottage cheese, eggs, flour and salt and pepper to taste in a bowl and mix well. Spoon spinach mixture into prepared baking dish and sprinkle with reserved American cheese. Bake for 45 to 60 minutes or until brown and bubbly. You may freeze for future use. *Makes 6 to 8 servings.*

Caffe Latte

Caffe latte is one part espresso, two parts warmed milk, plus frothed milk. This mild blend of milk and coffee is typically served in a tall glass. In Italy, it is a coffee drink that is enjoyed by children and adults alike.

For 2 servings: heat 2 cups milk in a saucepan over medium-low heat until milk is steaming. Using a frother, whip $1/4$ cup cold milk until foamy. Divide 1 cup espresso and warmed milk between two tall heatproof glasses. Spoon milk foam on top to taste.

Frothing Milk

A light, buoyant froth is easier to achieve with cold than hot milk, and with skim milk more easily than with 2 percent or whole milk. (You'll need at least $1/4$ cup milk to froth it properly.)

EGGPLANT ROLLITINI

. . . .

Dairy

This recipe requires a little bit of work, but the result is well worth the time.

2 eggs
3 tablespoons milk
3/4 cup all-purpose flour
2 cups seasoned bread crumbs
1 (1- to 1¹/₂-pound) eggplant, peeled and cut lengthwise into ¹/₄-inch slices
3 tablespoons vegetable oil
3 cups ricotta cheese
8 ounces mozzarella cheese, shredded
2 ounces Parmesan cheese, grated
2 eggs, lightly beaten
   Onion powder to taste
   Garlic powder to taste
   Salt and pepper to taste
1 (16-ounce) jar marinara sauce, divided

Preheat oven to 350 degrees. Whisk two eggs and milk in a shallow dish until blended. Place flour and bread crumbs on separate plates. Coat each eggplant slice with flour, dip in egg mixture and coat with bread crumbs. Heat oil in a skillet and fry coated slices until brown on both sides. Drain on paper towels.

Mix ricotta cheese, mozzarella cheese and Parmesan cheese in a bowl. Stir in two eggs and season to taste with onion powder, garlic powder, salt and pepper. Spread ¹/₂ of marinara sauce in a 9×13-inch baking dish. Arrange 1 fried eggplant slice on a plate and spread ²/₃ of slice with a layer of cheese mixture. Roll from filled end to enclose filling and arrange roll in prepared baking dish. Repeat process with remaining eggplant slices and remaining cheese mixture. Top with remaining marinara sauce and bake for 40 to 45 minutes or until golden brown and bubbly. *Makes 6 to 8 servings.*

Zucchini, Tomato and Mozzarella Tart

Dairy

This tart is unique because it uses puff pastry for the crust, which yields a lighter crust and is also very easy.

1/2 (17.3 ounce) package (1 sheet) frozen PEPPERIDGE FARM® Puff Pastry, thawed

1 1/2 cups (6 ounces) shredded mozzarella cheese

6 tablespoons plus 1/4 cup freshly shredded Parmesan cheese, divided

1/2 cup thinly sliced fresh basil

1/4 cup chopped green onions

1 tablespoon chopped fresh oregano

2 small zucchini, cut into thin rounds

3 to 4 plum tomatoes, thinly sliced

2 large eggs

1 cup half-and-half

1/2 teaspoon salt

1/4 teaspoon pepper

Preheat oven to 400 degrees. Roll out pastry dough to 1/8 inch thick. Trim edges to a 13-inch circle. Press pastry into a greased 9- to 10-inch springform pan. Chill 1 hour. Sprinkle mozzarella cheese over the bottom of crust and top with 6 tablespoons Parmesan cheese. Sprinkle basil, green onions and oregano on top. Arrange a layer of zucchini, then top with a layer of tomatoes, in concentric circles. Whisk eggs, half-and-half, salt and pepper in a medium bowl; pour over tomato layer. Sprinkle with remaining Parmesan cheese. Bake 45 to 60 minutes or until center is set and crust is golden brown. Serve warm or at room temperature. *Makes 4 to 8 servings.*

Cappuccino

Cappuccino is equal parts espresso, warmed milk and froth. A cappuccino is a treat to drink; a thick layer of froth tickles the nose, then gradually dissolves into the caramel-colored coffee. Indeed, its perfect balance—a nearly even blend of espresso and warmed milk—may account for its wide popularity. In Italy, where it was named for brown-and-white cowls of the Capuchin monks, it is the classic morning beverage.

For 2 servings, heat 1 cup milk in a saucepan over medium-low heat until steaming. Using a frother, whip 1/2 cup cold milk until foamy. Divide 1 cup espresso and warmed milk between two coffee cups. Spoon milk foam on top to taste.

ZUCCHINI FRITTATA
Dairy

Preheat oven to 350 degrees. Coat a 9×13-inch baking pan with nonstick cooking spray. Heat 2 tablespoons oil in a skillet and sauté 2 chopped onions until tender but not brown, stirring frequently. Stir in 4 thinly sliced unpeeled zucchini and 8 ounces thinly sliced mushrooms and cook until tender. Remove from heat. Add 8 ounces shredded mozzarella or pizza cheese, 4 lightly beaten eggs and salt and freshly ground pepper to taste to vegetable mixture and mix well. Pour egg mixture into the prepared baking pan and bake for 30 minutes or until light brown. Serve hot or chilled. *Makes 6 to 8 servings.*

VEGETABLE BUNDT FRITTATA
Dairy

What a great addition to a brunch spread.

2	cups (1-inch) pieces fresh asparagus or broccoli (about 1 pound)	2	cups (8 ounces) shredded Cheddar cheese, divided
	Salt to taste	2	small onions, chopped
12	eggs	1	carrot, grated
1	cup milk	1	teaspoon salt
1	cup all-purpose flour	1/4	teaspoon freshly ground pepper
1/2	teaspoon baking powder	2	scallions, chopped

Preheat oven to 375 degrees. Coat a 12-cup bundt pan with nonstick cooking spray. Steam asparagus in boiling salted water in a saucepan for 5 minutes or until tender-crisp and bright green; drain. Whisk eggs in a bowl until foamy. Add milk and continue whisking until blended. Stir in flour and baking powder. Add 1 1/2 cups cheese, asparagus, onions, carrot, salt and pepper and mix well.

Pour egg mixture into prepared pan and bake for 45 minutes or until golden brown. Cool in the pan on a wire rack. Frittata can be made in advance up to this point. Increase oven temperature to 500 degrees or preheat broiler. Invert cooled frittata onto an oven-safe plate and sprinkle with remaining 1/2 cup cheese and scallions. Bake or broil until cheese melts. Serve immediately. *Makes 12 to 16 servings.*

CHEESE-FILLED PORTOBELLO MUSHROOMS

Dairy

6 large portobello mushrooms, stems removed	1 tablespoon chopped fresh basil
3 tablespoons olive oil, divided	1 cup (4 ounces) shredded mozzarella cheese
1/2 teaspoon salt	1/2 cup (2 ounces) grated Parmesan cheese
1/4 cup chopped plum tomatoes	

Preheat oven to 400 degrees. Coat a baking sheet with nonstick cooking spray. Wipe mushroom caps with a damp paper towel and brush both sides with 2 tablespoons of olive oil. Sprinkle with salt. Arrange mushrooms stem side down on the prepared baking sheet. Bake for 20 to 25 minutes or until tender, brushing with additional olive oil and covering loosely with foil if the mushrooms dry out before cooked through. Remove from oven.

Heat remaining 1 tablespoon of olive oil in a medium skillet over medium heat and add tomatoes. Cook until sauce thickens, stirring frequently. Turn mushrooms over with metal spatula and layer each with equal portions of tomato sauce, basil, mozzarella cheese and Parmesan cheese. Broil for 3 minutes or until light brown and bubbly. Serve immediately. To serve as an hors d'oeuvre, cut mushrooms into quarters and arrange on colorful platter. *Makes 6 servings.*

Dessert Coffees
Combine 1/2 cup hot brewed coffee with one of the following flavorings and top with a dollop of whipped cream and a sprinkle of cinnamon or nutmeg.

For Cafe Alexander, add 1 tablespoon creme de cacao and 1 tablespoon brandy.

For Cafe Benedictine, add 2 tablespoons Benedictine and 1 tablespoon light cream.

For Cafe Caribe, add 1 tablespoon coffee liqueur and 1 tablespoon rum.

For Cafe Columbian, add 2 tablespoons coffee liqueur.

For Cafe Dublin, add 1 tablespoon Irish whiskey and 2 teaspoons sugar.

For Cafe Holland, add 2 tablespoons chocolate mint liqueur.

For Cafe Israel, add 2 tablespoons chocolate syrup and 2 tablespoons orange liqueur.

Roasted Eggplant and Bell Pepper Terrine

Dairy

*P*repare the terrine one day in advance and store, covered, in the refrigerator. Bring to room temperature before serving.

4 red bell peppers
2 eggplant, cut into
   $1/4$-inch slices
1 small shallot, minced
1 tablespoon balsamic
   vinegar
$1/2$ teaspoon salt

$1/8$ teaspoon freshly
   ground pepper
2 tablespoons extra-virgin
   olive oil
$1/4$ cup low-fat ricotta cheese
2 cups loosely packed fresh
   basil leaves
   Fresh basil for garnish

Roast bell peppers over gas flame or under a broiler until blackened. Remove to a deep bowl and let steam, covered with plastic wrap, for 10 to 15 minutes. Peel, seed and cut bell peppers into 1-inch strips.

Preheat oven to 400 degrees. Grease two baking sheets. Arrange eggplant slices in a single layer on prepared baking sheets and roast for 20 to 25 minutes or until tender and light brown, turning after 12

minutes. Remove to a wire rack to cool. Whisk shallot, vinegar, salt and pepper in a bowl until combined. Add olive oil gradually, whisking constantly until well combined.

Grease a 5×9-inch loaf pan and line with plastic wrap. Arrange $1/3$ of eggplant slices slightly overlapping in prepared loaf pan. Brush lightly with vinaigrette. Layer with $1/2$ of bell pepper strips slightly overlapping, $1/2$ of ricotta cheese and $1/2$ of basil. Brush with vinaigrette. Top with $1/2$ of remaining eggplant slices and brush lightly with vinaigrette. Layer with remaining bell peppers, remaining ricotta cheese, remaining basil and brush with vinaigrette. Top with remaining eggplant slices and brush with vinaigrette. Press firmly but gently to compress layers. Chill, covered tightly with plastic wrap, for 12 to 24 hours. Invert onto a platter and garnish with additional fresh basil. *Makes 10 to 12 servings.*

SHIITAKE MUSHROOM AND HERB STRATA

Dairy

· · · · · · · · · · · · ·

This is a great brunch recipe that will leave your guests "scrambling" for more!

- 2 tablespoons butter
- 1 pound fresh shiitake mushrooms, stemmed and coarsely chopped
- 1/2 cup chopped shallots
- 3/4 teaspoon dried rosemary, crushed
- 2 garlic cloves, minced
  Salt and pepper to taste
- 1 cup light cream
- 8 ounces cream cheese, cubed
- 8 eggs, lightly beaten
- 8 ounces mozzarella cheese, shredded
- 8 to 10 (1-inch) slices Italian bread (about 10 ounces)

Grease a 9×13-inch baking dish. Heat butter in a heavy skillet over medium-high heat and sauté mushrooms, shallots and rosemary for 5 minutes or until mushrooms and shallots are tender, stirring constantly. Add garlic and cook for 1 minute. Season to taste with salt and pepper. You may prepare in advance and let stand at room temperature.

Mix light cream and cream cheese in a saucepan and cook over medium-low heat until smooth, whisking frequently. Remove from heat and cool slightly. Whisk in eggs and then mozzarella cheese.

Arrange bread slices over bottom of prepared baking dish. Pour egg mixture over bread and sprinkle with mushroom mixture. Chill, covered with foil and topped with a pan filled with sugar, rice or canned goods, for 1 to 10 hours. This assures that the egg mixture penetrates the entire piece of bread. Preheat oven to 325 degrees. Bring strata to room temperature and bake for 45 minutes or until puffed and golden brown. *Makes 8 to 10 servings.*

POLENTA LASAGNA

Dairy

This is a nice change from traditional lasagna. The polenta is a great new flavor and a nice twist on a classic.

POLENTA SHORTCUT

You may substitute two 16-ounce tubes commercially prepared polenta for homemade polenta. Combine with onion mixture and proceed as directed in recipe.

2	tablespoons olive oil	2 (10-ounce) packages
1	onion, finely chopped	frozen chopped spinach,
1	garlic clove, minced	thawed and drained
7	cups water	4 cups ricotta cheese
	Salt to taste	2 cups shredded mozzarella
2	cups instant polenta	cheese, divided
7	tablespoons grated	Pepper to taste
	Parmesan cheese, divided	1 (32-ounce) jar
		marinara sauce

Heat olive oil in a large saucepan and sauté onion for 3 to 5 minutes or until tender. Add garlic and sauté for 1 minute longer. Add water and desired amount of salt to the onion mixture and bring to a boil. Add polenta gradually, stirring constantly. Reduce heat to low and cook for 3 to 5 minutes or until smooth and creamy, stirring constantly. Stir in 1/4 cup Parmesan cheese. Let stand for 2 hours or until set.

Preheat oven to 350 degrees and grease a 9×13-inch baking dish. Mix spinach with 3 tablespoons Parmesan cheese, ricotta cheese, 1 1/2 cups mozzarella cheese and salt and pepper to taste in a bowl. Spread a thin layer of marinara sauce in the prepared baking dish. Flatten the polenta a few tablespoons at a time and layer over the sauce until the bottom is completely covered. Top with 1/2 of cheese mixture, 1/2 of remaining marinara sauce, remaining polenta, remaining cheese mixture and remaining marinara sauce. Sprinkle with remaining 1/2 cup mozzarella cheese and bake for 1 hour or until brown and bubbly. *Makes 12 servings.*

VEGGIE BURGERS

Parve

1	cup cooked brown rice	1	rib celery, chopped
1	cup drained chick-peas, coarsely mashed	2	garlic cloves, minced
1/2	cup rolled oats		Salt, pepper and paprika to taste
1/4	cup fresh parsley, chopped		Soy sauce to taste
3	tablespoons vegetable oil		Buns or pitas
1	onion, chopped		Sliced tomatoes and onions

Preheat broiler or grill. Combine brown rice, chick-peas and oats in a bowl and mix well. Stir in parsley. Heat oil in a skillet and sauté onion until tender. Stir in celery and garlic and sauté for 2 to 3 minutes longer or until celery is tender. Add onion mixture to rice mixture and mix well. Season to taste with salt, pepper, paprika and soy sauce.

Shape rice mixture into patties and broil or grill until brown on both sides, turning once. Serve on buns or in pitas dressed with sliced tomatoes and sliced onions. *Makes 4 to 6 servings.*

Photograph for this recipe is on page 123.

LINGUINI, BASIL AND MUSHROOM FLAN

Dairy

	Nonstick cooking spray	1/2	teaspoon freshly ground pepper
3	cups sliced cremini mushrooms	2	cups (about 4 ounces) linguini, cooked, drained
1 1/4	cups thinly sliced leeks	1/3	cup chopped fresh basil
6	eggs	1/2	cup (2 ounces) shredded mozzarella cheese
1/2	cup milk		
2	teaspoons butter, melted		
3/4	teaspoon salt		

Preheat oven to 450 degrees. Heat cooking spray in a large nonstick skillet and sauté mushrooms and leeks for 6 minutes or until tender, stirring frequently. Whisk eggs in a bowl until blended. Add milk, butter, salt and pepper and whisk until well blended. Stir in mushroom mixture. Add cooked pasta, basil and cheese and mix well.

Pour egg mixture into greased skillet and cook for 4 minutes or until edge begins to set. Gently lift edge with spatula to allow the uncooked egg mixture to flow underneath the cooked portion. Cook for 5 minutes longer or until set. Cut into wedges and serve. *Makes 4 servings.*

GRATE NEWS!
A serrated knife can be a useful substitute when you do not have a cheese grater. Hold the cheese directly over the dish and scrape lightly with the serrated knife.

SAY CHEESE!

*Cheeses come in many varieties and flavors. Cheese generally begins as milk—
either cow, goat, or sheep—which is often cooked or curdled to start the chemical processes
that change it into cheese. Sometimes other ingredients are added to the process.
It then separates into liquid, called "whey," and solids, "curds." The whey is drained off and
curds are either allowed to drain or are pressed into different shapes. Here's a quick
reference to better understand cheeses and their flavors.*

HARD CHEESES are cured curds that have been pressed, then aged for at least 60 days. Examples of hard cheese include Parmesan, Pecorino, Swiss, and Kashkaval. These often have a mature flavor and a hard texture that grates well.

SEMI-SOFT/SEMI-FIRM cheeses are curds that are pressed and pasteurized, but not aged. Their texture is firm but sliceable. Examples include Mozzarella, Muenster, Havarti, Gouda, Monterey Jack, and Cheddar. The flavor of these cheeses is typically milder than that of a hard cheese.

BLUE-VEINED cheeses are injected or sprayed with spores of the mold from different penicilliums. These cheeses are aged, with the result that they have veins of flavorful blue or green mold. Blue-veined cheeses are made from either cow or sheep milk. Examples of blue-veined cheeses include Blue Cheese and Roquefort.

Some **SOFT CHEESES** are ripened. They are subjected to various bacteria, and then the cheese ripens from the outside. They can range in consistency from creamy and spreadable to crumbly. Examples of these cheeses include Brie, Camembert, Feta, and Goat Cheeses. They range in flavor from mild to more flavorful.

FRESH CHEESES are soft and commonly available. They include Ricotta, Mascarpone, Cream Cheese, Cottage Cheese, and Farmer Cheese. These cheeses are all mild in flavor.

MAKE YOUR OWN FUN

*For a fun night in, and a great activity for kids'
parties and sleepovers or an easy family gathering,
Make Your Own Pizza, page 185.*

CHOCOLATE FRENCH TOAST WITH RASPBERRY SAUCE

Dairy

Very easy to prepare and a real crowd pleaser.

RASPBERRY SAUCE
- 1/2 cup fresh raspberries
- 1 tablespoon fresh lemon juice
- 1/2 to 3/4 cup confectioners' sugar

FRENCH TOAST
- 2 cups milk
- 6 eggs
- 1 tablespoon sugar
- 1 teaspoon vanilla extract
- 3 tablespoons unsalted butter, divided
- 8 (1/2-inch) slices challah
- 4 ounces semisweet chocolate, finely chopped
- 1/2 cup fresh raspberries

For the sauce, combine raspberries, lemon juice and 1/2 cup of confectioners' sugar in food processor and process until combined. Taste and add remaining confectioners' sugar if desired. Strain sauce through a fine mesh strainer over a bowl, discarding solids.

For the toast, whisk milk, eggs, sugar and vanilla in shallow dish until blended. Heat some of the butter in a large heavy nonstick skillet over medium heat. Dip 1 bread slice into egg mixture until lightly soaked and place in hot butter. Sprinkle with 1/4 of chocolate. Dip another slice of bread into egg mixture and place over chocolate, forming a sandwich. Place in the skillet. Press gently with spatula to compress and cook until light brown. Turn and cook until brown on both sides, adding more butter as needed. Cut each diagonally into halves and then into quarters. Arrange in a shallow baking dish and keep warm in a 200-degree oven. Repeat process with bread, egg mixture and chocolate. Serve French toast with raspberries and sauce. *Makes 4 servings.*

Photograph for this recipe is on page 169.

MAKE YOUR OWN PIZZA

Dairy

For a fun night in, a great activity for kids' parties and sleepovers, or an easy family gathering, set up a make-your-own pizza station. This recipe is lots of fun, and everyone will have pizzas according to their specifications.

CRUST
- 1¼ cups warm (100 to 110 degrees) water
- 2 envelopes dry yeast
- 3 tablespoons olive oil
- 1 tablespoon honey
- 4 cups all-purpose flour, divided
- 2 teaspoons kosher salt
  Cornmeal
  Olive oil for brushing

PIZZA
- 4 cups marinara sauce
- 1 red onion, thinly sliced
- 6 plum tomatoes, sliced
- 1 pound fresh mozzarella cheese, shredded
- 8 ounces Cheddar cheese, shredded
- 1 bunch basil leaves, chopped
- 2 cups ricotta cheese
- 4 garlic cloves, sliced
- 4 ounces Parmesan cheese, grated
  Crushed red pepper flakes
- 1 red or yellow bell pepper, julienned
- 1 bunch broccoli, separated into small florets
- 2 cups fresh spinach leaves, chopped
- 2 cups thinly sliced white mushrooms or small portobello mushrooms
- ½ cup olive oil

For the crust, combine warm water, yeast, 3 tablespoons olive oil and honey in mixing bowl of an electric mixer fitted with dough hook. Add 3 cups of the flour and salt and beat until combined. Add remaining 1 cup flour until a soft dough forms, beating constantly. Knead at medium speed for 10 minutes or until smooth, adding flour if necessary to prevent the dough from sticking to bowl.

Knead dough on a lightly floured surface until smooth and elastic. Shape into a ball and place in greased bowl, turning to coat. Let rest, covered for 30 minutes. Divide dough into 3 equal portions for 3 large pizzas or into 6 portions for smaller pizzas. Shape each portion into a ball and arrange on a baking sheet. Let rest. Use immediately or chill for up to 4 hours. If chilled, bring to room temperature. Roll larger portions into 12-inch rounds and smaller portions into 8-inch rounds. Arrange rounds on baking sheets sprinkled with cornmeal. Brush with olive oil.

For the pizza, preheat oven to 500 degrees. Spread rounds with marinara sauce and top with desired toppings, piling high. Drizzle each pizza with olive oil and bake for 15 minutes or until crust is crisp and toppings are cooked through. *Makes 3 (12-inch) pizzas or 6 (8-inch) pizzas.*

Photograph for this recipe is on page 183.

PUMPKIN APPLE STREUSEL MUFFINS

Parve or Dairy

STREUSEL TOPPING
- $1/2$ cup sugar
- $1/4$ cup all-purpose flour
- 1 teaspoon ground cinnamon
- $1/4$ cup ($1/2$ stick) butter or margarine

MUFFINS
- $2^1/2$ cups all-purpose flour
- 2 cups sugar
- 1 tablespoon pumpkin pie spice
- 1 teaspoon baking soda
- $1/2$ teaspoon salt
- 1 cup canned pumpkin
- $1/2$ cup vegetable oil
- 2 eggs, lightly beaten
- 2 cups chopped peeled McIntosh apples

For the topping, mix sugar, flour and cinnamon in bowl. Cut in butter and blend until crumbly.

For the muffins, preheat oven to 350 degrees. Grease eighteen muffin cups or line with paper liners. Mix flour, sugar, pumpkin pie spice, baking soda and salt in a bowl and set aside. Beat pumpkin, oil and eggs in a bowl using an electric mixer until blended. Add flour mixture to pumpkin mixture and mix just until moistened. Fold in apples. Spoon batter into prepared muffin cups and sprinkle with topping. Bake for 35 to 40 minutes or until inserted toothpick comes out clean.

Makes $1^1/2$ dozen muffins.

Top to bottom:
Cranberry Orange Muffins with Cinnamon-Sugar Topping 187
Very Berry Bread 187 • Pumpkin Apple Streusel Muffins (this page).

VERY BERRY BREAD

Parve or Dairy

2 cups all-purpose flour	2 eggs
2 teaspoons baking powder	$1/2$ cup half-and-half or non-
$1/2$ teaspoon salt	dairy topping
$1/2$ cup (1 stick) butter or	2 teaspoons vanilla extract
margarine, softened	1 pound fresh strawberries,
$1^1/2$ cups plus 3 to 4 tablespoons	chopped
sugar, divided	6 ounces fresh blueberries

Preheat oven to 350 degrees. Mix flour, baking powder and salt together and set aside. Beat butter and $1^1/2$ cups sugar in a bowl using an electric mixer until blended. Beat in eggs, then flour mixture. Stir in half-and-half and vanilla. Fold in berries.

Spoon batter evenly into two greased 5×9-inch loaf pans and sprinkle with 3 to 4 tablespoons sugar. Bake for 35 to 45 minutes or until an inserted toothpick comes out clean. Cool slightly, then remove from pans. You may also bake in muffin cups but adjust baking time. *Makes 2 loaves.*

CRANBERRY ORANGE MUFFINS WITH CINNAMON-SUGAR TOPPING

Parve

$2^1/2$ cups all-purpose flour	2 eggs
2 teaspoons baking soda	1 tablespoon orange zest
$1^1/4$ cups sugar, divided	1 cup dried cranberries
$1/2$ cup (1 stick)	$1/4$ cup sugar
unsalted margarine	$1/2$ teaspoon ground
$3/4$ cup orange juice	cinnamon

Preheat oven to 350 degrees. Line twelve muffin cups with paper liners. Mix flour and baking soda together and set aside. Beat 1 cup sugar and margarine in mixing bowl using an electric mixer until smooth. Add orange juice, eggs and orange zest and beat until blended. Add flour mixture and stir just until moistened. Fold in cranberries.

Spoon batter into the prepared muffin cups. Combine $1/4$ cup sugar and cinnamon in a bowl and sprinkle evenly over tops of muffins. Bake for 20 to 25 minutes or until light brown and a wooden pick inserted in the center comes out clean. Cool in pan for 2 minutes. Remove muffins to wire rack to cool. *Makes 1 dozen muffins.*

Photograph for these recipes is on page 186.

SUCCESS WITH MUFFINS AND QUICK BREADS

Get it right every time with these guidelines:

Coat the bottom of individual muffin cups or loaf pans with nonstick cooking spray. Whisk dry ingredients together to combine thoroughly.

Make a well in the center of the dry ingredients; then stir in wet ingredients just to moisten. Do not overmix or muffins may be tough.

Bake until a toothpick inserted in the center comes out clean.

Cool briefly in the baking pan on a rack. Remove to a rack and cool completely.

SIDE DISHES

SAMPLER

FAMILY FRIENDLY
Soy Sauce Green Beans 191 • Green Beans with Cremini Mushroom Sauce 192
Roasted Cauliflower 193 • Creamed Spinach 193 • Bravas Potatoes 195
Herbed Mashed Potatoes 196 • Scalloped Potatoes with White Wine 196
Stuffed Zucchini 199 • Fall Starburst 200 • Ratatouille Tart 201
Brown Rice with Leeks and Mushrooms 202
Barley-Pine Nut Casserole 202 • Pear and Cranberry Crisp 203
Orzo with Caramelized Onion and Mushroom Sauté 206
Crunchy Top Pumpkin Bread 207 • Coriander Rice 209
Homemade Rice and 'Roni 210 • Corn Squash Muffins 211
Yerushalmi Kugel 211 • Snap-Crackle-Pop Apple Kugel 212

QUICK AND EASY
Roasted Cauliflower 193 • Creamed Spinach 193
Marinated Portobello Mushrooms 194
Bravas Potatoes 195 • Roasted Sweet Potatoes and Mushrooms 198
Brown Rice with Leeks and Mushrooms 202
Barley-Pine Nut Casserole 202 • Orange and Almond Couscous 203
Orzo with Caramelized Onion and Mushroom Sauté 206
Crunchy Top Pumpkin Bread 207 • Basmati Rice with Asparagus 209
Homemade Rice and 'Roni 210 • Corn Squash Muffins 211
Yerushalmi Kugel 211 • Pineapple Rounds 213

FREEZES WELL
Creamed Spinach 193 • Crunchy Top Pumpkin Bread 207
Corn Squash Muffins 211 • Yerushalmi Kugel 211 • Snap-Crackle-Pop Apple
Kugel 212 • Pineapple Rounds 213

Oven-Roasted Asparagus with Orange Almond Vinaigrette

Parve

For a pretty presentation, serve garnished with orange slices.

4   tablespoons olive oil, divided
1/4   cup slivered almonds
1/2   cup orange juice
1   teaspoon minced fresh thyme
2   tablespoons minced shallot
2   tablespoons red wine vinegar
    Kosher salt and pepper to taste
2   pounds asparagus, ends trimmed

Preheat oven to 500 degrees. Heat 2 tablespoons olive oil in a large skillet over medium heat and sauté almonds for 5 minutes or until golden brown. Add orange juice, thyme and shallot. Increase heat and simmer for 4 minutes or until thickened. Remove from heat and stir in vinegar and kosher salt and pepper to taste. Set aside. Coat asparagus with remaining 2 tablespoons olive oil and season with kosher salt and pepper to taste. Spread in a single layer on a baking sheet and roast for 10 minutes or until tender, turning occasionally. Top with orange almond vinaigrette.

Makes 6 to 8 servings.

COLD GREEN BEANS WITH DILL AND PECAN SAUCE

Parve

1¹/2 pounds fresh green beans	¹/2 cup (2 ounces) chopped pecans
3/4 cup chopped scallions	¹/4 cup olive oil or vegetable oil
3 tablespoons minced parsley	
3 tablespoons minced dill weed	3 tablespoons cider vinegar or wine vinegar
	Salt and pepper to taste

Steam green beans for 5 to 7 minutes or until tender and crisp. Rinse with cold running water to stop cooking. Drain well. Mix beans with scallions. Combine parsley, dill weed, pecans, olive oil, vinegar and salt and pepper to taste in a jar with a tight-fitting lid. Shake to combine. Pour over beans and toss to coat. *Makes 4 to 6 servings.*

SOY SAUCE GREEN BEANS

Parve

1 pound green beans, trimmed	2 tablespoons soy sauce
2 tablespoons olive oil	1 teaspoon cumin
	1 garlic clove, minced

Preheat oven to 450 degrees. Steam green beans in boiling water for 4 to 5 minutes. Drain and rinse with cold running water. Combine olive oil, soy sauce, cumin and garlic in a medium bowl and mix well. Add beans and toss to coat. Arrange beans and sauce on a baking sheet and cook for 45 minutes, stirring often.
Makes 4 servings.

STRAIGHT CUT
To cut scallions, string beans, or any food that is straight and linear, line up the pieces next to one another. Then just slice the entire line.

GREEN BEANS WITH CREMINI MUSHROOM SAUCE

Parve or Meat

T̲his is an updated version of the classic green bean casserole. The casserole can be assembled a day ahead of serving and refrigerated overnight. Let it return to room temperature before baking. Keep the fried shallots in an airtight container overnight. Recrisp in a 350-degree oven and let cool.

1 pound shallots, thinly sliced	Pinch of cayenne pepper
1/2 cup plus 3 tablespoons all-purpose flour	Black pepper to taste
1/2 cup vegetable oil for frying	1 pound cremini mushrooms caps, thinly sliced
Salt to taste	2 cups MANISCHEWITZ® Chicken Broth or bouillon
2 1/2 pounds green beans	1/2 cup nondairy creamer
2 tablespoons unsalted margarine	2 tablespoons fresh lemon juice
1 onion, thinly sliced	
1/2 teaspoon paprika	

Toss shallots with 1/2 cup flour; shake off any excess flour. Heat vegetable oil in a large skillet over medium heat and fry shallots in two batches for 3 minutes or until crisp. Transfer with a slotted spoon to paper towels, then season with salt to taste.

Steam green beans in salted water for 5 minutes or until just tender. Drain and rinse under cold running water; pat dry.

Preheat oven to 400 degrees. Heat margarine in a skillet over medium-high heat. Add onion and sauté for 5 minutes or until softened. Add paprika, cayenne and a large pinch of black pepper. Add mushrooms, cover and cook for 5 minutes or until softened. Uncover and stir in 3 tablespoons flour and then gradually add broth. Simmer, stirring, for 5 minutes, until lump-free and thickened. Stir in nondairy creamer, lemon juice and green beans. Cover and simmer for 5 minutes or until beans are heated through, stirring occasionally. Season with salt and black pepper to taste. Spoon into a large baking dish. Bake, covered with foil, for 20 minutes or until bubbling. Uncover, scatter shallots on top and serve. *Makes 10 servings.*

ROASTED CAULIFLOWER
. . . .
Parve

" *gave this recipe to a couple of friends and before I knew it, the whole town was making it!*"

2 to 3 heads cauliflower,
   cut into florets
1/2 cup olive oil

6 to 8 garlic cloves, crushed
   Kosher salt and pepper
   to taste

Combine all ingredients in a plastic bag and toss to coat the cauliflower. Marinate up to 12 hours. Preheat oven to 400 degrees. Spread cauliflower with marinating liquid on a large rimmed baking sheet. Roast in the upper part of the oven for 35 to 45 minutes or until cauliflower is golden brown, turning occasionally. *Makes 6 to 8 servings.*

CREAMED SPINACH
. . . .
Meat

" *hen you think about comfort food and old-time favorites, creamed spinach is certainly one food that comes to mind. It was the favorite family side dish in my husband's family and is always served in my home on holidays and by request on birthdays.*"

1/4 cup (1/2 stick) margarine
5 tablespoons quick mixing
   flour (or all-purpose flour)
1 cup nondairy creamer
2 cups MANISCHEWITZ®
   Chicken Broth

2 (10-ounce) packages
   frozen chopped spinach,
   thawed and drained
   Salt, pepper and garlic
   powder to taste

Melt margarine in a large saucepan and stir in flour, whisking until blended. Gradually pour in creamer and cook until thickened, whisking constantly. Whisk in soup and cook until mixture begins to thicken. Add spinach and salt, pepper and garlic powder to taste. Simmer over low heat for 5 to 10 minutes. Serve immediately or rewarm, covered. *Makes 6 to 8 servings.*

CAULIFLOWER PREP
Whether you plan to boil, steam, or roast this vegetable, start by giving your cauliflower a simple trim.

Although the leaves and stem are edible, they have a tough texture and stronger flavor than the florets.

Rinse cauliflower well just before using it. Snap off and discard tough outer leaves (or save them for the broth pot).

With a sharp knife, cut off the stem at the base of the head to remove the core.

Cut or break cauliflower into desired size florets.

MARINATED PORTOBELLO MUSHROOMS

Parve

These two recipes are both delicious but very different ways to serve portobello mushrooms.

$1/2$ cup olive oil	2 teaspoons minced garlic
$1/4$ cup red wine vinegar	2 teaspoons lemon juice
2 teaspoons soy sauce	2 pounds portobello
2 tablespoons honey	mushroom caps, sliced

Preheat oven to 350 degrees. Combine olive oil, vinegar, soy sauce, honey, garlic and lemon juice in a large bowl. Add mushrooms and toss to coat. Arrange in a roasting pan with marinade and roast, uncovered, for 20 minutes. *Makes 4 to 6 servings.*

ITALIAN PORTOBELLO MUSHROOMS

Parve

2 large or 4 small portobello mushrooms, stems removed	Arugula
	1 plum tomato, chopped
2 to 4 garlic cloves, sliced	2 tablespoons balsamic vinegar
Salt and pepper to taste	
$1/2$ cup plus 3 to 4 teaspoons olive oil, divided	1 teaspoon Dijon mustard

Preheat broiler. Line a baking sheet with foil and coat with nonstick cooking spray. Arrange mushrooms gill side up on prepared baking sheet and sprinkle with garlic and salt and pepper to taste. Drizzle with 3 to 4 teaspoons olive oil. Broil 6 inches from the heat source for 5 minutes. Caps will still be firm. Cut into $1/2$-inch slices. Place arugula on a serving platter. Arrange mushrooms over arugula. Top with tomato. Combine balsamic vinegar, Dijon mustard and $1/2$ cup olive oil in a bowl and mix well. Pour over mushrooms. *Makes 4 servings.*

BRAVAS POTATOES

Parve

I f you like spicy fries, try these peppery roasted potatoes.

1 tablespoon minced garlic
1/4 cup olive oil
2 teaspoons red pepper flakes
1 teaspoon kosher salt
2 pounds Yukon gold or
    red potatoes, cut into
    1-inch-thick wedges

Preheat oven to 400 degrees. Combine garlic, olive oil, pepper flakes and salt in a large bowl. Add potatoes and toss to coat. Spread potatoes in a single layer in a large baking sheet. Cover with foil and roast for 15 minutes to steam. Remove foil and roast for 30 minutes longer or until tender and brown, stirring once or twice. *Makes 4 servings.*

HERBED MASHED POTATOES

Parve

You can make these in advance, then dot with margarine to reheat.

5 pounds Yukon gold potatoes, peeled and quartered	3 to 4 garlic cloves, minced
	1½ cups nondairy creamer
Salt to taste	¼ cup flat leaf parsley, finely chopped
¼ cup olive oil	¼ cup dill weed, minced
4 cups chopped scallions (4 to 5 bunches)	Pepper to taste

Combine potatoes with enough salted water to cover by 1 inch in a large pot. Bring to a boil and simmer for 15 to 20 minutes or until potatoes are tender. Heat olive oil in a large skillet and sauté scallions and garlic for 5 to 8 minutes or until tender. Drain potatoes and return to pot. Pour in nondairy creamer and mash the potatoes with an immersion blender until smooth. Stir in scallion mixture, parsley, dill weed and salt and pepper to taste, mixing until well combined. *Makes 8 to 10 servings.*

SCALLOPED POTATOES WITH WHITE WINE

Parve

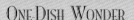

ONE-DISH WONDER

Turn this recipe into a one-dish meal! When the potatoes have baked, uncovered, for 40 minutes, top them with four or five 5-ounce white fish fillets seasoned with salt and pepper. Bake for 15 minutes longer; then garnish with parsley to serve.

½ cup olive oil	1¼ cups BARON HERZOG CHENIN BLANC® dry white wine
6 garlic cloves, minced	
1 teaspoon dried oregano	
2 teaspoons salt	½ cup water
5 pounds russet potatoes, peeled and thinly sliced into ¼-inch rounds	

Preheat oven to 450 degrees. Grease an 11×14-inch baking pan or two 9×13-inch pans. Combine olive oil, garlic, oregano and salt in a small bowl and whisk to combine. Arrange potato slices slightly overlapping in the prepared pan and drizzle evenly with olive oil mixture. Combine wine and water and pour over potatoes. Bake, covered, for 20 minutes. Uncover and bake for an additional 45 to 60 minutes or until the potatoes are tender and lightly browned. *Makes 8 to 10 servings.*

Sweet Potato Purée with Almond Streusel

Parve

STREUSEL

- 1/3 cup all-purpose flour
- 1/3 cup whole almonds
- 3 tablespoons dark brown sugar
- 2 teaspoons paprika
- 1/4 cup (1/2 stick) margarine, chilled and cut into pieces

SWEET POTATO PURÉE

- 4 pounds red-skin sweet potatoes
- 1/3 cup fresh orange juice
- 2 tablespoons dark brown sugar
- 2 tablespoons margarine, softened
- 1 1/2 teaspoons grated orange zest
- Salt and pepper to taste

For the streusel, combine all ingredients in order listed in a food processor. Pulse to blend until mixture forms small clumps. Spoon into a bowl and refrigerate for at least 1 hour and up to two days.

For the sweet potato purée, preheat oven to 375 degrees. Grease a 9×13-inch oval baking dish. Pierce potatoes in several places with a fork. Bake directly on the oven rack for 1 hour or until very tender. Cool and peel. Mash flesh in a bowl with orange juice, brown sugar, margarine and orange zest. Season with salt and pepper to taste. Spoon into the prepared baking dish. (Purée can be made up to one day ahead. Cover and chill.) Raise oven temperature to 400 degrees. Scatter streusel over potatoes. Bake for 40 minutes, until purée is hot and streusel is crisp. Cool for 5 minutes, then serve.

Makes 8 to 10 servings.

Photograph for this recipe is on page 89.

ROASTED SWEET POTATOES AND MUSHROOMS

Parve or Meat

$1/4$ cup MANISCHEWITZ® Chicken Broth or
   vegetable broth
3 tablespoons olive oil
2 tablespoons balsamic vinegar
2 pounds sweet potatoes, peeled and
   cut into 1-inch chunks
10 large shallots, peeled and cut into halves lengthwise
4 bay leaves
2 tablespoons plus 1 teaspoon chopped fresh marjoram
   Salt and pepper to taste
8 ounces large fresh shiitake mushrooms,
   stemmed and caps quartered
3 tablespoons chopped fresh parsley

Preheat oven to 400 degrees. Whisk broth, olive oil and vinegar in a small bowl. Combine sweet potatoes, shallots, bay leaves, 1 tablespoon of marjoram and half the broth mixture in a separate large bowl. Season with salt and pepper to taste. Add mushrooms, 1 tablespoon of marjoram, remaining broth mixture and salt and pepper to taste and combine until well blended.

Spread sweet potato mixture over a greased baking sheet. Roast for 30 minutes, until potatoes begin to soften, stirring occasionally. Add mushroom mixture, return to oven, and roast 30 minutes longer, until potatoes and mushrooms are tender, stirring occasionally. Spoon into a bowl; add parsley and remaining 1 teaspoon marjoram and mix well. *Makes 6 to 8 servings.*

PEAS WITH SPINACH AND SHALLOTS

Parve

1   tablespoon margarine
1   tablespoon vegetable oil
2   shallots, thinly sliced
2   garlic cloves, thinly sliced
1   (10-ounce) package
    frozen peas

1/4   cup water
  5   ounces baby spinach
3/4   teaspoon salt
1/4   teaspoon pepper

Heat margarine and oil in a large skillet over medium heat and sauté shallots and garlic for 6 minutes or until soft, stirring often. Add peas and water and cook for 5 minutes or until peas are tender. Stir in spinach, salt and pepper. Cook and toss for 1 minute, just until spinach wilts. *Makes 4 servings.*

STUFFED ZUCCHINI

Parve

6   zucchini
3   tablespoons olive oil
1   (10-ounce) package frozen chopped
    spinach, thawed and drained
2   onions, finely chopped
4   garlic cloves, minced
8   to 10 ounces button mushrooms,
    finely chopped
2   eggs, lightly beaten
    Salt and pepper to taste
    Paprika

Preheat oven to 350 degrees. Trim zucchini and boil in water to cover for 5 minutes. Drain and cool. Cut zucchini into halves lengthwise and scoop out pulp, leaving a 1/4-inch shell. Chop pulp. Heat olive oil in a large skillet and sauté zucchini, spinach, onions and garlic for 5 minutes. Add mushrooms and sauté for an additional 2 to 3 minutes. Add eggs and salt and pepper to taste and mix well. Spoon filling into zucchini shells and sprinkle with paprika. Bake for 30 minutes or until tender and set. *Makes 12 servings.*

PORTOBELLO MUSHROOM CAPS STUFFED WITH RATATOUILLE

Parve

Heat 1 tablespoon olive oil in a large skillet over medium heat and sauté 5 or 6 (4- to 5-inch) portobello mushroom caps, rounded side down. Cook for 10 minutes or until golden brown. Turn and cook for 6 minutes or just until tender. Turn over (cup side up) and fill with ratatouille filling (see Ratatouille Tart at right). Garnish with 1/4 cup chopped parsley and serve. *Makes 6 servings.*

FALL STARBURST

Parve

This dish will add a starburst of color to your table. It would be a wonderful dish for Sukkot or any fall gathering.

1 1/2 to 2 pounds butternut squash, cut into halves and seeds removed	4 Granny Smith apples, peeled, cored and sliced
1/2 cup (1 stick) margarine	1/4 cup granulated sugar
1/2 cup dark brown sugar	2 cups fresh cranberries
	1/4 cup granulated sugar
	Cinnamon-sugar

Boil squash in water to cover in a saucepan until tender. Cool until it can be handled and scoop out flesh, discarding peel. Purée squash with margarine and brown sugar in a food processor.

Cook apples and 1/4 cup granulated sugar in a saucepan for 8 to 10 minutes or until juices begin to be released and the sugar melts and coats the apples and set aside. Preheat oven to 350 degrees. Heat cranberries with 1/4 cup granulated sugar in a saucepan until berries soften and burst, stirring often. Arrange apples around the edge of a 9-inch French white ovenproof dish. Pour the squash purée in the center and top with the cranberries, leaving a small border of squash. (The cranberries may bleed onto the apples slightly.) Sprinkle with cinnamon-sugar and bake for 20 minutes. *Makes 6 to 8 servings.*

Photograph for this recipe is on page 89.

ZUCCHINI AND MUSHROOM BAKE

Parve

3 pounds zucchini, cut into 1/2-inch circles	1 tablespoon sugar
1/2 cup chopped onion	2 eggs
1 pound button mushrooms, sliced	3 tablespoons margarine
1/2 cup cornflake crumbs	2 teaspoons powdered chicken bouillon

Preheat oven to 350 degrees. Boil water in a large pot. Add zucchini slices and steam for 5 minutes; drain. Combine with remaining ingredients and mix well. Spoon mixture into a greased baking dish. Bake for 1 hour. *Makes 6 to 10 servings.*

RATATOUILLE TART

Parve

Here are two delicious ways to serve ratatouille. The tart makes a stunning presentation on the table and is a big crowd pleaser (even with the kids). The stuffed portobello mushrooms caps are also pretty on the table and are a lighter way to serve the ratatouille. The caps will present beautifully as an appetizer as well. (See sidebar on page 200.) If you don't like cooked bell pepper, omit it—the ratatouille will be just as good.

FILLING

5 to 6 tablespoons olive oil
1 large eggplant, peeled and cut into 1/2-inch cubes
1 large onion, chopped
2 garlic cloves, minced
1 green bell pepper, diced
3 to 4 zucchini, peeled and diced
1 teaspoon dried oregano
Salt, pepper and garlic powder to taste
2 (8-ounce) cans tomato sauce
1 tablespoon tomato paste

CRUST

1/2 (17.3-ounce) package frozen PEPPERIDGE FARM® Puff Pastry (1 sheet), thawed

TOPPING

6 small plum tomatoes, cut into 1/4-inch-thick rounds
2 zucchini, cut into 1/4-inch-thick rounds
1 tablespoon bread crumbs

For the filling, preheat oven to 350 degrees. Heat olive oil in a large skillet over medium-high heat and sauté eggplant, onion and garlic for 5 minutes until just soft, stirring often. Add bell pepper and zucchini and sauté for 5 to 10 minutes longer or until tender, stirring often. Season with oregano and salt, pepper and garlic powder to taste. Pour in tomato sauce and tomato paste. Reduce heat to low and simmer 5 minutes longer so flavors blend.

For the crust, roll pastry to a 12-inch circle on a floured surface. Press into a greased 10-inch tart pan with a removable bottom and trim the excess dough. Pour in filling.

For the topping, layer tomato and zucchini in overlapping, alternating concentric circles. These circles should completely cover the eggplant filling. Sprinkle with bread crumbs and bake for about 1 hour, until golden brown. *Makes 8 to 10 servings.*

Brown Rice with Leeks and Mushrooms

Parve

2 cups brown rice
4 cups water
2 teaspoons powdered bouillon
3 tablespoons vegetable oil

2 to 3 leeks, white parts only, sliced
1 to 2 garlic cloves, minced
8 to 10 ounces white mushrooms, sliced
Salt and pepper to taste

Combine rice, water and bouillon in a saucepan and bring to a boil. Cover, reduce heat and simmer until liquid is absorbed. Heat oil in a large skillet and sauté leeks and garlic for 5 minutes or until transparent. Add mushrooms and cook for 3 to 5 minutes longer or until mushrooms are tender. Combine rice and leek mixture and season with salt and pepper to taste. Serve warm. *Makes 6 to 8 servings.*

Barley-Pine Nut Casserole

Meat

6 tablespoons margarine, divided
1/2 cup pine nuts or slivered almonds
1 cup barley
1 onion, chopped

1/2 cup minced fresh parsley
1/4 cup minced chives
Salt and pepper to taste
3 1/2 cups beef broth or MANISCHEWITZ® Chicken Broth

Preheat oven to 375 degrees. Grease a 1 1/2-quart casserole. Heat 2 tablespoons margarine in a medium skillet and sauté pine nuts until lightly toasted. Remove from the skillet with a slotted spoon. Add remaining margarine to the same skillet over medium-high heat. Add barley and onion and sauté until tender. Remove from heat and stir in pine nuts, parsley, chives and salt and pepper to taste. Spoon into the prepared casserole.

Bring broth to a boil in a saucepan and pour into casserole. Bake for 1 hour or until liquid is absorbed. *Makes 4 to 6 servings.*

PEAR AND CRANBERRY CRISP

Parve

3 large pears (such as
   Anjou, Bosc or Bartlett),
   peeled, cored and sliced
1 cup fresh cranberries,
   rinsed and picked over
3/4 cup plus 2 to 4 tablespoons
   sugar
3/4 cup all-purpose flour
1/2 teaspoon nutmeg or
   cinnamon

1/4 teaspoon salt (optional)
1/2 cup (1 stick) cold
   margarine, cut into
   small pieces
1 cup coarsely chopped
   walnuts
1/2 cup old-fashioned or
   quick-cooking oats
   (not instant)

Preheat oven to 350 degrees. Arrange pears and cranberries in the bottom of a greased, shallow 1¹/₂-quart baking dish or 9-inch glass baking dish. Sprinkle fruit with 2 to 4 tablespoons sugar, depending on fruit's sweetness. Mix ³/₄ cup sugar with flour, nutmeg and salt in a large bowl. Cut in margarine with a pastry blender or two knives until mixture resembles large crumbs. Stir in walnuts and oats and mix well. Sprinkle over the fruit. Bake for 35 to 40 minutes or until filling is bubbly and top is light brown. Best served warm with cream or ice cream. *Makes 6 servings.*

ORANGE AND ALMOND COUSCOUS

Meat

1 tablespoon extra-virgin
   olive oil plus additional
   for toasting almonds
1/4 cup sliced almonds
1¹/2 cups MANISCHEWITZ®
   Chicken Broth

1¹/2 cups couscous
   Grated zest of 2 oranges
2 tablespoons
   chopped parsley

Heat olive oil in a medium saucepan. Add almonds and cook for 2 to 4 minutes or until light brown. Transfer almonds to a dish and set aside. Bring broth and remaining 1 tablespoon olive oil to a boil in same saucepan. Remove from heat and stir in couscous, orange zest and parsley. Cover and let stand for 5 minutes. Fluff couscous with a fork and toss in almonds. *Makes 4 to 6 servings.*

KNOW YOUR OATS

Oats taste good in desserts as well as hot cereals, soups, and stews; they are also high in fiber and good for you.

Rolled oats, made by warming and pressing hulled grains, come in old-fashioned, quick-cooking, and instant varieties. Steel cut, or Irish, oats are made by cutting toasted grains into small pieces.

For baking, it is better to use old-fashioned rolled oats. You can use quick-cooking oats, but instant oats are not recommended.

Oats are also great for thickening soups without adding a lot of extra fat or calories.

TWO GREAT KITCHEN COMPANIONS

GOODNESS FROM THE GROUND

Get to know mushroom varieties and start putting their great flavors and textures to work.

BUTTON MUSHROOMS are the variety most commonly available in supermarkets. They have a mild flavor and add a nice accent to sauces and salads.

CHANTERELLES are shaped like trumpets and are found, among other places, in the Pacific Northwest.

CREMINI MUSHROOMS are baby portobello mushrooms. They have the same meaty texture but are much smaller.

PORCINI MUSHROOMS can be found dried or fresh and are very fragrant and flavorful. They're often used in soups and sauces. They are usually imported from Italy.

PORTOBELLOS have very large caps and a meaty texture. They can be grilled and substituted for chicken or meat.

SHIITAKES are an Asian variety with a distinctive flavor. They're often found dried. The woody stem should be discarded or used to flavor broth.

CLEANING MUSHROOMS
No need for those specialty brushes; a clean, soft-bristled toothbrush provides a comfortable handle, and the small head slips easily under the gills to capture every stray bit of dirt. A run through the dishwasher cleans the soiled toothbrush.

LESS IS MORE
Dried mushrooms, such as shiitake and porcini, cost more than fresh mushrooms, but their flavor is so intense that fewer are required to flavor a recipe. They have the added advantage of being available all year round.

Don't refrigerate dried mushrooms. Stored in an airtight container, in a dark, cool spot, they will keep for up to a year. Large pieces are preferable to small, and caps are preferable to stems.

REHYDRATING DRIED MUSHROOMS
Rinse mushrooms under cold water to remove grit. Soak mushrooms in warm water until soft (about 30 minutes). Drain in a sieve lined with paper towels. Use the liquid in other recipes. To save time, you can also rehydrate dried mushrooms in the microwave. Place the rinsed mushrooms and water in a microwave-safe bowl and cover with plastic wrap. Microwave on high for 30 seconds. Let stand, covered, until mushrooms are soft, about 5 minutes.

ONE POTATO, TWO POTATO

Get great results when you use the right potato for the job.

RED BLISS: A low-starch, high-moisture potato with a supple, creamy texture; use for roasting and boiling.

ROUND RED: Like round white, these are perfect for boiling.

ROUND WHITE: Waxier than russets, use them for boiling, steaming, and roasting.

RUSSET: These high-starch, low-moisture spuds are best for baking, mashing, and fries.

YUKON GOLD: a medium-starch, all-purpose potato with a smooth, velvety texture, perfect for roasting and frying. They're also great in soups and stews.

EARTHY DELIGHTS

*Chanterelle mushrooms, portobello mushroom, shiitake mushrooms,
white button mushrooms, Red Bliss potatoes, sweet potatoes*

ORZO WITH CARAMELIZED ONION AND MUSHROOM SAUTÉ

Parve or Meat

4½ cups MANISCHEWITZ® Chicken Broth or bouillon	4 teaspoons dark brown sugar
2 cups orzo	8 ounces mushrooms, thinly sliced
3 to 4 tablespoons margarine	Salt and pepper to taste
2 onions, cut into thin wedges	

Boil broth in a large saucepan and add orzo. Cook until tender and most of the liquid is absorbed. Drain any remaining liquid. Heat margarine in a large skillet over high heat and sauté onions and brown sugar until onions are translucent. Reduce heat to low and simmer onions for 15 to 20 minutes, stirring occasionally. When onions are beginning to brown, add mushrooms and cook for 5 to 10 minutes longer until onions are golden brown and mushrooms are tender. Combine orzo with onion mixture and season with salt and pepper to taste. *Makes 6 to 8 servings.*

CRANBERRY NUT PIE

Parve

"I made this pie for my husband's family and everybody loved it. It has become a required side dish at the Thanksgiving and Sukkot tables ."

1 deep dish pie crust	TOPPING
	1 egg
FILLING	½ cup sugar
2½ cups fresh cranberries	½ cup all-purpose flour
1¼ cups packed dark brown sugar	⅓ cup margarine, melted
¼ cup chopped walnuts or pecans	

Preheat oven to 350 degrees. Prick crust all over with a fork. Bake for 15 minutes or until light golden brown.

For the filling, combine cranberries, brown sugar and walnuts in a bowl and mix well. Pour into baked pie crust.

For the topping, combine egg, sugar, flour and margarine in a separate bowl and mix well with a fork. Spread over filling. Place pie on a baking sheet to catch any filling that bubbles over. Bake for 45 minutes or until golden. *Makes 8 to 10 servings.*

LENTIL RICE (ENGEDRAH)

Parve

1/2	cup lentils	
1	cup uncooked rice	
2	cups water	
	Salt to taste	

1/4	cup olive oil
2	onions, chopped
	Pepper to taste

Fill saucepan halfway with water, add lentils and bring to a boil. Lower heat and simmer for 10 minutes or until lentils are tender; do not overcook or lentils will fall apart. Drain lentils and set aside. Place rice, 2 cups water and salt to taste in the saucepan. Cover and simmer over low heat for 20 minutes until liquid is absorbed.

Heat olive oil in a skillet over medium-low heat and sauté onions until deep golden brown. Combine rice, lentils and onions and season with additional salt and pepper to taste. *Makes 6 servings.*

CRUNCHY TOP PUMPKIN BREAD

Parve

BREAD
4	cups all-purpose flour
2	teaspoons baking soda
2	teaspoons baking powder
3/4	teaspoon salt
2	cups packed dark brown sugar
1	(15-ounce) can solid-pack pumpkin
1	cup apple juice
4	eggs

1/4	cup vegetable oil
2	teaspoons vanilla extract
	Ground cinnamon to taste

TOPPING
1/3	cup margarine, melted
3/4	cup packed dark brown sugar
1/4	cup all-purpose flour
1	cup POST GRAPE-NUTS Cereal

For the bread, preheat oven to 350 degrees. Combine flour, baking soda, baking powder and salt in a large bowl and mix well. Beat brown sugar, pumpkin, apple juice, eggs, oil, vanilla and cinnamon in a bowl with an electric mixer until well blended. Add dry ingredients and mix well. Divide batter evenly between two greased 5×9-inch loaf pans or three 3×6-inch loaf pans.

For the topping, combine margarine, brown sugar and flour and mix well. Fold in Grape-Nuts. Sprinkle over the loaves. Bake for 1 hour to 1 hour 10 minutes. The loaves freeze well. *Makes 2 or 3 loaves.*

Photograph for this recipe is on page 89.

To freeze stock, pour the stock into a coffee mug lined with a quart-sized sealable plastic bag. Seal the bag; place it on a cookie sheet and freeze. Once the stock is frozen, you can remove the bags from the cookie sheet and store wherever there is room.

NOT JUST FOR WATER

Ice cube trays are perfect for freezing small quantities of food or liquids that you cook with often—tomato paste or sauce, pesto, chicken or beef stock, wine, egg whites, coffee, or tea (perfect in iced coffee or iced tea).

WILD BLEND RICE SAUTÉ

Meat

A hearty and delicious dish! You should be able to find this blend of rices in a single package at the supermarket. If you can't find it, combine equal parts long grain brown rice, sweet brown rice, and wild rice.

1 cup wild rice blend
2 cups MANISCHEWITZ® Chicken Broth
3 tablespoons olive oil, divided
1/2 cup chopped celery

1 cup thinly sliced mushrooms
1/2 cup chopped red onion
2 garlic cloves, minced
2 tablespoons teriyaki sauce
1 tablespoon soy sauce

Rinse rice and combine with broth and 1 tablespoon olive oil in a large saucepan. Bring to a boil over medium-high heat. Reduce heat, cover, and simmer for 45 minutes. Remove from heat and let stand an additional 10 minutes. Fluff with a fork.

Heat remaining 2 tablespoons olive oil in a large skillet and sauté celery, mushrooms, onion and garlic for 5 to 7 minutes or until tender. Add teriyaki sauce and soy sauce and simmer until liquid is absorbed. Combine vegetables and rice and mix well. Serve warm.

Makes 4 servings.

BASMATI RICE WITH ASPARAGUS

Meat

2 cups MANISCHEWITZ®
   Chicken Broth
1 cup basmati rice
1 pound asparagus, cut into
   1 1/2- to 2-inch pieces
3 to 4 tablespoons
   lemon juice

3 tablespoons chopped
   fresh dill weed
1 garlic clove, minced
1/3 cup olive oil
   Salt and pepper to taste

Bring broth to a boil in a saucepan and add rice. Reduce heat and simmer, covered, until liquid is absorbed. Steam asparagus for 4 minutes, then rinse in cold water.

Combine lemon juice, dill weed, garlic and olive oil in a bowl and mix well. Toss asparagus, rice and dressing in a large bowl with salt and pepper to taste. Serve warm or at room temperature.

Makes 6 to 8 servings.

CORIANDER RICE

Meat

Don't be scared off by the unusual spices. This rice has a mild flavor and rich color.

1/4 cup olive oil
3/4 cup minced shallots
   (about 4 large shallots)
1 tablespoon ground
   coriander
1/2 teaspoon turmeric
2 cups long grain or
   basmati rice

4 cups MANISCHEWITZ®
   Chicken Broth
1 1/2 teaspoons salt
   Chopped fresh parsley
   for garnish

Heat olive oil in a large saucepan over medium heat and sauté shallots for 10 minutes or until tender and golden brown. Add coriander and turmeric and cook, stirring, for 1 minute longer. Add rice and stir until well coated. Add broth and salt and bring to a boil. Cover and reduce heat to simmer. Cook for 20 minutes until rice is tender and liquid is absorbed. Fluff rice and garnish with parsley.

Makes 8 to 10 servings.

Spanish Rice

Parve or Meat

3 tablespoons margarine	1 green or red bell pepper,
1 large onion, finely	diced (optional)
chopped	1 cup long grain rice
2 to 3 garlic cloves,	1 (8-ounce) can tomato
finely chopped	sauce
4 to 5 plum tomatoes,	3 cups MANISCHEWITZ®
seeded and diced	Chicken Broth or water

Heat margarine in a large saucepan over medium heat and sauté onion for 5 to 8 minutes until golden brown. Add garlic, tomatoes and bell pepper and sauté for 8 to 10 minutes longer until vegetables are soft and liquid is absorbed. Stir in rice, tossing to coat. Allow to brown slightly. Add tomato sauce and broth and bring to a boil. Cover, reduce heat, and simmer until rice is tender and liquid has evaporated. Stir occasionally to prevent sticking. *Makes 4 servings.*

The Long and Short of Rice

Long grain rice is light and fluffy. Use it for pilafs and curries. Short grain rice is softer and stickier. Use it for rice pudding and sushi.

Arborio rice slowly absorbs broth during cooking, with constant stirring. It is used for risotto.

Basmati rice is fragrant and nutty. Use it for pilafs and curries.

Brown rice still has the outer coating intact, so it takes longer to cook than white rice and has a nutty taste. Some favor it over white rice because it is considered healthier.

Homemade Rice and 'Roni

Meat

"A simple, easy recipe that your kids will love. When I make it, I know there won't be any leftovers!"

1 tablespoon vegetable oil
8 ounces vermicelli or spaghetti
1 cup uncooked long grain rice
1 small onion, chopped
2 cups MANISCHEWITZ® Chicken Broth
Salt and pepper to taste
1 tablespoon minced fresh parsley

Heat oil in a saucepan. Break pasta into 1/2- to 1-inch pieces and add to the oil. Sauté over medium heat until light brown. Add rice, onion and broth and mix well. Cook, covered, for 20 minutes. Add salt and pepper to taste. Fluff with a fork, sprinkle with parsley and serve. *Makes 4 to 6 servings.*

CORN SQUASH MUFFINS

Parve

"Credit for perfecting this recipe goes to my friend and neighbor. She reworked this recipe many times until she achieved perfection. Now her family (and mine) are so addicted to this delicious dish that we have to have it in constant supply."

1	cup cornmeal	2	eggs
1¼	cups all-purpose flour	1	cup soy milk or nondairy creamer
1½	cups sugar		
1½	tablespoons baking powder	¾	cup vegetable oil
½	teaspoon salt		Cinnamon
1	(10-ounce) package frozen winter squash purée		

Preheat oven to 350 degrees. Grease a muffin tin. Combine cornmeal, flour, sugar, baking powder and salt in a large bowl. Set aside. Combine squash, eggs, soy milk and oil in another bowl and mix well. Add dry ingredients and mix until well blended. Fill prepared muffin tin half full with batter. Sprinkle top with cinnamon. Bake for 25 minutes. *Makes 12 muffins.*

YERUSHALMI KUGEL

Parve

4¼	cups water	12	ounces fine noodles
¼	cup (½ stick) margarine	2	eggs
1	cup sugar	¼	cup packed dark brown sugar
2	teaspoons salt		
1	heaping teaspoon pepper	3	tablespoons vegetable oil

Preheat oven to 350 degrees. Combine water, margarine, sugar, salt and pepper in a large saucepan. Bring to a boil. Turn off heat, add noodles to pan and cover. Let stand 10 to 15 minutes.

Combine eggs, brown sugar and oil in a bowl. Beat with a fork. Add to the saucepan and mix well. Let stand 15 minutes longer.

Grease a bundt pan and pour in noodle mixture. Bake 1¼ hours until golden. Let cool, then remove from pan. *Makes 8 servings.*

SNAP-CRACKLE-POP APPLE KUGEL

Parve

APPLES

- 5 large McIntosh apples, peeled, cored and thinly sliced
- 1 teaspoon ground cinnamon
- 1/4 cup sugar
- 2 tablespoons all-purpose flour

FILLING

- 1/2 cup (1 stick) margarine, softened
- 2 eggs
- 1/2 cup sugar
- 1 teaspoon vanilla extract
- 3/4 cup all-purpose flour

TOPPING

- 1 1/2 cups crisp rice cereal, crushed
- 1/2 cup packed dark brown sugar
- 1/4 cup (1/2 stick) margarine, melted

For the apples, preheat oven to 350 degrees. Toss apples, cinnamon, sugar and flour in a large bowl. Spread over the bottom of a greased 9×13-inch baking dish.

For the filling, combine margarine, eggs, sugar, vanilla and flour in a medium bowl and mix with a spoon until well blended and smooth. Pour over apple mixture, spreading to cover apples.

For the topping, combine rice cereal, brown sugar and margarine in a medium bowl and mix well. Sprinkle over filling. Bake, uncovered, for 45 minutes until golden brown. *Makes 12 to 15 servings.*

Mashed Sweet Potatoes and Pears

Parve

5 pounds sweet potatoes
(sometimes labeled yams)

6 tablespoons margarine,
divided

5 large firm Bartlett pears,
cored and cut into
1/3-inch-thick slices,
divided

3/4 cup (or more) pear juice

1/4 cup sugar

1/2 teaspoon ground cinnamon

1/4 teaspoon cardamom
Pepper to taste

Preheat oven to 400 degrees. Pierce sweet potatoes with a fork and bake on a baking sheet for 1 hour or until tender. Reduce oven temperature to 350 degrees. Heat 2 tablespoons margarine in a large nonstick skillet over medium heat and sauté pears about 5 minutes or until tender. Add pear juice. Reduce heat to medium-low, cover and simmer until pears are very tender, adding more juice if needed. Purée pears in a food processor. Peel sweet potatoes. Beat sweet potatoes with remaining 1/4 cup (4 tablespoons) margarine with electric mixer until smooth. Add in pear purée, sugar, cinnamon, cardamom and pepper, mixing well. (Can be prepared to this point a day in advance. Cover and chill.) Spoon into a greased baking dish and bake for 20 minutes or until heated through. Garnish for serving with additional pear slices in the center. *Makes 8 to 10 servings.*

Pineapple Rounds

Parve

1/2 cup (1 stick) margarine

5 slices white bread, crusts
removed

1 (20-ounce) can crushed
pineapple, drained

1/2 cup sugar

4 eggs

1/4 cup cornflake crumbs

1/4 cup packed dark brown
sugar

1/4 cup ground pecans

Preheat oven to 350 degrees. Grease a muffin tin. Melt margarine in a medium bowl. Break bread into small pieces, adding to the margarine; mix well. Add pineapple, granulated sugar and eggs and mix well. Spoon into the prepared muffin tin. Combine cornflakes, brown sugar and pecans in a bowl. Spoon a little of the mixture on each pineapple round. Bake for 40 minutes. *Makes 12 large or 18 small rounds.*

LEEK AND MUSHROOM STUFFING

Parve or Meat

"A friend asked whether I had any good side dishes for her to try during the holidays, as she was having a lot of company. I gave her this recipe. No sooner were the holidays over than my phone was ringing—her guests were calling me for the recipe."

1 1/2	cups hot water	6	garlic cloves, minced
1/2	ounce dried porcini mushrooms	2	cups SEGAL'S CHARDONNAY® dry white wine
1/2	cup (1 stick) margarine		
1	pound fresh shiitake mushrooms, stems discarded and caps sliced	1	tablespoon fresh thyme, chopped
		1	large challah, broken into small pieces
1	pound button mushrooms, sliced	1	egg, lightly beaten
1 1/2	cups sliced leeks, white and light green parts only	1	cup MANISCHEWITZ® Chicken Broth or bouillon

Preheat oven to 350 degrees. Combine hot water and porcini mushrooms in a bowl and let stand for 30 minutes or until mushrooms are soft. Remove mushrooms with a slotted spoon, reserving liquid.

Heat margarine in a large skillet over medium-high heat and sauté shiitake mushrooms and button mushrooms for 10 minutes. Add leeks and garlic and sauté for 5 minutes longer. Add wine, thyme and porcini mushrooms and cook for 5 minutes or until most of the wine evaporates, stirring occasionally. (Recipe can be prepared to this point a day in advance and refrigerated.) Spoon mixture into a large bowl. Add challah and egg and mix well.

The stuffing can be baked in the turkey or in a greased 9×13-inch baking pan. If the mixture seems dry, it can be moistened with either broth or the reserved liquid from porcini mushrooms. Cover the pan and bake for 40 minutes. Uncover and bake for 20 minutes longer. *Makes 10 to 12 servings.*

Photograph for this recipe is on page 89.

Traditional Chestnut Stuffing

Parve or Meat

This traditional stuffing is a staple at the Thanksgiving table but delicious all year long.

7	cups crushed saltines
3	to 4 tablespoons vegetable oil
4	cups diced onions
2	cups diced celery
2 1/2	cups sliced mushrooms
1 1/2	cups cooked, chopped and shelled chestnuts plus whole chestnuts for garnish
1	tablespoon salt
1/4	cup minced parsley
1	teaspoon garlic powder
2	teaspoons poultry seasoning
1/2	teaspoon pepper
1/2	cup MANISCHEWITZ® Chicken Broth or bouillon
	Chopped fresh parsley for garnish

ROASTING CHESTNUTS

Preheat oven to 400 degrees. With a sharp knife, cut an "X" on the flat side of each chestnut shell. Spread the chestnuts in a single layer in a shallow baking pan. Roast for about 20 minutes or until tender. Remove from the oven. When the chestnuts are cool enough to handle, peel them with a paring knife.

Preheat oven to 350 degrees. Crush saltines in a sealable plastic bag, breaking them into small pieces but not crumbs. Heat oil in a large skillet over medium-high heat and sauté onions, celery, mushrooms and chopped chestnuts for 7 to 10 minutes until vegetables are tender. Stir in salt, parsley, garlic powder, poultry seasoning, pepper and crackers and mix well.

To cook in the turkey, stuff the mixture into a turkey and roast along with the turkey. To serve, remove from the turkey and add some pan drippings for additional flavor.

To cook stuffing separately, add broth, mixing well. Spoon stuffing into a greased 9x13-inch baking dish and bake, covered, for 45 minutes. For extra color and interest, garnish with whole chestnuts and chopped parsley. *Makes 10 servings.*

Photograph for this recipe is on page 89.

DESSERTS

SAMPLER
. . . .

FAMILY FRIENDLY
Fresh Fruit Trifle 218 • Warm and Soothing Apple Crisp 219
Pear Tarte Tatin 223 • Strawberries and Cream Pie 224 • Grandma's Apple Pie 226
Marbleized Chocolate Chip Cookie Tart 230 • Classic Cheesecake 232 • Banana Cake 237
Berry Bundt Cake 237 • Chocolate Cheese Cupcakes 238 • Coffee Cake Muffins 238
Decorated Black and White Cake 239 • Chocolate Babka 240 • Warm Chocolate Soufflés 243
Decadent Creamy Pound Cakes 247 • Chocolate Sour Cream Pound Cake 247
Streusel Pound Cake 248 • Pull-Apart Cake 249 • Almond Crisps 250
Secret Recipe Chocolate Chip Cookies 251 • Chocolate Chip Peanut Butter Cookies 252
Crinkle Cookies 254 • Oatmeal (Coconut) Cookies 255 • Ginger Cookie Press Cookies 255
Lemon or Cream Meringue Nests 257 • Classic Refrigerator Sprinkle Cookies 259
Palmiers and Twists 261 • Apricot Pinwheels 262 • Double-Decker Confetti Brownies 265
Cranberry Sticks 266 • My Mother's Mandelbread 266
Peanut Butter S'More Stacks 267 • Strawberry Streusel Bars 268
White Chocolate Pretzel Clusters 268 • Whoopie Pies 269 • Flavorful Krispie Treats 270
Quick Praline Bars 270 • Chocolate Raisin Nut Clusters 271 • Flavored Popcorns 273

FREEZES WELL
Apricot Rugelach 220 • Banana Cake 237 • Berry Bundt Cake 237
Chocolate Cheese Cupcakes 238 • Coffee Cake Muffins 238 • Chocolate Babka 240
Warm Chocolate Soufflés 243 • Decadent Creamy Pound Cakes 247
Chocolate Sour Cream Pound Cake 247 • Streusel Pound Cake 248
Secret Recipe Chocolate Chip Cookies 251 • Chocolate Chip Peanut Butter Cookies 252
Oatmeal (Coconut) Cookies 255 • Ginger Cookie Press Cookies 255
Butter Pecan Cookies 258 • Classic Refrigerator Sprinkle Cookies 259 • Palmiers and Twists 261
Chocolate Chocolate Chocolate Biscotti 263 • Sinfully Delicious Cookies 264
Double-Decker Confetti Brownies 265 • Cranberry Sticks 266 • My Mother's Mandelbread 266

SPECIAL OCCASION
Apricot Rugelach 220 • Strawberries and Cream Pie 224 • Caramel Nut Tart 231
Espresso Cheesecake 233 • Crunchy Almond Confetti Cake 236
Decorated Black and White Cake 239 • Chocolate and Hazelnut Meringue Cake 241
Cinnamon Roll-Up Cookies 253 • Sinfully Delicious Cookies 264

FRESH FRUIT TRIFLE

Parve

This is a wonderfully light dessert. It is colorful, has a nice crunch, and makes a nice centerpiece for any dessert spread.

BERRY SAUCE
- 3 to 4 tablespoons confectioners' sugar
- 1/2 teaspoon orange extract
- 1/2 cup frozen orange juice concentrate
- 1 (12-ounce) package frozen strawberries
- 1 (10-ounce) package frozen raspberries

HONEY NUT CRUNCH
- 8 ounces honey-glazed pecans, coarsely chopped
- 3/4 cup packed dark brown sugar
- 8 ounces honey-glazed almonds, coarsely chopped
- 6 tablespoons margarine, melted
- 1 1/2 cups quick-cooking oats
- 1 teaspoon ground cinnamon

FRUIT FILLING
- 1 (15-ounce) can pineapple chunks
- 3 red Delicious apples
- 1 large Granny Smith apple
- 1 yellow Delicious apple
- 4 large oranges, peeled and cut into chunks

For the sauce, process confectioners' sugar, orange extract, orange juice concentrate and berries in a blender or food processor until smooth; chill.

For the crunch, preheat oven to 350 degrees. Combine pecans, brown sugar, almonds, margarine, oats and cinnamon in a bowl and mix well. Spread on a baking sheet and bake for 5 to 10 minutes or until crisp. Break into very small pieces. When cool, store in an airtight container until needed.

For the filling, drain pineapple and reserve juice. Cut unpeeled apples into chunks. Combine pineapple chunks and oranges in a separate bowl.

To assemble, place a tall glass in the center of a trifle bowl. Fill glass with sauce, pouring any remaining sauce into the bottom of the bowl. Spoon 2/3 of the apple mixture into the bowl. Spread pineapple mixture over apples and top with remaining apple mixture. Sprinkle with crunch. Serve any remaining crunch in a bowl with the trifle. *Makes 12 servings.*

PERFECT PINEAPPLE TWO WAYS

Parve

For sliced pineapple or pineapple chunks, remove leafy crown and trim both ends of the pineapple so it will stand erect. Cut pineapple lengthwise into quarters. Place each quarter peel side down on a work surface and slide a knife between the peel and flesh to remove peel. Stand quarters upright and slice off the core portion. Slice or chop the pineapple as desired. *Makes 6 to 8 servings.*

WARM AND SOOTHING APPLE CRISP

Parve or Dairy

*T*his family favorite is the perfect blend of sweet and tart and is a cinch to prepare. It is enjoyed by all and will become a tradition in your home, too.

CRISP TOPPING

- 1 cup all-purpose flour
- 1/2 cup packed dark brown sugar
- 1/2 cup (1 stick) margarine or butter

FILLING

- 3 pounds McIntosh apples, peeled and sliced, about 10 apples
- 1/4 cup all-purpose flour
- 3/4 cup sugar
- 1 tablespoon cinnamon

For the topping, mix flour, brown sugar and margarine in a bowl until crumbly.

For the filling, preheat oven to 350 degrees. Coat a 9×13-inch baking dish with nonstick cooking spray. Combine apples with flour, sugar and cinnamon in a bowl. Spread in the prepared baking dish. Sprinkle evenly with topping. Bake for 1 hour or until apples are bubbling. Serve warm with vanilla ice cream or Vanilla Sauce (page 223). *Makes 12 servings.*

ZINGY WATERMELON AND MANGO

Parve

*T*his is a simple but deliciously refreshing summer fruit dessert.

- 1 (4-pound) piece seedless watermelon
- 3 or 4 ripe mangos
  Juice of 2 limes
- 1 teaspoon freshly grated lime zest
- 1/2 teaspoon sugar

Cut watermelon and mangos into bite-size pieces. Combine with lime juice, lime zest and sugar in a bowl; toss together, coating well. Chill until serving time. *Makes 8 to 10 servings.*

SERVING PIECES

As an alternative way to serve fresh berries or nuts, melt 24 ounces of chocolate chips and paint three coats of the chocolate over the inside of a lunch-size paper bag. Let stand until firm and tear off the bag to produce a beautiful, edible serving container. You can also use a small cardboard box lined with foil; when the chocolate is firm, lift it gently from the box by the foil and peel off the foil.

APRICOT RUGELACH

Dairy

RUGELACH PASTRY
- 1 cup (2 sticks) unsalted butter, softened
- 8 ounces PHILADELPHIA Cream Cheese, softened
- 1/4 cup sugar
- 1/4 teaspoon kosher salt
- 1 teaspoon vanilla extract
- 2 cups all-purpose flour

RAISIN NUT FILLING
- 6 tablespoons sugar
- 1/4 cup packed light brown sugar
- 3/4 cup raisins
- 1 cup walnuts, finely chopped
- 1/2 teaspoon ground cinnamon

ASSEMBLY
- 1/2 cup apricot preserves
- 3 tablespoons sugar
- 1 teaspoon ground cinnamon

For the pastry, beat butter with cream cheese with electric mixer until light and fluffy. Add sugar, salt and vanilla and mix well. Add flour and mix at low speed just until combined. Shape into a ball on a floured surface and cut the ball into quarters. Wrap in plastic wrap and chill for 1 hour.

For the filling, combine sugar, brown sugar, raisins, walnuts and cinnamon in a bowl and mix well.

To assemble and bake, preheat oven to 350 degrees. Line a baking sheet with baking parchment paper. Roll each portion of the pastry into a 9-inch circle on a floured surface. Spread each circle with 2 tablespoons apricot preserves and 1/2 cup filling; press filling lightly into the pastry. Cut each circle into 16 wedges. Roll wedges from wide end to center, enclosing the filling. Tuck under the points and place on the prepared baking sheet. Sprinkle with a mixture of sugar and cinnamon. Bake for 15 to 20 minutes or until light brown.
Makes 64 cookies.

RASPBERRY NUT TART

Parve

2 cups almonds, sliced
2/3 cup sugar
1/2 cup plus 2 tablespoons margarine, chilled and chopped
1 1/4 cups all-purpose flour
1/4 teaspoon salt
2 tablespoons beaten egg
3/4 cup raspberry jam
1 container fresh raspberries

Preheat oven to 400 degrees. Reserve 1/4 cup of the almonds for topping. Process remaining 1 3/4 cups almonds with sugar in a food processor until finely ground. Add margarine, flour and salt and process to the consistency of sand. Add 1 cup of the mixture to reserved almonds in a bowl. Add egg to remaining ground almond mixture and pulse until mixture begins to clump together. Press mixture into the bottom and up the side of a greased 9-inch tart pan with removable bottom. Bake for 15 minutes.

Stir raspberry jam and spread over cooled crust. Arrange fresh raspberries over jam. Break apart reserved almond mixture, forming small clusters. Sprinkle almond clusters over raspberries. Bake for 15 minutes longer. Cool in pan on a wire rack. Loosen side of tart from pan with a knife and remove side. *Makes 8 servings.*

TART TIPS

To crush raspberries and remove the seeds without a sieve, use a flour sifter instead.

EASY AS PIE CRUST

Use a teaspoon or the bottom of a ramekin or drinking glass to press crumbs into a buttered springform pan or tart pan with a removable bottom to create a clean edge.

RUSTIC FRUIT TART

Parve

FOR GREAT DOUGH

Chill ingredients. Refrigerating flour and other ingredients in addition to the butter results in flakier pastry.

After you prepare the dough, shape as needed and make it level on top. Cover completely with plastic wrap.

Refrigerate dough for at least one hour or up to a day. Remove from the refrigerator and let stand until softened, but don't let dough become too soft; it rolls best when cold and firm.

Pressing dough makes it easier to roll the dough sheet to an even thickness. Before you begin rolling, place the rolling pin on the dough and place hands on the rolling pin about an inch from either side of the edge. Press down until your knuckles touch the work surface. Make indentations all over until the dough is an even thickness.

The free-form nature of the crust for this delicious tart is easy to make. The recipe includes two filling choices: the plums add a wonderful tart flavor, while the pears offer a sweeter flavor.

TART PASTRY
- 1 cup all-purpose flour
- 1/4 teaspoon sugar
- 1/4 teaspoon salt
- 1/4 cup vegetable oil
- 1/4 cup ice water
- 3/4 teaspoon vanilla extract

PLUM FILLING
- 7 to 8 ripe plums, sliced
- 2 1/2 tablespoons all-purpose flour
- 10 tablespoons sugar, divided

PEAR FILLING
- 1/2 cup water
- 1 cup plus 2 tablespoons late-harvest riesling or dessert wine, divided
- 1/2 cup plus 1 tablespoon sugar, divided
- 3 large Anjou pears, peeled, cored and thinly sliced
- 1 tablespoon all-purpose flour

For the pastry, mix flour, sugar and salt in a bowl. Mix in half the oil with a fork until mixture resembles meal. Add remaining oil and mix well. Combine water and vanilla and add to flour mixture, mixing until well blended. Form into a ball, wrap up and chill for 1 hour. Roll dough into a 15-inch circle on a floured surface. Place on a baking sheet and chill for 10 minutes.

For the plum filling, preheat oven to 400 degrees. Toss plums with flour and 3 tablespoons of sugar in a bowl. Arrange over the pastry circle, leaving a 3-inch edge. Sprinkle with 4 tablespoons of sugar. Fold the edge of the pastry over plums and brush with water. Sprinkle the edge with remaining 3 tablespoons sugar. Bake for 45 minutes or until light brown, pushing the plums down gently with a spoon so juices bubble up to cover the plums. Cool on a wire rack.

For the pear filling, preheat oven to 400 degrees. Bring water with 1 cup wine and 1/2 cup sugar to a boil in a saucepan. Boil until syrup is reduced to 1/2 cup. Add pears and cook for 5 minutes. Drain, reserving pears and syrup separately. Toss pears with flour and 1 tablespoon sugar. Spread over the center of the pastry circle. Drizzle half the reserved syrup over pears. Fold edge of pastry over pears, enclosing pears and juices. Bake for 35 to 45 minutes or until crust is golden brown and pears are tender. Whisk remaining 2 tablespoons wine into remaining syrup. Cut tart into wedges. Drizzle with syrup. *Makes 8 servings.*

Photograph for this recipe is on page 217.

PEAR TARTE TATIN

Parve

3   to 4 tablespoons
   margarine, softened

4   or 5 ripe pears, peeled
   and cut into halves

2   tablespoons fresh
   lemon juice

$^1/_3$ cup sugar

$^1/_3$ cup packed dark
   brown sugar

$^1/_2$ teaspoon ground
   cinnamon

$^1/_2$ (17.3-ounce) package
   frozen PEPPERIDGE
   FARM® Puff Pastry
   (1 sheet), thawed

Preheat oven to 425 degrees. Spread margarine over the bottom of a 10- or 11-inch ovenproof skillet. Brush each pear half with lemon juice. Combine sugar, brown sugar and cinnamon in a bowl and sprinkle in prepared skillet. Arrange pears cut side up in skillet with wider end to outer edge. Simmer over medium-high heat for 8 to 10 minutes or until syrup thickens and caramelizes. Remove from heat.

Roll puff pastry into a 13-inch circle $^1/_8$ inch thick. Place over pears and tuck in edge slightly around pears. Bake for 30 minutes or until pastry is puffed and golden brown. Let stand for several minutes. Place a serving platter over skillet and invert tortetta onto platter. *Makes 8 servings.*

VANILLA SAUCE

Parve

6   egg yolks

3/4 cup sugar

2   cups nondairy creamer

2   tablespoons vanilla extract

Whisk egg yolks and sugar together in a saucepan. Cook over low heat until light and fluffy, whisking constantly; remove to a bowl. Combine nondairy creamer and vanilla extract in the same saucepan. Bring to a boil over low heat, whisking constantly; reduce heat. Add egg mixture and simmer for 15 to 20 minutes or until creamy, whisking constantly; do not boil. Cool to room temperature. Chill until custard consistency. Let stand at room temperature for 30 minutes before serving. *Makes 2$^1/_2$ cups.*

**HERZOG LATE
HARVEST WHITE
RIESLING
(WHITE,
CALIFORNIA)**

Pleasantly sweet, with rich, ripe concentrated fruit flavors highlighting this delicious easy drinking wine that pairs well with rich desserts.

DECORATING PIE PASTRY

For a decorative perforated piecrust, roll chilled dough 1/8 inch thick and punch holes in it with a 1/4-inch round pastry tip. Do this quickly so the holes will retain their shape.

For a lattice piecrust, roll half the dough into an 11-inch circle. Cut the circle into 1/2-inch strips with a sharp knife or pastry wheel.
Arrange five strips 1 inch apart across the pie filling. Place five strips at right angles to the first strips. Trim the ends if needed and fold the edge of the bottom crust over the strips to build up the edge. Seal and crimp the edges.

SLICING STRAWBERRIES

To slice a strawberry evenly, remove the stem, place it lengthwise in an egg slicer, and press down firmly.

STRAWBERRIES AND CREAM PIE

Parve or Dairy

"*Every year my friend invites a group over to watch the Wimbledon tennis matches. She always serves this pie along with Champagne to continue the established British tradition.*"

FLAKY PASTRY
- 1 1/4 cups all-purpose flour
- 1/4 cup sugar
- 1/2 cup (1 stick) margarine or butter
- 1 egg yolk
- 1 tablespoon (or more) ice water

STRAWBERRY AND WHITE CHOCOLATE MOUSSE FILLING
- 1 1/4 cups heavy cream or nondairy topping, divided
- 6 ounces white chocolate, chopped
- 1/2 teaspoon vanilla extract
- 2 egg whites
- 1/4 teaspoon cream of tartar
- 16 ounces fresh strawberries, thinly sliced lengthwise

For the pastry, preheat oven to 375 degrees. Lightly grease a 10-inch tart pan with a removable bottom. Mix flour and sugar in a food processor. Add margarine and process to coarse meal consistency. Add egg yolk and water and process until clumps form, adding additional water if needed. Press together and shape into a disk. Put disk between two sheets of waxed paper and roll into a 13-inch circle. Press into the prepared pan; fold in the overhang and press into the side to form a double thickness. Pierce all over with a fork and place in the freezer for 30 minutes.

Line pastry with foil and weight with pie weights or dried beans. Bake for 25 minutes or until set. Remove weights and foil and bake for 20 minutes longer or until golden brown. Cool on a wire rack.

For the filling, bring 1/4 cup of cream to a boil in a saucepan. Remove from the heat and add white chocolate, stirring until melted and smooth. Stir in vanilla. Cool for 15 minutes. Beat remaining 1 cup cream with electric mixer until soft peaks form and set aside. Clean and dry bowl from mixer and beat egg whites and cream of tartar until stiff peaks form. Fold chocolate and whipped cream into egg whites. Spoon into prepared crust and smooth with a spatula. Arrange strawberries in concentric circles on the top. Chill for 8 hours or longer. *Makes 8 servings.*

Strawberry Rhubarb Crisp

Parve or Dairy

OAT TOPPING

1 cup all-purpose flour
1/2 cup rolled oats
1/3 cup sugar
1/3 cup packed dark
   brown sugar
1 teaspoon ground
   cinnamon
1/4 teaspoon salt
1/2 cup (1 stick) margarine or
   butter, melted

FILLING

4 cups (1-inch) pieces
   fresh rhubarb
2 cups strawberry halves
2 Granny Smith apples,
   peeled and sliced
1/2 cup sugar
2 tablespoons cornstarch

For the topping, mix flour, oats, sugar, brown sugar, cinnamon and salt in a bowl. Add melted margarine and mix until crumbly.

For the filling, preheat oven to 350 degrees. Grease a 9×13-inch baking dish. Combine rhubarb with strawberries, apples, sugar and cornstarch in a bowl and toss to mix well. Spoon into prepared dish and sprinkle evenly with topping. Bake for 35 to 40 minutes or until rhubarb is tender and topping is golden brown. *Makes 12 servings.*

Strawberry Whip

Parve

"You will really enjoy this light and refreshing dessert. It was given to me by my dearest longtime friend. It became a staple during the summer months and on Passover, and now everyone looks forward to the day the Strawberry Whip makes its appearance."

1 egg white
1 pint strawberries, washed,
   hulled and chopped
1/2 to 1 cup sugar

Orange shells (optional)
Ladyfingers (optional)
Strawberries for garnish
Mint leaves for garnish

Beat egg white at high speed with electric mixer until fluffy. Add chopped strawberries and sugar and beat until stiff peaks form and mixture increases in volume. You can freeze mixture in a bowl, in scooped-out orange shells or in a springform pan lined around the side with ladyfingers. Serve garnished with additional strawberries and mint, if desired. *Makes 6 servings.*

STRAWBERRY RHUBARB SAUCE

Strawberries and rhubarb also make a delicious sauce to serve with a fruit tart or fresh fruit, or as a garnish for any dessert. Combine a 16-ounce package of frozen rhubarb, 2 pints of halved strawberries, 1 cup water, 1/2 to 3/4 cup sugar and 2 or 3 cinnamon sticks in a saucepan. Cover and cook over low to medium heat for 30 minutes or until tender. Remove the cinnamon sticks and purée the fruit.

GRANDMA'S APPLE PIE
· ·
Parve or Dairy

*"*We are made up of people from all backgrounds and regions, but one thing that we all share is traditions. The contributor of this recipe converted to Judaism. His family roots are in the south, and this is his traditional hometown classic apple pie. His grandma always made each pastry separately to be sure that it was divided perfectly."*

CRUST

  3 cups all-purpose flour, divided
  4 teaspoons sugar, divided
  1 cup vegetable oil, divided
  1/4 cup water or milk, divided

FILLING

  6 large Granny Smith apples, peeled, cored and sliced
  1/2 teaspoon vanilla extract (optional)
  3/4 to 1 cup sugar
  1 teaspoon ground cinnamon
  1 teaspoon sugar

PASTRY TIPS

To reduce pastry shrinkage, wrap the dough in baking parchment or waxed paper and chill for 20 to 30 minutes before rolling it out. For a one-crust pie or tart, place the rolled dough in the pan and line with baking parchment. Weight the shell with dried beans, pie weights or uncooked rice. Bake at 400 degrees just until firm; then remove the weights. Bake for 3 to 5 minutes longer or until golden brown.

For the crust, preheat oven to 400 degrees. Combine half of the crust ingredients in the order listed and mix by hand to form a soft dough. Place the dough in an ungreased pie dish and press dough along the bottom of the dish, then up the side. Combine remaining half of the crust ingredients in the order listed and mix by hand to form a soft dough ball. Set aside.

For the filling, spread apples in the pastry-lined pie dish and sprinkle with vanilla, if desired. Mix 3/4 cup to 1 cup sugar with cinnamon in a bowl. Sprinkle over apples. Roll remaining dough into a circle between two pieces of waxed paper. Remove one piece of waxed paper and invert the pastry onto the pie. Peel off remaining waxed paper, trim the edge and pinch the edge at 1/4-inch intervals to seal. Cut five 1-inch slits in the top to vent and sprinkle with 1 teaspoon sugar. Bake for 30 minutes. Reduce oven temperature to 350 degrees and bake for about 30 minutes or until crust is golden brown. *Makes 6 to 8 servings.*

Note: You can prepare the apples for this pie and other apple desserts in advance and toss them with a small amount of lemon juice to keep them from oxidizing and browning.

You can prepare the crust pastry in one batch and divide it.

Balsamic-Glazed Strawberries

Parve

3 tablespoons balsamic
   vinegar
3 tablespoons dark
   brown sugar
3 tablespoons orange juice

1 teaspoon grated
   orange zest
1 pint strawberries,
   cut into quarters

Combine vinegar, brown sugar, orange juice and orange zest in a small heavy saucepan. Heat over medium heat until sugar is dissolved and simmer for 1 minute, stirring constantly. Remove from heat and add strawberries, tossing to coat evenly. Store in the refrigerator until serving time. *Makes 4 servings.*

Note: These are a wonderful accompaniment to Almond Lattice Meringues or Fresh Fruit Sorbet.

Fresh Fruit Sorbet

Parve

Serve this layered with chopped fresh fruit in Champagne glasses and topped with Mango Sauce (at right) or your favorite sauce.

3/4 to 1 cup sugar
1   cup water
1   cup puréed fruit, such as mangos,
     raspberries, peaches, kiwifruit,
     apricots, cherries or strawberries

Combine sugar and water in a saucepan and bring to a boil. Reduce heat and simmer for 5 minutes. Remove from the heat and cool completely. Combine with fruit purée. Place in a plastic freezer container and mix well. Freeze for approximately 1 hour, stirring every 10 minutes to break up the ice crystals as they form. *Makes 4 servings.*

Mango Magic

Mango Sauce
is a delicious
accompaniment to
any fresh fruit and is
particularly nice with
pineapple,
strawberries, or
sorbets.

To prepare this
simple sauce, process
2 chopped mangos
with the juice of
1 lime, 1/2 cup orange
juice and 1/4 cup
sugar in a food
processor until
smooth. Chill until
time to serve.

BLACK RUSSIAN FROZEN DESSERT

Parve

CHOCOLATE PEANUT
BUTTER CRUNCH

 12 ounces semisweet
       chocolate
 1/2 cup cornflake crumbs
 1/3 cup smooth or crunchy
       peanut butter

DESSERT

 16 ounces nondairy topping,
       thawed
  2 cups (scant) sugar
  1 tablespoon vanilla
       sugar, or 1 teaspoon
       vanilla extract
  3 eggs
 2 1/2 tablespoons instant coffee
       granules dissolved in a
       small amount of hot water
  5 teaspoons Kahlúa, or
       to taste

For the crunch, melt chocolate in a double boiler. Remove from heat and stir in cornflake crumbs and peanut butter. Spread 1/8 to 1/4 inch thick on a baking sheet lined with foil. Freeze until firm.

For the dessert, beat nondairy topping with the whisk attachment of an electric mixer for 6 minutes or until soft peaks form. Add sugar, vanilla sugar, eggs, coffee and Kahlúa, mixing at low speed. Spoon into a bowl.

Cover chocolate crunch with waxed paper and crush into tiny pieces with a mallet, hammer or the back of a knife. Fold into the coffee mixture. Freeze until firm. Serve as soon as removed from the freezer, as it thaws quickly. *Makes 8 servings.*

CHOCOLATE TOFFEE PIE

Parve

This is a great way to end a meal.

OAT CRUST

- 2¹/₂ cups rolled oats
- 1¹/₃ sticks margarine
- 1 cup packed dark brown sugar
- 1 teaspoon vanilla extract

CHOCOLATE FILLING

- 4 ounces semisweet chocolate
- 1 cup (2 sticks) margarine
- 2 cups confectioners' sugar
- 4 eggs
- 2 teaspoons vanilla extract

TOFFEE TOPPING

- 8 ounces parve whipped topping
- 1 tablespoon sugar
- 1 teaspoon instant coffee granules dissolved in a small amount of water
- 1 tablespoon vanilla extract
- 1 tablespoon Kahlúa (optional)

For the crust, preheat oven to 350 degrees. Combine oats, margarine, brown sugar and vanilla in a bowl and mix well. Press over the bottom of a greased 9×13-inch baking pan. Bake for 15 minutes. Cool on a wire rack.

For the filling, melt chocolate and margarine in a double boiler and mix well. Stir in confectioners' sugar, eggs and vanilla. Spread over the cooled crust. Freeze for 1 hour.

For the topping, beat whip topping at high speed with electric mixer until stiff peaks form. Stir in sugar, coffee, vanilla and Kahlúa. Spread over the chocolate mixture. Freeze until firm. *Makes 8 servings.*

Marbleized Chocolate Chip Cookie Tart

Parve

2¼	cups all-purpose flour	2	eggs
½	teaspoon baking soda	1	teaspoon salt
1	cup (2 sticks) unsalted	2	teaspoons vanilla extract
	margarine, softened	1½	cups (9 ounces) semisweet
½	cup sugar		chocolate chips, divided
1	cup packed light		
	brown sugar		

Preheat oven to 350 degrees. Grease and flour a 10-inch tart pan with a removable bottom. Mix flour and baking soda together and set aside. Beat margarine with sugar and brown sugar at medium speed with electric mixer until light. Add eggs, salt and vanilla and beat at low speed for 1 minute or until smooth. Stir in flour mixture and mix until just combined. Fold in half the chocolate chips.

Spread dough in the prepared pan. Sprinkle with remaining chocolate chips. Bake for 3 minutes. Run a knife through the dough to mix in melted chocolate and marbleize. Bake for 30 minutes or until edge is golden brown and center is almost set. Cool in the pan for 20 minutes. Use any remaining dough to make cookies. Serve drizzled with Fudge Sauce (recipe below). *Makes 8 servings.*

Note: Adorn your dessert with long orange or lemon peel twists.

Photograph for this recipe is on page 235.

Fudge Sauce

Parve

12	ounces (2 cups)	1	teaspoon unsweetened
	semisweet chocolate chips		baking cocoa
1	cup (2 sticks) margarine	1	teaspoon sugar
1	teaspoon water	2	tablespoons dark
			corn syrup

Melt chocolate chips in a saucepan over medium heat or in the microwave in a microwave-safe bowl. Add margarine, water, baking cocoa, sugar and corn syrup and mix well. Allow to cool to room temperature. *Makes 8 servings.*

CARAMEL NUT TART

Parve

CINNAMON CRUST

- 1 1/2 cups all-purpose flour
- 2 tablespoons sugar
- 1 teaspoon ground cinnamon
- 1/4 teaspoon salt
- 1/2 cup (1 stick) unsalted margarine, chilled and cut into 1/2-inch pieces
- 1 teaspoon vanilla extract
- 3 tablespoons (about) ice water

CARAMEL NUT FILLING

- 1 1/4 cups sugar
- 1/4 cup water
- 2/3 cup nondairy topping
- 3 tablespoons unsalted margarine, cut into small pieces
- 1 tablespoon honey
- 1 teaspoon vanilla extract
- 3/4 cup walnuts, chopped
- 3/4 cup pecans, chopped
- 1/3 cup slivered blanched almonds
- 1 ounce white chocolate, chopped

For the crust, combine flour, sugar, cinnamon and salt in a food processor. Add butter and pulse until mixture resembles coarse meal. Mix in vanilla. Add ice water 1 tablespoon at a time, pulsing to form moist clumps. Shape into a ball and flatten into a disk. Wrap in plastic wrap and chill for 2 hours or until firm.

Preheat oven to 375 degrees. Grease a 9-inch tart pan with a removable bottom. Roll pastry disk into a 12-inch circle and place in the tart pan. Fold in the overhang and press against the side to form a high double edge. Pierce with a fork and place in the freezer for 15 minutes. Bake for 20 minutes or until light brown. Cool on a wire rack.

For the filling, increase oven temperature to 400 degrees. Combine sugar and water in a medium saucepan. Cook over medium-low heat until sugar dissolves. Increase heat and boil for 9 minutes or until a deep amber color, swirling the saucepan and brushing down the side of the pan occasionally with a pastry brush; do not stir. Reduce heat to medium and gradually whisk in the topping; mixture will bubble up. Cook until smooth, stirring constantly. Stir in margarine, honey and vanilla. Mix in walnuts, pecans and almonds. Pour into the cooled crust. Bake for 20 minutes or until filling bubbles all over. Cool on a wire rack.

Melt white chocolate in a double boiler, stirring until smooth. Drizzle over the tart with a fork. Let stand at room temperature for 30 minutes or up to 8 hours. *Makes 8 servings.*

CLASSIC CHEESECAKE

Dairy

Multiple versions of cheesecake were submitted for the book, eventually narrowed down to three. The competition was so serious that the final testing was held at the school board meeting. This was the unanimous winner!

GRAHAM CRACKER CRUST
10 whole cinnamon
     graham crackers
     (20 squares)
 6 tablespoons (3/4 stick)
     butter, melted

CHEESECAKE FILLING
 1 cup sugar
 3 tablespoons cornstarch
32 ounces PHILADELPHIA
     Cream Cheese, softened
 1 extra-large egg
1/2 cup heavy cream
 1 teaspoon vanilla extract

For the crust, process graham crackers in a food processor until finely crushed. Mix graham cracker crumbs and butter in a bowl. Press over the bottom of a greased 10-inch springform pan.

For the filling, preheat oven to 450 degrees. Mix sugar and cornstarch together. Beat cream cheese with electric mixer until smooth. Add sugar mixture and mix until light. Mix in egg. Add cream and vanilla gradually and mix until smooth. Pour filling into the prepared crust. Cover the outside of the pan tightly with foil. Place in a larger baking pan filled halfway with water. Bake for 35 to 45 minutes or until the top is golden brown. Cool on a wire rack; chill for 3 hours to overnight. Place on a serving plate and remove the side of the pan. Top as desired.
Makes 16 servings.

Note: You can garnish with 2 tablespoons melted seedless raspberry jelly spread on top of cake and add fresh berries and a mint leaf, if desired. This can also be baked in individual miniatures. Using a generous tablespoon of crumbs, press into a muffin pan, covering the bottom and side. Refrigerate while preparing filling. Prepare filling and spoon into crust. Bake for 10 to 15 minutes.

ESPRESSO CHEESECAKE

Dairy

"When I was trying to convince my brother to agree to one of my unreasonable demands, I offered to make him this cheesecake as a means of persuasion, and it worked! Now I offer it as a proven weapon to bend the will of the most reluctant!"

CHOCOLATE COOKIE CRUST
- 1¹/₂ cups crushed chocolate wafers
- 5 tablespoons unsalted butter, melted

ESPRESSO FILLING
- 1 tablespoon instant espresso powder
- 2 teaspoons vanilla extract
- 24 ounces PHILADELPHIA Cream Cheese, softened
- 1 cup plus 2 tablespoons sugar
- 3 eggs
- 1 cup sour cream

ESPRESSO TOPPING
- 1 cup heavy cream
- 2 tablespoons sugar
- ¹/₂ teaspoon instant espresso powder
- 1 teaspoon vanilla extract
- Chocolate-covered coffee beans for garnish

For the crust, remove the ring of a 9-inch springform pan. Cover the bottom with heavy-duty foil, leaving a 2-inch overhang all around. Carefully attach the springform ring so that you do not tear the foil. Wrap the foil halfway up the outside of the pan. Lightly butter the insides of the pan. Tightly wrap the outside of the pan using two large pieces of foil. Mix chocolate wafer crumbs and butter in a bowl. Press evenly over the bottom of the prepared pan. Chill until time to fill.

For the filling, preheat oven to 325 degrees. Dissolve espresso powder in vanilla. Beat cream cheese with electric mixer until creamy. Beat in sugar gradually. Beat in eggs one at a time. Add sour cream, then espresso mixture, mixing well. Spoon into prepared pan and smooth the top. Place in a larger pan and fill halfway with boiling water. Bake for 1¹/₄ hours or until the center is just firm. Turn off the oven and let cheesecake stand in the oven with the door ajar for 1 hour. Cool, covered with foil, on a wire rack. Chill for 4 hours or longer. Loosen cheesecake from the pan with a knife; remove the side of the pan.

For the topping, combine cream with sugar, espresso powder and vanilla in a mixing bowl. Beat at medium speed just until soft peaks form. Reserve 1 cup of the mixture and spread the remainder evenly on the cheesecake. Spoon reserved cream mixture into a pastry bag fitted with a medium star tip. Pipe in rosettes around the outer edge and garnish with chocolate-covered coffee beans. *Makes 16 servings.*

TIPS FOR PREPARING YOUR BEST CAKE YET

Level the top of a cake to create a clean silhouette. Hold the cake steady with a hand on top, and use a serrated knife to remove a thin horizontal slice at the top to level a domed appearance. You can also invert the layer and use the flat base as the top.

Before frosting a cake, place several narrow strips of waxed paper around the edge of the serving platter. Place the cake on the serving platter, frost, and then gently pull out the waxed paper.

To apply a smooth frosting, first coat the entire cake with a thin layer of frosting and let it set briefly. Then apply the remaining frosting and decorations.

To ensure a completely smooth layer of frosting on cakes or cupcakes, dip the spatula regularly into hot water and dry it before continuing.

Wrap a cooled, freshly baked cake in foil and freeze overnight. Remove from the freezer and frost it immediately to prevent it from crumbling as you frost it.

Preparing cake pans helps keep the cake from sticking. First grease the pan, and then add a layer of baking parchment. Grease the parchment, sprinkle with flour, and rotate the pan to distribute the flour evenly. Tap out excess flour.

Baking parchment should not be too large or it may wrinkle the cake. Use the pan as a guide, and cut around the parchment for the right size.

GET SMART ABOUT CHOCOLATE GARNISHES

The chocolate for garnishes should be melted slowly, as it burns easily. If using the microwave, heat it at 50 percent power. On the stove, use a double boiler. Remove it from the heat when the chocolate is melted a little more than halfway and stir until completely melted. If it begins to harden when mixed with liquid, add a small amount of vegetable oil, using one tablespoon for every six ounces of chocolate.

Dress up your cake or dessert with delicate **CHOCOLATE DRIZZLES.** Melt chocolate and pour into a pastry bag or sealable plastic bag with a small corner snipped off. Drizzle the chocolate over the dessert or serving plates for a spectacular look. You can also drizzle the chocolate designs onto waxed paper and chill them until firm. Remove to the dessert with a metal spatula.

TO MAKE CHOCOLATE LEAVES, use nontoxic lemon leaves from the florist. Make sure the leaves have a bit of stem so you can hold them. Wash and dry them well. Use a paintbrush to paint melted chocolate on the underside of each leaf; do not allow to run over the edge, as that will make it difficult to peel. Let stand on waxed paper or baking parchment until firm; peel off the leaf.

TO SHAVE CHOCOLATE, it should be at room temperature. For fine shavings, use the coarse side of the grater. For larger shavings, peel off curls with a vegetable peeler.

TO MAKE CHOCOLATE CURLS, pour melted chocolate onto a foil-lined baking sheet. Let stand until cooled but not hard. Place a large knife at a 45-degree angle to the chocolate, and use a sawing motion to remove thin curls. These can be arranged in concentric circles on a dessert with the thinner ends toward the center.

Celebrate life's special occasions. From the top down then clockwise: Cinnamon Roll-Up Cookies 253
Marbleized Chocolate Chip Cookie Tart 230 • Decorated Black and White Cake 239
Almond Crisps 250 • Chocolate Torte 244 • Whoopie Pies 269 • Double-Decker Confetti Brownies 265
Classic Refrigerator Sprinkle Cookies 259 • Chocolate and Hazelnut Meringue Cake 241

CRUNCHY ALMOND CONFETTI CAKE

Parve

ALMOND TOPPING
1 egg white
1¼ cups sliced almonds
2 tablespoons sugar

CAKE
7 eggs, separated
¼ teaspoon cream of tartar
1½ cups sugar, divided
1½ cups (9 ounces) semisweet chocolate chips
2¼ cups cake flour
1 teaspoon baking powder
½ teaspoon salt

½ cup vegetable oil
⅔ cup water
2 tablespoons almond liqueur (optional)
1 teaspoon vanilla extract
½ to 1 teaspoon almond extract

ALMOND GLAZE
1½ cups confectioners' sugar
½ teaspoon almond extract
1 to 2 tablespoons nondairy creamer

For the topping, preheat oven to 325 degrees. Beat egg white with a fork in a medium bowl for 30 seconds or until foamy. Add almonds and mix to coat well. Sprinkle with sugar and mix until well coated. Spread in a single layer on an ungreased nonstick baking sheet. Bake for 5 minutes. Stir with a wooden spoon and bake for 5 to 8 minutes longer. Stir again and let stand; almonds will become crisp as they cool.

For the cake, beat egg whites and cream of tartar at medium speed with electric mixer until foamy. Beat at high speed until mixture begins to hold its shape. Add ½ cup sugar gradually and beat until soft peaks form. Place in a separate bowl and set aside.

Wash and dry the bowl of mixer. Pulse chocolate chips in a food processor until partially grated. Sift cake flour, 1 cup sugar, baking powder and salt into a mixing bowl. Make a well in the center and add oil, egg yolks, water, liqueur and flavorings to the well. Beat at medium speed for 3 minutes or until smooth and thick. Fold in chocolate chips.

Gradually fold in egg whites with a rubber spatula. Spread evenly in a deep 9½- or 10-inch tube pan. Bake for 1¼ hours or until firm when gently pressed and any cracks on the top appear dry. Loosen from the pan with a knife and remove to a serving plate.

For the glaze, combine confectioners' sugar and almond extract in a small bowl. Add just enough creamer to make a thick smooth glaze. Reserve 2 tablespoons of the glaze. Drizzle remaining glaze over the cake, allowing it to drip down the side and center. Sprinkle with the topping and drizzle with the reserved glaze. *Makes 16 servings.*

BANANA CAKE

Parve

2 ripe bananas, peeled
   and sliced
2 eggs
1/2 cup vegetable oil
1/2 cup plus 1 tablespoon
   orange juice

1³/4 cups all-purpose flour
1¹/2 cups sugar
1 teaspoon baking soda
1 teaspoon vanilla extract
   Cinnamon-sugar to taste

Preheat oven to 325 degrees. Grease a loaf pan. Mash bananas in a bowl using a fork. Add eggs, oil and orange juice in a mixing bowl and mix well. Add flour, 1¹/2 cups sugar, baking soda and vanilla and mix until smooth. Sprinkle top with cinnamon-sugar. Bake for 1 hour and 20 minutes or until toothpick comes out clean. Cool on a wire rack. *Makes 8 servings.*

BERRY BUNDT CAKE

Parve

Credit for this cake goes to a kosher bed-and-breakfast in Newport, Rhode Island. Three school families filled up that six-room inn for a delightful Shabbat weekend—touring fabulous mansions, attending services at the historic Touro Synagogue, and clambering over the Cliff Walk.

3 cups all-purpose flour
2 cups sugar
1 tablespoon baking powder
1 teaspoon ground
   cinnamon (optional)
1/4 cup orange juice
4 eggs
1 cup vegetable oil

2 teaspoons vanilla extract
3 cups blueberries or
   raspberries, or a mixture
   of both
   Confectioners' sugar or
   lemon glaze for garnish
   (see sidebar)

Preheat oven to 350 degrees. Grease and flour a bundt pan. Combine flour, sugar, baking powder and cinnamon in a bowl; mix well and set aside. Beat orange juice, eggs, oil and vanilla with electric mixer until smooth. Add flour mixture and mix until smooth. Spread half the batter into the prepared pan and sprinkle blueberries over the batter; top with remaining batter. Bake for 50 to 60 minutes or until a tester comes out nearly clean. Cool in the pan on a wire rack and remove to a serving plate. Garnish with confectioners' sugar.
Makes 16 servings.

POURING CAKE BATTER

Pour cake batter evenly around the edge of the cake pan rather than in the center. This will avoid a raised center and allows it to bake evenly.

BERRY CAKE BONUS

For a lemon cake variation, add 1¹/2 teaspoons lemon extract to the Berry Bundt Cake batter and drizzle the baked cake with a mixture of 1 cup confectioners' sugar and the juice of 1 lemon.

To enjoy Berry Bundt Cake all year, buy blueberries in season, wash and dry them well and spread them on a baking sheet. Freeze until firm and measure into 1 cup portions. Store in the freezer in sealable plastic bags until needed.

DESSERT SHORTCUT
You can create a dessert by placing a plain baked cheesecake in a mixing bowl and adding one cup of heavy cream. Beat until mixture is smooth and the consistency of mousse. Spoon into a pastry bag fitted with a star tip and pipe into miniature graham cracker crusts or chocolate cups. Chill until serving time.

BUTTERCREAM FROSTING FACTS
Buttercream frosting may separate during mixing. Continue to beat it until it is thick and creamy. To make it extra creamy, especially on humid days, chill it for an hour and then beat it again.

CHOCOLATE CHEESE CUPCAKES
Dairy

$1^1/2$ cups all-purpose flour	1 tablespoon vinegar
$1^1/4$ cups sugar, divided	1 teaspoon vanilla extract
$^1/4$ cup baking cocoa	8 ounces PHILADELPHIA
1 teaspoon baking soda	cream cheese, softened
$^1/2$ teaspoon salt	1 egg
1 cup water	1 cup (6 ounces) miniature
$^1/3$ cup vegetable oil	chocolate chips (optional)

Preheat oven to 350 degrees. Grease and flour muffin cups. Mix flour, 1 cup sugar, cocoa, baking soda and salt with an electric mixer. Add water, oil, vinegar and vanilla and mix until smooth; set aside. Combine cream cheese, egg, $^1/4$ cup sugar and chocolate chips in a mixing bowl. Beat with electric mixer until well mixed. Spoon enough cocoa batter into each muffin cup to cover bottom. Spoon 1 heaping tablespoon cheese filling in center of each cup. Add enough remaining chocolate batter to fill each cup $3/4$ full. Bake for 20 to 25 minutes or until the cupcakes test done. *Makes 14.*

Photograph for this recipe is on page 245.

COFFEE CAKE MUFFINS
Dairy

Coffee Cake Muffins are a great solution when you have to take your coffee and breakfast to go.

$1^1/4$ cups sugar, divided	1 teaspoon baking soda
$^1/2$ cup chopped nuts	$^1/2$ cup (1 stick) butter, softened
1 teaspoon ground cinnamon	2 eggs, lightly beaten
$1^1/2$ cups all-purpose flour	1 cup sour cream
$1^1/2$ teaspoons baking powder	1 tablespoon vanilla extract

Preheat oven to 350 degrees. Grease 24 muffin cups. Mix $^1/4$ cup sugar, nuts and cinnamon in a bowl and set aside. Mix flour, baking powder and baking soda together. Beat butter and 1 cup sugar with electric mixer until light. Beat in the eggs and sour cream. Add flour mixture and vanilla and mix until blended. Spoon half the batter into the muffin cups, filling half full. Sprinkle with half the nut mixture. Repeat with remaining batter and nut mixture. Bake for 20 minutes or until a tester comes out clean. *Makes 2 dozen.*

DECORATED BLACK AND WHITE CAKE

Parve or Dairy

This cake requires some effort, but makes a stunning presentation on the dessert table.

CHOCOLATE CAKE

2	cups all-purpose flour
1	cup sugar
3/4	cup packed brown sugar
2/3	cup baking cocoa
1 1/2	teaspoons baking powder
1/2	teaspoon baking soda
1/2	teaspoon salt
1 1/2	cups nondairy creamer or milk
1/2	cup (1 stick) margarine or butter, softened
2	eggs
2	teaspoons vanilla extract

CHOCOLATE FROSTING

2 1/2	cups confectioners' sugar
1/2	cup nondairy creamer or light cream
1	teaspoon vanilla extract
1	cup (2 sticks) margarine or butter, softened
6	ounces semisweet chocolate, melted and cooled

ASSEMBLY

	Vanilla Frosting (at right)
3	or 4 packages rolled wafer cookies

For the cake, preheat oven to 350 degrees. Grease two 9-inch cake pans. Combine flour, sugar, brown sugar, baking cocoa, baking powder, baking soda and salt in a bowl. Add creamer, margarine, eggs and vanilla. Beat at low speed with electric mixer until the ingredients are moistened. Beat at high speed for 3 minutes or until smooth. Spread in prepared pans. Bake for 30 minutes or until a tester comes out clean. Cool on wire racks.

For the chocolate frosting, wash and dry mixer bowl and combine confectioners' sugar, creamer and vanilla. Add margarine and beat until smooth; do not overbeat. Fold in melted chocolate. You can store this frosting for up to three days in the refrigerator and bring to room temperature before spreading.

To assemble, generously spread some chocolate frosting between layers and lightly over the top and side of the cake. Score the top of the cake into 8 wedges (like a pizza). Spoon the remaining chocolate frosting into a pastry bag fitted with a number 27 star tip. Starting at the center, pipe rosettes onto alternating wedges, increasing the number of rosettes as you fill the wedge, filling completely. Clean and dry the bag and fill with Vanilla Frosting (see sidebar). Pipe vanilla rosettes on the alternate wedges. Press cookies lightly around the side of the cake and tie a sheer gold ribbon around the cookies. *Makes 8 to 16 servings.*

Photograph for this recipe is on page 235.

VANILLA FROSTING

Parve or Dairy

Combine one 16-ounce package confectioners' sugar, 1/2 cup (1 stick) margarine or butter and 1 teaspoon vanilla extract in a mixing bowl and beat until smooth. Add 3 to 4 tablespoons nondairy creamer or milk to make the desired consistency, mixing well.

WHITE CAKE

Parve

To substitute a white cake for the Chocolate Cake in this recipe, combine 3 cups flour, 2 cups sugar, 1 cup vegetable oil, 1 teaspoon baking powder, 3/4 cup orange juice, 4 eggs and 1 teaspoon vanilla in a mixing bowl and proceed as for the Chocolate Cake.

MIXING TIPS
Use a large mixing bowl to have plenty of room for mixing and keeping the batter from spattering out of the bowl.

Begin and end the mixing process with the dry ingredients. Blend at low speed and mix until smooth.

Scrape the bowl often with a spatula to incorporate the ingredients evenly.

CHOCOLATE BABKA
. . . .
Parve or Dairy

Once you try this, you will never go back to store-bought babka.

DOUGH
- 2 tablespoons dry yeast
- $1/3$ cup warm water
- $1/2$ cup sugar
- $5 1/2$ to 6 cups all-purpose flour
- $1/2$ cup plus 6 tablespoons vegetable oil
- 1 cup milk, soy milk or nondairy creamer
- $2/3$ teaspoon salt

CHOCOLATE FILLING
- $1/2$ cup baking cocoa
- 1 cup sugar
- 1 teaspoon ground cinnamon (optional)

BABKA TOPPING
- 2 tablespoons butter or margarine
- 6 tablespoons all-purpose flour
- 6 tablespoons sugar

For the dough, preheat oven to 350 degrees. Grease two 5×9-inch loaf pans. Combine yeast, warm water and sugar in a bowl. Cover and let stand for 10 minutes to proof the yeast. If bubbles do not form, your yeast is not active and you should not continue. Beat yeast mixture, flour, $1/2$ cup oil, milk and salt with an electric mixer to form a smooth dough. Divide into 2 portions and roll each portion into an 8×12-inch rectangle on a lightly floured surface. Brush each surface with 3 tablespoons oil.

For the filling, mix baking cocoa, sugar and cinnamon in a bowl. Sprinkle over the dough, leaving a 1-inch border on all sides. Roll tightly from the short side like a jelly roll. Repeat with remaining rectangle and filling. Place seam side down in the loaf pans.

To top and bake, combine butter, flour and sugar in a bowl and mix well. Sprinkle on the loaves. Let rise for 30 minutes. Bake for 35 to 40 minutes or until golden brown. Freeze well. *Makes 2 loaves.*

CHOCOLATE AND HAZELNUT MERINGUE CAKE

Parve

This is just as good without the meringue topping. Bake the chocolate cake without the meringue for forty to forty-five minutes or until it is slightly firm to the touch and begins to crack.

CAKE

10	tablespoons unsalted margarine, softened
3/4	cup packed light brown sugar
6	eggs, separated
12	ounces bittersweet chocolate, melted and cooled
1	tablespoon rum (optional)
1	tablespoon vanilla extract
	Pinch of salt

HAZELNUT MERINGUE

1	cup hazelnuts
4	ounces bittersweet chocolate, coarsely chopped
1	tablespoon cornstarch
4	egg whites
1/4	teaspoon cream of tartar
1	cup superfine sugar

ABOUT THIS CAKE

Cake is just as good without the meringue topping. Bake the chocolate cake until it is crackling and slightly firm, 40 to 45 minutes.

Use the largest spatula you can and as few strokes as possible when folding the egg whites into the chocolate mixture to maintain the light, airy consistency.

Rub the hazelnuts vigorously inside a folded towel while still warm.

For the cake, preheat oven to 350 degrees. Grease a 9-inch springform pan with a 3-inch side. Line bottom with baking parchment; grease and flour parchment. Beat margarine and brown sugar with electric mixer until light. Beat in egg yolks 1 at a time. Add melted chocolate, rum and vanilla and mix well. Beat egg whites and salt with a whisk attachment in a clean mixing bowl until soft peaks form. Fold into the chocolate mixture gradually. Spread in prepared pan and bake for 25 minutes.

For the meringue, spread hazelnuts in a single layer on a rimmed baking sheet. Toast for 10 to 15 minutes or until toasted and fragrant and skins begin to crack. Rub inside a towel while still warm to remove skins. Cool and chop coarsely. Mix hazelnuts, chopped chocolate and cornstarch in a small bowl. Beat egg whites with cream of tartar with electric mixer, using a whisk attachment until frothy. Add superfine sugar gradually, beating for 8 minutes or until stiff peaks form. Fold in hazelnut mixture. Remove cake from oven and spread meringue mixture on top of cake and return to oven. Bake for 25 to 30 minutes longer or until the meringue is light brown and firm. Cool for 30 minutes. Loosen cake from the side of the pan with a knife and place the cake on a serving plate; remove the side of the pan.
Makes 12 servings.

Photograph for this recipe is on page 235.

CHOCOLATE ROULADE
· · · · · · · · · · · · · · · · · · · ·
Parve or Dairy

5 *eggs, separated*	*Unsweetened baking cocoa*
1 *cup sugar*	2 *cups sweetened whipped*
6 *ounces (1 cup) semisweet*	*cream or nondairy*
chocolate	*topping*
3 *tablespoons brewed*	
black coffee	

Preheat oven to 350 degrees. Grease a 10×15-inch baking pan and line with baking parchment paper; grease the parchment paper. Beat the egg whites until stiff. Wash and dry the mixer and beat egg yolks with electric mixer until fluffy, adding sugar gradually. Melt chocolate with coffee in a saucepan over low heat. Add to the egg yolks gradually. Fold in the egg whites.

Spread evenly in the prepared pan. Bake for 15 minutes; do not overbake. Remove from oven and cover with a damp towel for 20 minutes. Remove towel and dust cake with baking cocoa. Invert onto waxed paper and remove the baking parchment paper. Spread with whipped cream. Lift the long side of the waxed paper and flip about 2 inches of cake onto itself to assist in rolling the cake to enclose the filling. Dust top with cocoa. The cake may crack as you roll it. Use confectioners' sugar, whipped cream or frosting to cover any cracks. *Makes 12 servings.*

CHOCOLATE INTELLIGENCE

Store chocolate in a dry place and keep it away from anything with strong odors.

Different brands of chocolate and cocoa vary dramatically in taste, color, and texture. Chocolate is processed from cacao beans. The more cacao that chocolate contains, the more bitter it will be. For example, a good-quality bittersweet chocolate can be 70 percent cacao. Semisweet chocolate is about 50 percent cacao and has more sugar; it can often be substituted for bittersweet chocolate without significantly affecting the flavor or texture. White chocolate is not true chocolate because it contains cocoa butter rather than cacao.

WARM CHOCOLATE SOUFFLÉS

Parve

For advance preparation, make the soufflés, but freeze them unbaked. Bake directly from the freezer for eighteen to twenty minutes. Or, desserts can be baked shortly before Shabbos and put directly on the warm (not very hot) area on the warming tray.

TRUFFLES

- 8 ounce good-quality semisweet chocolate
- 1 (8-ounce) container nondairy topping

CAKES

- 1 cup (2 sticks) margarine
- 8 ounces semisweet chocolate
- 4 eggs
- 4 egg yolks
- 3/4 cup sugar
- 3/4 cup flour, sifted

For the truffles, chop chocolate into small nuggets. Heat nondairy topping until very hot, but do not boil. Pour over chocolate and stir until completely melted and combined. Let mixture stand, covered, for 8 to 12 hours until firmed up. With a scoop or melon baller, scoop the mixture into small balls.

For the cakes, preheat oven to 400 degrees. Melt margarine with semisweet chocolate in a saucepan or microwave. Beat eggs, egg yolks and sugar with electric mixer until light colored. Mix in melted chocolate, then fold in flour by hand.

Grease 8 ramekins. Pour batter into each ramekin until 3/4 full. Place a truffle in the center of each ramekin. Bake for 12 minutes. Cool slightly and dust with confectioners' sugar. Serve immediately.

Makes 8 soufflés.

THE CORRECT AMOUNT

Liquid versus dry

Pair the right tool with the right ingredient. Measure liquids in clear measuring cups. To get the best reading, measure at eye level. Scoop dry ingredients into graduated cups, using the appropriate size for your measuring needs.

A Triangle of Temptation

To make chocolate wedges, melt 1 cup semisweet chocolate chips or white chocolate chips with 1 tablespoon shortening in the microwave. Spread it evenly inside a waxed paper-lined springform pan the size of the cake you want to decorate. Let stand until firm and remove the side of the pan. Chill for 30 minutes. Heat the blade of a knife in hot water and wipe dry. Cut the circle quickly but gently into 16 wedges. Overlap the wedges to cover the top of a cake. You can make both dark and white chocolate wedges and alternate on the cake.

CHOCOLATE TORTE

Parve or Dairy

CAKE

1/2	cup dark corn syrup
1/2	cup margarine
5	ounces semisweet chocolate
3/4	cup sugar
3	eggs
1	teaspoon vanilla extract
1	cup all-purpose flour
1	cup chopped nuts (optional)

CHOCOLATE GLAZE

3	ounces semisweet chocolate
1	tablespoon margarine
2	tablespoons dark corn syrup
1	tablespoon nondairy creamer or milk
1/4	cup confectioners' sugar Additional confectioners' sugar

For the cake, preheat oven to 350 degrees. Grease and flour a 9-inch springform pan. Bring corn syrup and margarine to a boil in a saucepan, stirring occasionally. Remove from the heat and add chocolate, stirring until melted and smooth. Mix in sugar. Beat in eggs one at a time. Add vanilla. Blend in flour gradually. Stir in nuts. Spread in the prepared pan and bake for 30 minutes. Cool completely on a wire rack.

For the glaze, melt chocolate with margarine in a saucepan, stirring to mix well. Remove from the heat and stir in corn syrup, creamer and 1/4 cup confectioners' sugar. Place cake on a serving plate and remove the side of the pan. Spread glaze evenly over the top and side of the torte. Sprinkle with additional confectioners' sugar.
Makes 8 servings.

Photograph for this recipe on page 235.

Note: When preparing a dark colored cake, use cocoa powder to dust the greased pan instead of flour. To decorate a dark colored cake, sift confectioners' sugar over the top. For an even more elegant touch, place a stencil over the confectioners' sugar and then dust with cocoa powder.

CHOCOLATE TURTLE PIE

Dairy

COOKIE CRUST

About 22 chocolate
sandwich cookies
1/4 cup (1/2 stick) butter,
melted

CARAMEL FILLING

20 caramel candies
1/4 cup heavy cream
2 cups pecan pieces

CHOCOLATE TOPPING

3/4 cup semisweet
chocolate chips
1/4 cup heavy cream

For the crust, preheat oven to 375 degrees. Process cookies in a food processor until broken into fine crumbs. Mix cookie crumbs with butter in a bowl. Press over the bottom and side of a 9-inch tart pan with a removable bottom. Bake for 10 minutes. Cool on a wire rack.

For the filling, melt caramel candies in a heavy saucepan over low heat, stirring to blend well. Stir in cream. Remove from the heat and mix in pecans. Spread evenly in the prepared crust. Chill in the refrigerator for 10 minutes or until set.

For the topping, melt chocolate in a double boiler over simmering water. Stir in cream. Drizzle over the pie. Chill for 1 hour or longer. Bring to room temperature to serve. *Makes 6 servings.*

*Clockwise from top: Classic Cheesecake 232 • Apricot Rugelach 220
Cheesecake Miniatures 232 • Chocolate Cheese Cupcakes 238
Chocolate Turtle Pie (this page).*

**GAMLA MUSCAT
(WHITE, ISRAEL)**
Well-balanced and
refreshing, with sweet
lingering flavors that
pair nicely with creamy
pastries and desserts.

ORANGE POPPY SEED CAKE

Parve

*T*he orange flavor is a nice twist to the traditional lemon in poppy seed
cake and goes nicely with the earthy flavor of the seeds.

CAKE

3	cups all-purpose flour
1	tablespoon baking powder
	Pinch of salt
5	eggs
1½	cups sugar
1	cup vegetable oil
1½	tablespoons finely grated orange zest
1	tablespoon vanilla extract

¾	cup orange juice
⅔	cup poppy seeds

ORANGE GLAZE

¼	cup orange juice
¼	cup sugar
3	tablespoons margarine

For the cake, preheat oven to 350 degrees. Grease and flour a
10-inch springform pan. Mix flour, baking powder and salt together
and set aside. Beat eggs and sugar with electric mixer until light. Beat
in oil, orange zest and vanilla. Add dry ingredients alternately with
orange juice, beginning with dry ingredients and mixing well after
each addition. Fold in poppy seeds. Spread evenly in the prepared
pan. Bake for 1 hour or until a tester comes out nearly clean.

For the glaze, combine orange juice, sugar and margarine in a small
saucepan. Cook over low heat for 3 to 4 minutes or until thickened,
stirring frequently. Pierce holes in cake as soon as it comes out of the
oven and pour glaze gradually over the cake. Cool on a wire rack and
place on a serving plate; remove the side of the pan. *Makes 12 servings.*

DECADENT CREAMY POUND CAKES

Dairy

For best results, bake these cakes at least a day before serving. Wrap them in plastic wrap and store them until serving time. They also freeze well.

1 1/2 cups (3 sticks) unsalted butter, softened	6 eggs
8 ounces cream cheese, softened	1 teaspoon vanilla extract
	3 cups all-purpose flour
3 cups sugar	2 teaspoons salt

Preheat oven to 350 degrees. Coat two 5x9-inch loaf pans with nonstick cooking spray. Beat butter and cream cheese with electric mixer until smooth. Add sugar and beat for 5 minutes or until light and fluffy. Beat in eggs one at a time. Mix in vanilla. Add flour and salt half at a time, mixing at low speed just until moistened after each addition.

Spread in the prepared loaf pans and tap pans on the work surface to remove any air bubbles. Bake for 1 to 1 1/4 hours or until a tester comes out clean and the tops are golden brown; tent with foil if necessary to prevent overbrowning. Cool in the pans for 10 minutes. Remove to a wire rack to cool completely. *Makes 16 servings.*

CHOCOLATE SOUR CREAM POUND CAKE

Dairy

2 1/2 cups all-purpose flour	5 eggs
1 cup baking cocoa	2 teaspoons vanilla extract
1 teaspoon baking soda	1 cup sour cream
1/2 teaspoon salt	1 cup boiling water
1 1/2 cups (3 sticks) butter, softened	Confectioners' sugar (optional)
3 cups sugar	

Preheat oven to 350 degrees. Grease and flour a 10-cup bundt pan. Sift flour, cocoa, baking soda and salt together and set aside. Beat butter with electric mixer until light. Add sugar and beat until fluffy. Beat in eggs one at a time. Mix in vanilla. Add dry ingredients one-third at a time, alternating with sour cream and mixing well after each addition. Beat in water gradually. Spread evenly in the prepared pan. Bake in the lower third of the oven for 1 hour or until a tester comes out clean. Cool in the pan for 15 minutes. Invert onto a wire rack to cool completely. Sprinkle lightly with confectioners' sugar. *Makes 16 servings.*

BAKING WITH BUTTER OR MARGARINE

Butter and margarine should be allowed to come to room temperature to soften for baking; this makes for a smoother batter and a lighter and more tender finished product. Creaming the butter whips in tiny air bubbles, which expand during baking for a smoother texture. It takes four to seven minutes to properly cream butter or margarine with sugar.

If butter is to be melted, it should be heated just until it starts to liquefy, removed from the heat, and stirred to finish melting. Chilled butter or margarine is used in pastries. Usually it is cut into small pieces to allow it to be "cut into" the dry ingredients without being completely incorporated. As the pastry bakes, the butter will melt to create little air pockets and give the crust its flakiness.

FLOP-PROOF POUND CAKES

For a flop-proof pound cake, butter and eggs must be at room temperature. Even though a small amount of baking powder can be added to avoid heaviness, creaming the butter and sugar at medium speed is what aerates the cake and gives it a light texture. Add the eggs one at a time and beat well after each addition to allow complete absorption.

WHY A BUNDT PAN?

The bundt pan, a tube pan with a fluted side, was invented for a Hadassah group writing a cookbook. The design was created to ensure even cooking—the hollow central tube conducting heat to the center of the cake and the fluted side conducting heat from the outside. It is especially useful for heavier batters, such as pound cakes and nut cakes.

STREUSEL POUND CAKE

Parve

2   *cups all-purpose flour*
1   *teaspoon baking powder*
1/4 *teaspoon salt*
1   *cup (2 sticks) unsalted margarine, softened*
2   *cups plus 4 teaspoons sugar, divided*
2   *eggs*
1   *cup nondairy creamer*
1   *teaspoon vinegar*
1   *teaspoon vanilla extract*
1   *cup chopped pecans*
1   *teaspoon ground cinnamon*

Preheat oven to 350 degrees. Grease and flour a bundt pan. Sift flour, baking powder and salt together and set aside. Beat margarine and 2 cups sugar with electric mixer until light. Beat in eggs one at a time. Add creamer, vinegar and vanilla and mix just until blended (do not overmix). Add dry ingredients and mix just until blended. Spread 1/3 of the batter in the prepared pan.

Mix pecans, cinnamon and remaining 4 teaspoons sugar in a bowl. Sprinkle three-fourths of the pecan mixture over the batter in the pan. Top with remaining cake batter and sprinkle with remaining pecan mixture. Bake for 1 hour. Cool in the pan for 15 minutes. Invert onto a platter. *Makes 16 servings.*

PULL-APART CAKE

. . . .

Parve

No matter how many scrumptious desserts are served, there is always one that disappears the fastest. The Pull-Apart Cake, a favorite with young and old, is literally torn into pieces. Aside from the popularity of the recipe, the other advantage is the ease with which it is made: even the kids can do it.

2 (15-ounce) packages KINERET frozen challah dough	1 tablespoon ground cinnamon
3/4 cup sugar	1/2 cup (1 stick) margarine, melted
3/4 cup packed brown sugar	

Defrost challah dough until it is just beginning to rise. Grease a bundt pan or tube pan. Mix sugar, brown sugar and cinnamon in a small bowl. Shape dough into walnut-size balls. Dip balls into melted margarine and roll in cinnamon-sugar mixture, coating evenly. Arrange loosely in the prepared pan, allowing room to rise. Sprinkle any remaining cinnamon-sugar on the top.

Preheat oven to 350 degrees. Let the dough rise for 30 minutes. Place the pan on a baking sheet and bake for 30 to 35 minutes or until golden brown. Cool completely in the pan on a wire rack.
Makes 12 to 16 servings.

Note: You can also make this in a 9×13-inch pan—it is not as pretty but as delicious and an easier cleanup.

ABOUT SUGAR

Brown sugar is made by combining sugar with molasses. Dark brown sugar has a higher molasses content than light brown sugar, giving it a more pronounced molasses flavor, a deeper color, and a higher moisture content.

Granulated sugar is the most widely used type of sugar for baking and cooking.

Superfine sugar has finer crystals, making it the choice for meringues and finer-textured cakes, such as angel food.

Confectioners' sugar is also called powdered sugar. It is made by grinding granulated sugar to a fine powder, then sifting. A little cornstarch is added to prevent caking. It is used primarily for frostings and dusting.

ALMOND CRISPS

Parve

*A*lmond Crisps are a great addition to the dessert table. They look very elegant and tickle the palates of all ages.

COOKIES

- 3/4 cup all-purpose flour
- 1 teaspoon baking powder
- 1/2 teaspoon salt
- 1/2 cup (1 stick) unsalted margarine, softened
- 1 cup packed light brown sugar
- 1 egg
- 1 teaspoon vanilla extract
- 1/2 cup finely chopped almonds

CHOCOLATE COOKIE GLAZE

- 6 ounces semisweet chocolate, chopped, or 1 cup chocolate chips
- 1 teaspoon vegetable shortening

For the cookies, preheat oven to 400 degrees. Sift flour, baking powder and salt together and set aside. Beat margarine at high speed with electric mixer until light. Add brown sugar and beat until fluffy. Beat in egg and vanilla on low speed until smooth . Add dry ingredients and mix or stir until smooth. Stir in almonds. Drop by level teaspoonfuls 2 inches apart onto ungreased nonstick cookie sheets. Bake for 5 minutes or until golden brown. Cool on the pan on a wire rack.

For the glaze, combine chocolate and shortening in a double boiler or microwave-safe bowl. Melt over barely simmering water or microwave on High for 1 minute and stir to blend well. Drizzle over cooled cookies from the tines of a fork. Remove to a wire rack and cool for 1 hour. *Makes 1 1/2 dozen.*

Photograph for this recipe is on page 235.

SECRET RECIPE
CHOCOLATE CHIP COOKIES

Parve

1/2 cup rolled oats	3/4 cup packed dark brown sugar
2 1/4 cups all-purpose flour	1 teaspoon lemon juice
1 1/2 teaspoons baking soda	2 teaspoons vanilla extract
1/4 teaspoon ground cinnamon	2 eggs
1/2 teaspoon salt	3 cups (18 ounces) semisweet chocolate chips
1 cup (2 sticks) margarine, softened	1 1/2 cups chopped walnuts (optional)
3/4 cup sugar	

Preheat oven to 350 degrees. Line two baking sheets with baking parchment. Process rolled oats in a food processor until finely ground. Combine with flour, baking soda, cinnamon and salt in a bowl. Beat margarine with sugar, brown sugar, lemon juice and vanilla with electric mixer until light. Beat in eggs. Add dry ingredients and mix well. Fold in chocolate chips and walnuts. Drop by tablespoonfuls 2 inches apart onto the prepared pans. Bake for 16 minutes or until light brown. Remove to a wire rack to cool. Store in an airtight container. *Makes 2 dozen.*

EASY CHOCOLATE MOUSSE
Dairy

Combine 1 large bar milk chocolate with a few drops of hot water in a microwave-safe dish and microwave until melted, stirring once or twice. Cool slightly. Beat 2 cups whipping cream in a mixing bowl until stiff peaks form and fold in melted chocolate. Microwave 1 large bar milk chocolate in a microwave-safe dish (without water) until melted, stirring once or twice. Cool slightly and fold into whipped cream mixture. Chill, covered, until serving time. *Makes 6 to 8 servings.*

CHOCOLATE CHIP PEANUT BUTTER COOKIES

Dairy

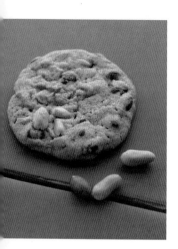

"What would a collection of chocolate chip cookies be without one made with peanut butter? You can divide the amount of chocolate chips and peanuts by using any proportion you want, as long as the total equals three cups. I like to use salted peanuts when I make these cookies. The yin and yang of sweet and savory makes a tantalizing balance of flavors."

3/4 cup lightly packed very fresh dark brown sugar

1/2 cup quick (1-minute) oatmeal

1/3 cup granulated sugar

13/4 cups all-purpose flour, spooned in and leveled

1/2 teaspoon baking soda

1/2 teaspoon salt

1 cup (2 sticks) unsalted butter, slightly firm

1 cup creamy peanut butter

2 tablespoons light corn syrup

1 large egg

2 teaspoons pure vanilla extract

3 cups total chocolate chips and salted cocktail peanuts (see Headnote)

Position the shelves in the upper and lower thirds of the oven. Heat oven to 375 degrees. Place brown sugar, oatmeal, and granulated sugar in the work bowl of a food processor fitted with a steel blade and process for 2½ to 3 minutes, stopping occasionally to pulse. The oatmeal should be finely ground and powdery. In a medium bowl, strain together flour, baking soda, and salt. Set aside.

In the large bowl of electric mixer fitted with a paddle attachment, mix butter on medium-low speed until smooth and lightened in color, about 1 minute. Mix in peanut butter and corn syrup until combined. Add oatmeal mixture in 3 additions and mix for 2 minutes, and then add egg and vanilla and mix for 1 minute longer. Scrape down bowl as needed. Reduce mixer speed to low, and then add dry ingredients, one-half at a time, and mix *just* until blended. Using a large rubber spatula, fold in the chocolate chips and peanuts.

Form into balls slightly smaller than a golf ball and place on cookie sheets about 3 inches apart. Flatten slightly to a thickness of 3/8 inch and a diameter of 2½ inches. Scrape down the sides of the bowl occasionally to ensure even distribution of chocolate chips and peanuts. Bake cookies for 9 to 10 minutes, or until edges *begin* to turn golden brown. To ensure even baking toward the end of baking time, rotate the pans top to bottom and front to back. *Do not overbake*.

Remove the cookies from the oven and let stand for 2 minutes. Using a thin metal spatula, carefully loosen. When firm enough to handle, transfer to cooling racks. Store in an airtight container. These cookies may be frozen. *Makes about 4 dozen.*

CINNAMON ROLL-UP COOKIES

Parve

3 cups all-purpose flour
2 teaspoons baking powder
1/2 teaspoon salt
1 teaspoon plus
   2 tablespoons ground
   cinnamon, divided

1 cup (2 sticks) margarine,
   softened
1 cup packed light
   brown sugar
2 eggs
1 teaspoon vanilla extract
6 tablespoons sugar

Mix flour, baking powder, salt and 1 teaspoon cinnamon together and set aside. Beat margarine and brown sugar with electric mixer until light. Beat in eggs and vanilla. Add dry ingredients and mix well. Chill for 1 hour or longer.

Mix sugar and remaining 2 tablespoons cinnamon together. Spread chilled dough into an 8×10-inch rectangle on waxed paper with a rubber spatula. Sprinkle with most of the cinnamon-sugar mixture, leaving a 1-inch edge. Roll into a log and sprinkle with remaining cinnamon-sugar. Wrap in plastic wrap and chill for 4 hours or longer.

Preheat oven to 350 degrees. Spray cookie sheets with nonstick cooking spray or line with baking parchment paper. Remove from plastic and cut cookie dough into 1/4-inch slices and arrange on the prepared cookie sheets. Bake for 8 minutes or until light brown on top. Cool on cookie sheets for 4 minutes and remove to wire racks to cool completely. *Makes 3 dozen.*

Photograph for this recipe is on page 235.

BAKING PARCHMENT
Baking parchment is treated with silicone and is used to line baking surfaces. It keeps foods from sticking and makes cleanup a breeze. It is a heatproof and grease-resistant surface sold in two forms—white, or bleached, and brown, or unbleached. To keep it in place, dot the corners of the baking pan with margarine and place the baking parchment in the pan. It can also be used to steam food such as chicken or fish. Just place the ingredients inside and fold to enclose the packet.

BAKING COOKIES

Preparing the Ingredients

Measure the flour by scooping it into a dry measuring cup and leveling it with the straight edge of a knife. Eggs and butter at room temperature are easier to add to the dough; you should remove them from the refrigerator about 2 hours before they are needed. Butter can also be cut into small pieces and microwaved very briefly just to soften but not melt it.

Mixing Dough

For the lightest cookies, mix only until the flour has been incorporated; do not overwork the dough when rolling it.

Shaping Cookies

Rolling out the dough between sheets of waxed paper cuts out the need for lots of extra flour to prevent sticking. If the dough becomes too soft to handle when rolling or cutting, refrigerate it for a few minutes before proceeding. If using a cookie cutter, dip it in flour before each cut. ➤

CRINKLE COOKIES

Parve

These cookies bake light and high and are almost like a brownie in a cookie format.

2¹/₃ cups (or more) all-purpose flour	³/₄ cup vegetable oil
³/₄ cup baking cocoa	4 eggs
2 teaspoons baking powder	2 teaspoons vanilla extract
¹/₂ teaspoon salt	1¹/₂ cups (9 ounces) chocolate chips
2 cups sugar	Confectioners' sugar

Mix flour, baking cocoa, baking powder and salt in a bowl until blended. Beat in sugar, oil, eggs and vanilla with electric mixer. Fold in chocolate chips. Chill for 4 hours.

Preheat oven to 350 degrees. Shape dough into small balls and roll in confectioners' sugar. Place on cookie sheets and bake for 12 to 15 minutes or until set. Cool on a wire rack. *Makes 3 dozen.*

GLAZED LEMON COOKIES

Parve

It is important to apply the glaze to the cookies when they are still very warm so it will spread easily and thinly.

2¹/₂ cups all-purpose flour	1 cup (2 sticks) margarine
1¹/₂ cups sugar	2 eggs
1¹/₂ teaspoons cream of tartar	1 tablespoon plus ¹/₄ cup lemon juice
1 teaspoon baking soda	2¹/₂ cups confectioners' sugar
¹/₄ teaspoon salt	
1 tablespoon grated lemon zest plus extra for garnish	

Preheat oven to 400 degrees. Mix flour, sugar, cream of tartar, baking soda, salt, 1 tablespoon lemon zest, margarine, eggs and 1 tablespoon lemon juice with electric mixer at low speed until well blended, scraping the bowl frequently. Drop by rounded teaspoonfuls 2 inches apart onto ungreased cookie sheets. Bake for 6 to 8 minutes or until the edges are light brown.

Mix confectioners' sugar and remaining ¹/₄ cup lemon juice in a small bowl. Spread over warm cookies and garnish with additional lemon zest, if desired. *Makes 5 dozen*

Oatmeal (Coconut) Cookies

Parve

*Y*ou don't have to mention that there is coconut in these. They have been served to people who don't like coconut, and they love them!

2 cups all-purpose flour	1 cup sugar
2 teaspoons baking powder	1 cup packed dark
2 teaspoons baking soda	brown sugar
1 teaspoon salt	2 eggs
1 cup (2 sticks) margarine, softened	2 cups rolled oats
	1 cup shredded coconut

Preheat oven to 350 degrees. Mix flour, baking powder, baking soda and salt together. Beat margarine, sugar and brown sugar with electric mixer with a paddle attachment until just combined. Beat in eggs. Add flour mixture and mix well. Add a mixture of oats and coconut; mix to form a dough. Shape into small balls and arrange on an ungreased cookie sheet lined with baking parchment paper. Press with the bottom of a glass to flatten slightly. Bake for 10 to 12 minutes or until golden brown. Remove to a wire rack to cool. *Makes 4 dozen.*

Ginger Cookie Press Cookies

Parve

2 cups all-purpose flour	1 cup (2 sticks) unsalted
1^1/$_2$ teaspoons ground ginger	margarine
1 teaspoon ground cinnamon	^{3}/$_4$ cup packed light brown sugar
^{1}/$_4$ teaspoon salt	1 tablespoon grated orange zest

Preheat oven to 350 degrees. Mix flour, ginger, cinnamon and salt together. Beat margarine with brown sugar and orange zest at high speed with electric mixer until light. Add dry ingredients and mix at low speed until smooth. Pack into a cookie press fitted with the desired design plate. Press 1^1/$_2$ inches apart onto an ungreased cookie sheet. Bake for 15 minutes or just until firm to the touch. Cool on a wire rack. *Makes 2^1/$_2$ dozen.*

Baking Cookies in the Oven

Always preheat the oven to the correct temperature. To ensure even baking, rotate the cookie sheets from front to back about halfway through the baking time; if you have cookie sheets on more than one rack, switch them on the racks.

Storing Cookies

Baked cookies will keep for several days in airtight containers at room temperature. To freeze unbaked cookies, shape them as desired and place on a cookie sheet lined with baking parchment or waxed paper. Cover with plastic wrap and freeze until firm. Transfer them to sealable plastic freezer bags and return to the freezer. There is no need to thaw the cookies before baking.

ALMOND LATTICE MERINGUES

Parve

Lattice meringues are a great complement to any fruit dessert and make a beautiful presentation. Prepare one recipe of Meringue batter (this page). Spoon into a pastry bag fitted with a plain round tip. Pipe into 3 vertical 3-inch strips 1 inch apart on a foil-lined cookie sheet. Pipe 3 horizontal strips across the first strips to form a lattice. Repeat the process with the remaining batter. Crush 1/3 cup lightly toasted sliced almonds and sprinkle over the lattices. Bake at 225 degrees for 30 to 40 minutes or until very light brown. Let stand in the oven for 8 hours to dry.

Photograph for this recipe is on page 257.

CHOCOLATE CHIP MERINGUES

Parve

3 egg whites	1/2 cup (3 ounces)
1/4 cup sugar	chocolate chips

Preheat oven to 300 degrees. Line a cookie sheet with foil, placing the shiny side down. Beat egg whites at medium speed with electric mixer until soft peaks form. Add sugar gradually and beat at high speed until stiff. Fold in chocolate chips just until mixed. Spoon by teaspoonfuls onto the prepared cookie sheet. Bake for 30 minutes. Turn off the oven and let the meringues stand in the oven, without opening the door, for 2 to 8 hours. *Makes 4 dozen.*

MERINGUES

Parve

3 large egg whites	3/4 cup sugar
1/8 teaspoon cream of tartar	1/2 teaspoon vanilla extract

Preheat oven to 275 degrees. Line a cookie sheet with foil and set aside. Beat egg whites and cream of tartar at high speed with electric mixer until soft peaks form. Add sugar, 2 tablespoons at a time, beating for 2 to 4 minutes until stiff peaks form and sugar dissolves. Beat in vanilla. Spoon meringue into a large pastry bag fitted with a large star tip. Pipe the cookies into small spiral mounds about 1 1/2 inches in diameter on the prepared cookie sheet. Bake for 20 to 30 minutes or until color is just beginning to turn (do not let meringues darken). Turn off the oven and let meringues stand in the closed oven overnight to completely dry. Store in an airtight container.
Makes 4 dozen small kisses or 8 to 12 dessert meringues.

Photograph for these recipes is on page 257.

LEMON OR CREAM MERINGUE NESTS

Parve

1   recipe Meringue batter (page 256)
1   package lemon pudding and pie filling mix
    Juice of 2 lemons
    Whipped topping
    Sliced strawberries and/or mint sprigs for garnish

Preheat oven to 225 degrees. Line 2 cookie sheets with foil. Prepare meringue batter and spoon into a pastry bag fitted with a star tip. Pipe into 3-inch circles, then pipe a rim around the edge of the circles to form nests. You can also spoon by $^1/_3$ cupfuls onto the cookie sheets and smooth into nests with the back of a spoon. Bake for 30 to 40 minutes or just until they begin to color. Turn off the oven and let the meringues stand in the oven for 8 hours to dry completely.

Prepare lemon pie filling using the package directions and adding lemon juice. Cool to room temperature and spoon into the shells. Garnish with strawberries and/or mint. You can also fill with sweetened whipped topping, if preferred. *Makes 8 servings.*

From top right, Apricot Pinwheels 262 • Palmiers 261
Lemon or Cream Meringue Nests (this page)
Almond Lattice Meringues 256 • Strawberry Meringues 258
Chocolate Chip Meringues 256 • Cinnamon Twists 261

EGG WHITES

Light and airy beaten egg whites are the secret to a delicious dessert or even a fluffy frittata. The beating increases the volume of the egg whites and affects their consistency; the longer they are beaten, the stiffer they become.

When separating the eggs, be careful not to let any yolk fall into the bowl, for inclusions will decrease the volume of the beaten egg white. Eggs are easiest to separate when they are cold, but they should be room temperature before beating.

The right bowl is also important. Stainless steel and copper bowls yield the best results. Avoid plastic, which can retain traces of grease even when washed.

You can store unbeaten egg whites, tightly covered, for up to four days or freeze them in ice cube trays. Transfer to a freezer bag and store for up to six months. Thaw for eight hours in the refrigerator to use.

**DRAMA ON A
PLATE**

Use a geometrically
shaped platter or plate
(square or triangle). Cut
a piece of paper into
either strips or a shape.
Place the paper on the
plate and generously
dust with either
confectioners' sugar or
cocoa powder (or both
but each dusted
separately). Carefully
remove the paper.
When removed, a
design will be visible
on the plate. This is a
great way to divide
a plate or serving
platter into quadrants.
Dessert items can
then be placed into
specific sections.

STRAWBERRY MERINGUES

Parve or Dairy

*Y*ou can prepare the meringues, filling, and garnish in advance for this
dessert, but you need to assemble it just before serving to keep the
meringues from getting soggy.

1   recipe Meringue batter (page 256)
1   pint strawberries, chopped, plus 12 strawberries, chopped,
      for garnish
1   cup heavy cream, or nondairy whipped topping
1/4 cup confectioners' sugar

Preheat oven to 225 degrees. Line two cookie sheets with foil.
Prepare meringue batter and spoon into a pastry bag fitted with a star
tip. Pipe into strips 1 inch wide and 3 inches long on the prepared
cookie sheets. Bake for 20 to 30 minutes or just until they begin to
color. Turn off the oven and let meringues stand in the oven for 8 hours
to dry completely. Beat 1 pint strawberries, cream and confectioners'
sugar with electric mixer until thick and fluffy. Spread mixture on half
of the meringue strips and top with the remaining strips. Garnish tops
with additional strawberries. *Makes 12.*

Photograph for this recipe is on page 257.

BUTTER PECAN COOKIES

Parve

1 1/2 cups pecans
1   cup (2 sticks) margarine,
      softened
2/3   cup sugar plus extra
      for rolling

2   cups all-purpose flour
2   teaspoons vanilla extract
1/4 teaspoon salt

Preheat oven to 350 degrees. Spread pecans on a baking sheet
and toast for 6 minutes, watching carefully to prevent burning.
Chop pecans. Beat margarine with 2/3 cup sugar with electric mixer for
1 minute or until light. Add flour, vanilla and salt and mix to form a
dough. Fold in pecans. Shape into balls and roll in remaining sugar.
Place 3 inches apart on cookie sheets and press with the bottom of a
glass to flatten. Bake for 15 minutes or until golden brown. Cool on
wire racks. *Makes 2 1/2 dozen.*

CLASSIC REFRIGERATOR SPRINKLE COOKIES

Parve

These cookies are real crowd pleasers. Customize them to your taste by coating with nuts for adults and colorful sprinkles for children. Double the recipe and freeze the extra to bake later.

1 cup (2 sticks) margarine, softened	2 cups all-purpose flour
1 cup sugar	2 teaspoons baking powder
1 egg	1/2 to 1 cup colored or
1 teaspoon vanilla extract	chocolate sprinkles

Beat margarine and sugar with electric mixer until light. Add egg and vanilla and beat until smooth. Add flour and baking powder and beat at low speed for 1 to 2 minutes. Shape into two logs about 2 inches in diameter on plastic wrap. Pour sprinkles on the logs and add remaining sprinkles to the plastic wrap, rolling logs over sprinkles to coat surface. Seal in the plastic wrap and chill for 2 to 8 hours.

Preheat oven to 350 degrees. Spray cookie sheets with nonstick cooking spray or cover with baking parchment paper. Cut logs into 1/4-inch slices and place 1 inch apart on the cookie sheets. Bake for 8 to 10 minutes or until edges are golden brown. Cool on wire racks and store in airtight containers. Keep unbaked logs chilled until baking time. *Makes 2 dozen.*

Photograph for this recipe is on page 235.

COOKIE BONUS

When you prepare any cookie dough, double the recipe and shape the extra dough into a log on plastic wrap. Wrap tightly and store in the freezer. For cookies at any time, thaw the log for fifteen to twenty minutes, slice into even rounds, and bake as instructed.

Ruby Jewel Miniatures

Parve

2   egg yolks
1   teaspoon vanilla extract
2 1/4   cups all-purpose flour
2/3   cup sugar
1   cup (2 sticks) unsalted margarine, chilled and cut into small pieces
1/3   cup (about) seedless raspberry jam or other thick jam
    Confectioners' sugar

Whisk egg yolks and vanilla together in a bowl. Process flour and sugar in a food processor until mixed. Add margarine 2 or 3 pieces at a time, processing constantly until crumbly. Add egg yolk mixture and process constantly until mixture forms a ball. Shape into a disk on plastic wrap. Wrap tightly and chill for 1 hour. Preheat oven to 350 degrees. Line 5 dozen miniature muffin cups with paper liners or grease them. Shape dough into 3/4-inch balls with lightly floured hands; place in the lined cups. Make an indentation in the center of each ball with the floured tip of a wooden spoon handle. Spoon jam into a pastry bag or plastic bag with the corner cut off. Pipe or squeeze 1/4 teaspoon of jam into the indentations. Bake for 15 to 20 minutes or until the edges are golden brown. Cool in cups on wire racks. Sprinkle with confectioners' sugar. *Makes 5 dozen.*

Note: You can also place the dough balls 1 inch apart on baking parchment-lined cookie sheets and prepare and bake as above. Loosen warm cookies with a thin spatula and remove to wire racks. Sift confectioners' sugar over the cookies through a fine-mesh sieve.

Palmiers and Twists

Parve

Palmiers and Twists are delicious served together or separately.

JOSEPH ZAKON
MUSCATINI
(RED, CALIFORNIA)
Delightfully fresh,
effervescent, and
semisweet, with
outstanding fruity
aromas and flavors that
pair well with pastries.

PALMIERS
1 (17.3-ounce) package
 frozen PEPPERIDGE
 FARM® Puff Pastry,
 thawed

CHOCOLATE FILLING
3/4 cup chocolate spread
3 tablespoons sugar or
 cinnamon-sugar

APRICOT FILLING
3/4 cup apricot preserves
 Cinnamon-sugar

TWISTS
1 cup sugar
1 1/2 tablespoons ground
 cinnamon
1 (17.3-ounce) package
 frozen PEPPERIDGE
 FARM® Puff Pastry,
 thawed

For the palmiers, preheat oven to 350 degrees. Roll each sheet of puff pastry to a 10×16-inch rectangle on a floured surface.

For chocolate palmiers, spread rectangle with half the chocolate spread. Sprinkle with half the sugar or cinnamon-sugar. Repeat with remaining puff pastry sheet and ingredients.

For apricot palmiers, spread rectangle with half the preserves. (If it is difficult to spread preserves, microwave them for 30 seconds.) Sprinkle with cinnamon-sugar. Repeat with remaining puff pastry sheet and ingredients.

Roll one of the long sides toward the center and repeat with the other side until they meet. Repeat with remaining sheet. Cut into 3/4-inch slices with a sharp knife. Place cut side down on an ungreased baking sheet. Bake for 15 minutes or until golden brown. *Makes 3 1/2 dozen.*

For the cinnamon twists, preheat oven to 350 degrees. Mix sugar with cinnamon in a bowl. Cut each sheet of puff pastry into thirds and roll each piece into a 4×16-inch rectangle. Cut into 1-inch strips vertically. Twist strips in the bowl of cinnamon-sugar while coating and place on an ungreased baking sheet. Bake for 15 to 20 minutes or until golden brown. *Makes 5 to 6 dozen.*

Photograph for this recipe is on page 257.

ALMOND COFFEE SQUARES

Parve

12 eggs, separated
2¹/2 cups sugar
16 ounces ground almonds
8 ounces parve semisweet
    chocolate

2 tablespoons instant
   coffee granules
1 cup (2 sticks) unsalted
   margarine
   Whole almonds for garnish

Preheat oven to 350 degrees. Grease a 9×13-inch baking pan. Beat egg whites with 1¹/2 cups sugar at high speed with electric mixer until stiff peaks form. Fold in ground almonds gradually. Spread in the prepared pan and bake for 25 to 30 minutes or until set.

Microwave chocolate with coffee granules in a microwave-safe dish for 1 to 2 minutes or until melted. Stir to blend well and cool.

Wash and dry mixer and beat egg yolks with 1 cup sugar with electric mixer until light. Beat in margarine. Add chocolate mixture and mix well. Spoon over hot baked layer and bake for 15 to 18 minutes longer or until set. Cool on a wire rack. Cut into squares. You can also cut this into small squares, place in small baking cups and top each with an almond. They can be frozen until needed. *Makes 2 dozen.*

APRICOT PINWHEELS

Parve

1 (17.3-ounce) package
   frozen PEPPERIDGE
   FARM® Puff Pastry,
   thawed

1 cup apricot preserves
   Cinnamon-sugar

Roll out each sheet of pastry to an 8×16-inch rectangle on a lightly floured surface. Cut each into half lengthwise and then cut each half into 4 squares for a total of 8 squares. Spread 1 to 2 tablespoons of apricot preserves in the center of each square. Make a diagonal cut from each corner of the square to within ³/4 inch of the center, using a sharp knife. Fold over every other point to the center, overlapping them slightly and sealing the points together. This will create the shape of a pinwheel. Place on a baking sheet covered with baking parchment paper and sprinkle cinnamon-sugar on the top. Bake for 30 to 40 minutes or until golden brown. *Makes 16 servings.*

Photograph for this recipe is on page 257.

CHOCOLATE CHOCOLATE CHOCOLATE BISCOTTI

Dairy

2 cups all-purpose flour, spooned in and leveled

1/3 cup strained Dutch-processed cocoa powder, spooned in and leveled

1 tablespoon baking powder

3 large eggs
 Pinch of salt

1 cup sugar

1 teaspoon vanilla extract

1/2 cup (1 stick) unsalted butter, melted and cooled to tepid

1 cup coarsely chopped walnuts

12 ounces semisweet chocolate chips

CHOCOLATE GLAZE

1/3 cup water

1/3 cup light corn syrup

1 cup sugar

8 ounces fine-quality bittersweet or semisweet chocolate, chopped

Position shelves in the upper and lower thirds of the oven. Heat oven to 350 degrees. Lightly dab corners of 10×15-inch pans with butter and line them with baking parchment. Set aside.

Whisk together flour, cocoa, and baking powder. Set aside.

In the bowl of electric mixer fitted with a whip attachment, beat eggs and salt on medium speed until lightened in color, about 2 minutes.

Gradually add sugar, taking about 2 minutes, then beat in vanilla. Pour tepid butter down the side of the bowl and beat for 30 seconds longer.

Remove bowl from mixer and, using an oversize rubber spatula, stir in walnuts and chocolate chips. Fold in dry ingredients in 3 additions, mixing only until combined. The dough will be very soft. For ease of handling, let the dough rest for 10 minutes to thicken.

Drop dough by heaping spoonfuls onto prepared pans and form four logs, measuring about 12 inches long and 2 inches wide. Flour your hands lightly and even the sides as best you can. It's okay if the logs are somewhat irregular. Bake for 20 to 25 minutes, or until set on top. To ensure even baking, rotate the pans top to bottom and front to back toward the end of baking time. Let cool for at least 20 minutes.

Lower the oven temperature to 325 degrees. Using a serrated knife, cut the logs on the diagonal into 1/2-inch-thick slices. Turn slices cut side up and return to the oven for 12 minutes. Turn the biscotti over and bake for 7 minutes longer or until crisp.

While the biscotti are toasting, make the glaze. Place the water, corn syrup and sugar in a heavy 2-quart saucepan. Bring to a boil over low heat, stirring occasionally. Remove from the heat and add chocolate. Let stand for 2 to 3 minutes, then whisk to smooth. While the biscotti are still warm, dip the ends in glaze and set on parchment-lined pans to dry. *Makes 6 dozen.*

SINFULLY DELICIOUS COOKIES

Dairy

2 cups (4 sticks) unsalted
butter, softened
16 ounces cream cheese,
softened

4 cups all-purpose flour
1 small can apricot or
raspberry fruit filling
1 cup confectioners' sugar
1 teaspoon vanilla sugar

Beat butter and cream cheese with electric mixer. Add flour and beat until mixture forms a ball. Wrap in plastic wrap and chill for 6 hours or longer. Preheat oven to 350 degrees. Line a cookie sheet with baking parchment paper or grease lightly. Roll dough into a square 1/8 inch thick on a lightly floured surface. Cut into 2-inch squares. Spoon fruit filling onto squares, leaving edges uncovered. Bring top and bottom edges to the center to cover filling and press edges to seal. Place on cookie sheet and bake for 20 minutes. Mix confectioners' sugar and vanilla sugar in a bowl. Roll warm cookies in the sugar mixture and cool on wire racks. Store in airtight containers. *Makes 4 dozen.*

HEART-SHAPED BROWNIES

Use a 2 1/2-inch heart-shaped cookie cutter for beautiful heart-shaped brownies. Dust them with baking cocoa for an extra touch. But don't let the brownie scraps go to waste. Mold them into 1-inch balls and roll them in baking cocoa, confectioners' sugar, or chopped nuts.

CAPPUCCINO BROWNIES

Parve

1 cup all-purpose flour
1 1/2 teaspoons ground
cinnamon
1/4 teaspoon salt
1/2 cup (1 stick) margarine
4 ounces semisweet
chocolate, chopped
1 1/2 cups sugar

1 tablespoon instant
espresso powder
2 teaspoons vanilla extract
4 eggs
3/4 cup chocolate chips
16 chocolate-covered
coffee beans

Preheat oven to 325 degrees. Grease a 9×9-inch baking pan. Mix flour, cinnamon and salt together. Melt margarine with chocolate in a large saucepan over low heat, stirring to blend well. Cool slightly and whisk in sugar, espresso powder, vanilla and eggs. Add dry ingredients and mix just until combined. Fold in chocolate chips. Spread in prepared pan and bake for 30 to 40 minutes or just until a wooden pick comes out with a few crumbs attached; do not overbake. Cool for 10 minutes. Score top into sixteen squares and place a chocolate-covered coffee bean in the center of each square. Cool completely and cut into squares. You can freeze these brownies. *Makes 16.*

DOUBLE-DECKER CONFETTI BROWNIES

Parve

2¹/₂ cups all-purpose flour, divided
2¹/₂ teaspoons baking powder
 ¹/₂ teaspoon salt
 ³/₄ cup (1¹/₂ sticks) margarine, softened, plus
      1 tablespoon margarine, melted, divided
  1 cup sugar
  1 cup packed light brown sugar
  3 eggs
  1 teaspoon vanilla extract
 ¹/₃ cup baking cocoa
  1 cup semisweet miniature chocolate chips, divided

Preheat oven to 350 degrees. Grease a 9×13-inch baking pan lightly. Mix 2¹/₄ cups flour with baking powder and salt in a medium bowl. Beat ³/₄ cup margarine, sugar and brown sugar with electric mixer until light. Beat in eggs and vanilla. Add dry ingredients and mix well. Remove and reserve half the batter. Blend cocoa with remaining 1 tablespoon melted margarine in a small bowl. Add to batter remaining in bowl and mix well. Spread in prepared pan.

Fold ¹/₄ cup flour and half the chocolate chips into reserved batter. Spread over first layer in the baking pan. Sprinkle with remaining chocolate chips. Bake for 25 to 30 minutes or until edges start to pull away from sides of pan. Cool on a wire rack and cut into squares. *Makes 2 dozen.*

Photograph for this recipe is on page 235.

THE RIGHT FLOUR

Flours are not interchangeable. Cake flour is light and soft, for airy cookies and cakes.

If you substitute all-purpose flour for cake flour, your cake may be too heavy. All-purpose flour is perfect for pie dough; cake flour is too crumbly, while bread flour might make the dough too tough to roll. Bread flour, with its high protein content, gives loaves the desired form and texture. There is an exception: you can switch from bleached to unbleached flour as desired. It is best to measure flour by dipping the measuring cup into the canister until it overflows and then leveling the top. You might actually have less flour if you spoon it into the cup.

CRANBERRY STICKS

Dairy

2¹/₂	cups all-purpose flour	1¹/₂	cups sugar
1	teaspoon baking powder	2	eggs
¹/₂	teaspoon salt	¹/₂	teaspoon almond extract
¹/₂	cup (1 stick) unsalted butter	1¹/₂	cups dried cranberries

Preheat oven to 350 degrees. Line a large heavy baking sheet with baking parchment paper. Mix flour, baking powder and salt in a medium bowl. Beat butter, sugar, eggs and almond extract with electric mixer until smooth. Add dry ingredients and mix well. Fold in cranberries.

Shape dough into 2 logs 1×2¹/₂×9 inches on a baking sheet. Bake for 35 minutes or until golden brown; logs will spread as they cook. Cut into ¹/₂-inch slices and arrange cut side down on the baking sheet. Bake for 5 to 10 minutes longer or until light brown. Cool on the baking sheet on a wire rack. You can freeze the sticks in an airtight container. *Makes 3 dozen.*

MY MOTHER'S MANDELBREAD

Parve

3	eggs	2¹/₂	cups all-purpose flour
³/₄	cup sugar	1	teaspoon baking powder
³/₄	cup vegetable oil	¹/₂	cup chocolate chips
¹/₂	teaspoon lemon juice	¹/₂	cup walnuts (optional)
¹/₄	teaspoon salt		Cinnamon-sugar
1	teaspoon vanilla extract		

Preheat oven to 350 degrees. Grease a baking sheet. Beat eggs, sugar, oil, lemon juice, salt and vanilla with electric mixer until smooth. Add flour and baking powder and mix well. Stir in chocolate chips and walnuts.

Shape into two logs on prepared baking sheet. Sprinkle with cinnamon-sugar. Bake for 30 to 45 minutes or until golden brown. Cut logs into slices and place cut side down on baking sheet. Sprinkle with additional cinnamon-sugar. Bake for 5 minutes longer. *Makes 3 dozen.*

Note: If you are not using nuts, double the chocolate chips.

PEANUT BUTTER S'MORE STACKS

Parve

BROWNIE

- 4 ounces semisweet or bittersweet chocolate, coarsely chopped
- $1/2$ cup (1 stick) unsalted margarine
- $1^1/2$ cups sugar
- 4 eggs
- 1 teaspoon vanilla extract
- $1/2$ cup all-purpose flour
- $1/4$ teaspoon salt

PEANUT BUTTER FILLING

- $1^1/2$ cups creamy peanut butter
- $1/2$ cup confectioners' sugar
- 1 teaspoon vanilla extract

PEANUT TOPPING

- $1/4$ cup sugar
- $1/4$ cup light corn syrup
- 4 egg whites
- $1/4$ cup water
- $1/2$ cup unsalted roasted peanuts for garnish

For the brownie, preheat oven to 350 degrees. Spray a 9×13-inch baking pan with nonstick cooking spray. Melt chocolate with margarine in a saucepan over low heat, stirring to blend well. Cool to lukewarm. Beat sugar, eggs and vanilla at high speed with electric mixer for 2 minutes or until thick and smooth. Beat in flour and salt at low speed. Add chocolate mixture and mix well. Spread in prepared pan and bake for 20 minutes or until a tester comes out with moist crumbs. Cool completely on a wire rack.

For the filling, combine peanut butter, confectioners' sugar and vanilla in a mixing bowl; mix until smooth. Spread over cooled baked layer.

For the topping, preheat oven to 400 degrees. Beat sugar, corn syrup, egg whites and water at high speed with electric mixer until stiff. Spread gently over peanut butter layer. Bake for 5 minutes or until golden brown. Cool to room temperature. Garnish with the unsalted peanuts and cut into small rectangles. *Makes 3 dozen.*

KIDS COOKING

A number of the recipes in this book lend themselves to being prepared by or with children. Here are some useful tips to ensure success:

Read the recipe together with your child to make sure he or she understands it.

Prepare all the equipment and ingredients before beginning to cook.

Wash hands well, roll up sleeves, and pin back hair before beginning.

Turn any pot handle in toward the center of the stovetop to avoid bumping into it.

Kids of all ages can help—the younger kids can pour in measured ingredients, crack eggs over a bowl, or break up crackers or vegetables. ➤

STRAWBERRY STREUSEL BARS

Parve

1 cup (2 sticks) margarine, softened
3/4 cup sugar
2 cups all-purpose flour
1 egg
1/2 to 3/4 cup chopped pecans
1 (10-ounce) jar strawberry preserves or other preserves

Preheat oven to 350 degrees. Grease a 7×11-inch baking pan. Beat margarine and sugar at low speed with electric mixer until smooth, scraping the bowl frequently. Add flour and egg and beat for 2 to 3 minutes or until crumbly. Stir in pecans. Reserve 1 cup of crumb mixture. Press remaining crumb mixture into prepared baking pan.

Spread preserves over bottom layer, leaving a 1/2-inch border on all sides. Crumble reserved mixture over the top. Bake for 40 to 50 minutes or until light brown. Cool on a wire rack and cut into bars. You can freeze these for up to one month. *Makes 2 dozen.*

WHITE CHOCOLATE PRETZEL CLUSTERS

Parve

12 ounces parve white chocolate chips
1 (16-ounce) package pretzel twists or thin sticks broken into small pieces

Melt white chocolate chips in a microwave-safe bowl for 1 minute or until melted, stirring in the middle. Combine with pretzels in a bowl and mix well. Spoon by teaspoonfuls onto a baking sheet and chill until firm. Store in an airtight container. *Makes 2 dozen.*

Photograph for this recipe is on page 273.

WHOOPIE PIES

Parve or Dairy

COOKIES

- 2 cups all-purpose flour
- 1 cup sugar
- 1/2 cup baking cocoa
- 1 teaspoon baking soda
- 1/4 teaspoon salt
- 3/4 cup milk or nondairy creamer
- 6 tablespoons margarine or butter, melted
- 1 egg
- 1 teaspoon vanilla extract

MARSHMALLOW CREME FILLING

- 6 tablespoons margarine or butter, softened
- 1 cup confectioners' sugar
- 7 or 8 ounces marshmallow creme
- 1 teaspoon vanilla extract

For the cookies, preheat oven to 350 degrees. Grease 2 large cookie sheets. Mix flour, sugar, baking cocoa, baking soda and salt in a large bowl. Add milk, margarine, egg and vanilla and mix with a wooden spoon until smooth. Spoon by heaping tablespoonfuls 2 inches apart onto prepared cookie sheets, placing twelve on each sheet. Bake for 12 to 14 minutes or until toothpick comes out clean when inserted. Remove to wire racks to cool.

For the filling, beat margarine with electric mixer until light. Add confectioners' sugar gradually and beat at low speed until smooth. Beat in marshmallow creme and vanilla. Spread 1 rounded tablespoon of filling on the flat side of half the cookies and top with remaining cookies. *Makes 1 dozen pies.*

Note: Peanut Butter Cream Filling can also be used to fill the cookies. Combine 1/4 cup softened butter or margarine, 1/2 cup confectioners' sugar, 1/2 cup peanut butter and 1/2 teaspoon vanilla in a mixing bowl and beat until smooth. Fill as above.

Photograph for this recipe is on page 235.

Try not to focus on the food looking perfect. Remember, they are just learning and you don't want to discourage them from trying again!

Focus on teamwork. It is a good lesson for them to learn, one that they will use in other aspects of life.

Take the opportunity to reinforce lessons that they have learned in school, such as fractions, addition, and subtraction. Cooking and measuring can become a math game.

The use of a timer or clock also reinforces time-telling skills.

Most of all, have fun and be safe!

FLAVORFUL KRISPIE TREATS

Parve

The question is, which flavor do they like best? It is usually a toss-up between the classic treats and the fruity ones. Make all three and see which ones win in your house.

1/2 cup (1 stick) margarine
12 ounces marshmallow creme

7 to 8 cups toasted rice cereal

Spray a 9×13-inch pan with nonstick cooking spray. Melt margarine in a large saucepan over medium heat. Add marshmallow creme and mix with a spoon until smooth. Remove from heat and fold in enough cereal to make the desired consistency. Press into prepared pan. Let stand until cool and firm and cut into squares. *Makes 32.*

For Fruity Krispies, substitute POST FRUITY PEBBLES Cereal for half the plain rice cereal.

For Chocolate Krispies, substitute POST COCOA PEBBLES Cereal for half the plain rice cereal.

QUICK PRALINE BARS

Parve

Here is a recipe that will be an instant hit on your table. Only you need to know how easy they are to prepare!

12 cinnamon or plain graham cracker rectangles
3/4 cup packed dark brown sugar

3/4 cup (1 1/2 sticks) margarine
1 teaspoon vanilla extract
3/4 chopped pecans

Preheat oven to 350 degrees. Arrange graham crackers in a single layer in a 10×15-inch baking pan, covering bottom of pan completely. Bring brown sugar and margarine to a boil in a saucepan. Boil for 1 minute, stirring constantly. Stir in vanilla. Pour evenly over graham crackers, spreading to cover completely. Sprinkle with pecans. Bake for 10 minutes or until bubbly. Cool for 30 minutes and break into bars. *Makes 12.*

CHOCOLATE RAISIN NUT CLUSTERS

Parve

If you are a lover of peanut chews, this recipe is for you! Even if you are not a raisin fan, don't leave them out—they give the clusters a pleasant chewy consistency.

2 (15-ounce) bittersweet chocolate bars, broken into pieces	3/4 cup confectioners' sugar
1¼ cups light corn syrup	2 teaspoons vanilla extract
	3/4 to 1 cup raisins
	2 cups roasted peanuts

Line a baking sheet with waxed paper. Melt chocolate in a double boiler over low heat or in a microwave-safe dish in the microwave. Combine chocolate and corn syrup in a bowl until smooth. Add confectioners' sugar, vanilla, raisins and peanuts and mix. Spoon by tablespoonfuls onto the prepared baking sheet and chill until serving time. Freezes well. *Makes 4 dozen.*

Photograph for this recipe is on page 273.

CANDIED PECANS

Parve

1 cup packed brown sugar	¼ cup coffee liqueur
1½ teaspoons salt	4 cups small pecan halves
2 egg whites	

Preheat oven to 325 degrees. Line a shallow baking pan with foil. Mix brown sugar and salt in a small bowl. Whisk egg whites and liqueur in a large bowl. Add pecans, stirring to coat evenly. Add brown sugar mixture and mix well. Spread in a single layer in the prepared pan. Bake for 20 to 25 minutes or just until pecans are toasted and crisp, stirring from the outer edges toward the center every 10 minutes. Remove to a waxed-paper lined tray to cool. *Makes 4 cups.*

Photograph for this recipe is on page 273.

PIQUANT ALMONDS

Parve

2¹/₂ cups almonds	1 tablespoon honey
¹/₄ cup sugar	1 tablespoon water
1¹/₂ teaspoons kosher salt	1 teaspoon olive oil
1 teaspoon cayenne pepper	

Preheat oven to 350 degrees. Spread almonds in a rimmed baking sheet. Bake for 10 minutes or until toasted and fragrant. Combine sugar, kosher salt and cayenne pepper in a large bowl. Combine honey, water and olive oil in a large skillet. Cook over medium heat for 1 minute, stirring to mix well. Add almonds and toss to coat evenly. Combine almonds with sugar mixture without scraping extra glaze into the bowl; toss to coat well. Spread in a single layer on waxed paper to cool. *Makes 2¹/₂ cups.*

SPICED NUTS

Parve

¹/₂ cup olive oil	1 teaspoon sweet paprika
³/₄ cup packed brown sugar	2 teaspoons hot paprika, or
2 tablespoons maple syrup	to taste
1 teaspoon finely chopped fresh rosemary	¹/₂ teaspoon coarse salt
1 teaspoon onion seeds	1¹/₃ pounds mixed almonds, pecans, cashews and
1 teaspoons fennel seeds	peanuts
1 teaspoon cumin seeds	

Preheat oven to 275 degrees. Line a baking sheet with baking parchment. Combine olive oil, brown sugar, maple syrup, rosemary, onion seeds, fennel seeds, cumin seeds, sweet paprika, hot paprika and coarse salt in a large bowl and mix into a paste. Add nuts and mix to coat well. Spread on prepared baking sheet. Bake for 1¹/₂ hours, stirring once after 45 minutes. Turn off oven and let nuts stand in oven with door ajar until cool; nuts will become crisp as they cool. Store cooled nuts in an airtight container. *Makes 1¹/₃ pounds.*

Photograph for these recipes is on page 273.

FLAVORED POPCORNS

Parve or Dairy

*F*lavored popcorn is a real favorite! Below are some of our unique and tasty popcorn recipes. For a greater variety and selection of popcorn flavors, visit our corporate sponsor, DALE & THOMAS POPCORN™ in their stores or online at www.daleandthomas.com.

HOT AND SPICY POPCORN
1¹/₂ teaspoons paprika
¹/₂ teaspoon ground cumin
³/₄ teaspoon kosher salt
   Cayenne pepper and black pepper to taste
8 to 10 cups freshly popped popcorn
2 tablespoons vegetable oil

SWEET AND CINNAMONY POPCORN
2 tablespoons sugar
1 teaspoon ground cinnamon
¹/₂ teaspoon kosher salt
8 to 10 cups freshly popped popcorn
2 tablespoons butter or margarine, melted

CHEESY POPCORN
¹/₄ cup (1 ounce) grated Parmesan cheese
³/₄ teaspoon kosher salt
¹/₄ teaspoon pepper
8 to 10 cups freshly popped popcorn
2 tablespoons olive oil

For Hot and Spicy Popcorn, mix paprika, cumin, kosher salt, cayenne pepper and black pepper in a bowl. Toss popcorn with oil in a large bowl. Add seasonings and toss to coat evenly.

For Cheesy Popcorn, mix cheese, kosher salt and pepper in a bowl. Toss popcorn with olive oil in a bowl. Add cheese mixture and toss to coat evenly.

For Sweet and Cinnamony Popcorn, mix sugar, cinnamon and kosher salt in a bowl and set aside. Coat hot popcorn with melted butter or margarine. Toss with the cinnamon-sugar, coating evenly. *Makes 8 to 10 cups.*

Pick-up treats! Pictured here are
Candied Pecans 271 • Chocolate Raisin Nut Clusters 271
Flavored Popcorn (this page)
White Chocolate Pretzel Clusters 268 • Spiced Nuts 272.

Traditional

MENU SAMPLER

SHABBAT

Night Menu

Creamy White Bean Soup 38
Balsamic Chicken 83
Dutch Oven Brisket 109
Roasted Cauliflower 193
Bravas Potatoes 195
Grandma's Apple Pie 226

Day Menu

Colorful Fish Pâté 29
Crunchy Nutty Salad 70
Lemon-Pistachio Chicken 90
Slow-Cooking
Country-Style Stew 120
Cold Green Beans with
Dill and Pecan Sauce 191
Orzo with Caramelized Onion
and Mushroom Sauté 206
Corn Squash Muffins 211
Almonds Crisps 250
Whoopie Pies 269

ROSH HASHANAH

Bubbie's Fricassee 19
Apricot-Glazed Turkey 104
Sweet and Savory Brisket 110
Stuffed Zucchini 199
Basmati Rice with
Asparagus 209
Snap-Crackle-Pop
Apple Kugel 212
Mashed Sweet Potatoes
and Pears 213
Rustic Fruit Tart 222
Decorated Black and
White Cake 239
Palmiers and Twists 261
Taiglach 278

SUKKOT

Sweet Potato Leek Soup 51
Tomato and Spinach Bisque 52
Autumn Salad 60
Squash and Apple-Stuffed
Turkey Breast 102
Herbed Standing Rib Roast 114
Green Beans with
Cremini Mushroom Sauce 192
Barley-Pine Nut Casserole 202
Pear and Cranberry Crisp 203
Warm and Soothing
Apple Crisp 219
Warm Chocolate Soufflés 243
Oatmeal (Coconut) Cookies 255

SHEMINI ATZERET/ SIMCHAT TORAH

Stuffed Wrappers with
Meat and Rice 25
Deli Meat Salad 64
Asian Salad 74
Sun-Dried Tomato and
Artichoke Chicken 97
Succulent Spareribs 117
Oven-Roasted Asparagus with
Orange-Almond Vinaigrette 190
Marinated Portobello
Mushrooms 194
Yerushalmi Kugel 211
Chocolate Torte 244
Pull-Apart Cake 249
Ruby Jewel Miniatures 260
Double-Decker
Confetti Brownies 265
White Chocolate Pretzel
Clusters 268

CHANUKAH

Sicilian Stuffed Rice Balls 16
Crispy Fried Fish 134
Eggplant Rollitini 174
Fruity Applesauce 284

PURIM

Todd's Merguez 15
Lahamagine 18
Yebra Sweet or Simple 22
Yebra with Chick-Peas 23
Barzargan 33
Mediterranean
Chick-Pea Soup 43
Georgian Pomegranate
Chicken 95
Soy Sauce Green Beans 191
Lentil Rice 207
Crunchy Almond
Confetti Cake 236
Classic Refrigerator
Sprinkle Cookies 259

SHAVUOT

Seared Tuna and
Avocado Tartare 31
Refreshing Summer Minted
Honeydew Soup 45
Salmon with Tomatoes
and Shallots 139
Mushroom Roll-Ups 164
Vegetable Bundt Frittata 176
Espresso Cheesecake 233
Sinfully Delicious Cookies 264
Cheese Blintz Loaf with
Banana Berry Topping 291

PASSOVER

Menu List on page 282

DELICIOUS CHALLAH

Parve

"I started baking challah about three years ago. Excited anticipation still fills my home as the smell of this freshly baked bread wafts through the rooms. Reciting the additional prayer adjacent to this recipe will enhance this special mitzvah. You will create the feeling of comfort and joy to all who grace your table."

1/4	cup dry yeast	8	eggs
4	cups warm (110-degree) water	5	pounds plus 2 cups bread flour
2	cups plus 1 tablespoon sugar	2	egg yolks
2	tablespoons salt	2	to 3 tablespoons water
2	cups vegetable oil		Poppy seeds, sesame seeds and cinnamon-sugar

Combine yeast, water and 1 tablespoon of sugar in a bowl and let stand for 5 to 10 minutes or until foamy. Place remaining sugar, salt, oil, eggs and flour in the bowl of an oversized electric mixer. Add yeast mixture. Blend at slow speed until well combined. Continue mixing at medium speed for 5 minutes.

Place dough in a stockpot or very large bowl. Cover and let rise in a warm draft-free location for 2 to 3 hours or until doubled in size. Remove a small portion of dough to "burn" and make the appropriate blessing on.

Preheat oven to 350 degrees. Line two to three baking sheets with parchment paper. Divide dough into eight equal portions. Cut each portion into three pieces. Roll each piece into a rope, keeping the center thicker and the ends thinner. Braid the pieces, then place on a prepared baking sheet. Let rise for 30 minutes.

Combine egg yolks and water and brush challahs with the mixture. Sprinkle with poppy seeds, sesame seeds or cinnamon-sugar, if desired. Bake for 30 to 35 minutes or until golden brown. Baked challahs freeze well. *Makes 8 loaves.*

Note: For more information on the blessing of the separation of challah, see *The Kosher Palette* or consult your rabbi.

Photograph for this recipe is on page 275.

ADDITIONAL PRAYER FOR BAKING CHALLAH

The mitzvah of hafrashat challah, the separating of the challah, is one of the three mitzvot entrusted especially to Jewish women. Observing the mitzvah of challah, our sages tell us, "will cause a blessing to rest on your house." The woman, so influential in shaping the values and attitudes of her family members, brings blessings upon her home and family through this mitzvah and instills faith in G-d within those around her. This mitzvah is easy to do, but an understanding of the guidelines for its fulfillment is necessary.

Below is a prayer, translated into English, which is said by the woman as she holds a small piece of separated dough in her hand.

"Our G-d and G-d of our fathers:

Let my Challah be accepted as an offering, on the mizbeich (altar). My mitzvah should be accepted as if I had done it perfectly."

"Long ago the Cohen was given the offering and for it the giver was forgiven of sin. So, too, should G-d forgive my sin. I should be like a newborn child. May I be able to honor my beloved Sabbaths and Holidays. May G-d grant me that my husband and my children and I be nourished by G-d, and that my children be protected by the loving G-d, may he be blessed, with great mercy and with great compassion. May the Challah be as if I brought a maaser—a tithe. Just as I perform my mitzvah of Challah with my whole heart, so may G-d protect me from pain and discomfort all my days."

COCOSH
· · · · · · · ·
Parve

*O*nce the roll is formed, you can cut it into individual buns. You can also substitute powdered chocolate drink mix for the cocoa and sugar.

2	softball-size balls of challah dough, ¹/₈ of challah recipe, opposite	²/₃	cup sugar
		¹/₃	cup unsweetened baking cocoa
6	to 8 tablespoons margarine, softened	1	egg yolk
		1	tablespoon water

Preheat oven to 325 degrees. Roll out each dough ball on a floured surface into a rectangle. Roll dough as thin as you can. Spread liberally with softened margarine. Combine sugar and cocoa in a bowl. Sprinkle half of the mixture over margarine on each rectangle.

Roll up jelly roll-style, stretching the dough so it forms more layers. Place on a greased jellyroll or baking pans with sides—it does ooze. Beat egg yolk and water and brush the mixture over the rolls. Bake for 20 to 25 minutes until light golden brown. *Makes 4 servings.*

Photograph for this recipe is on page 275.

BREAD MACHINE WHOLE WHEAT CHALLAH
Parve

This challah is lighter and not as sweet as Delicious Challah. Pastry flour is suggested because it results in a lighter challah. The ratio of flours can be adjusted to taste. If you like a sweeter challah, add 1 to 2 more tablespoons honey and ¹/₄ teaspoon vanilla.

Combine 4 tablespoons light olive oil, 2 tablespoons honey, 2 large eggs, ³/₄ cup room temperature water, 2 cups bread machine white flour, 1 cup whole wheat pastry flour or regular whole wheat flour, 1¹/₄ teaspoons salt, 1 tablespoon sugar and 2¹/₂ teaspoons yeast in the bread machine in the order listed. Program for regular dough; make medium loaves.

REVIVING HONEY

To revive crystallized honey, place the open jar in a saucepan filled with 1 inch of water. Heat over very low heat until honey becomes smooth, stirring often. Or microwave on High for 15-second increments, stirring often, until honey is liquified.

ROSH HASHANAH

The Jewish New Year, Rosh Hashanah, is one of the most symbolic festivals of the holiday cycle. The sweetness of the apples, honey, tzimmes, and honey cake that we eat all relate to our hopes for a sweet, happy new year. The smells and tastes evoke the comforting feeling of years gone by, along with the sweetness of many joyful years to come.

TAIGLACH (HONEY BALLS)

Parve

These sweets can be shaped two ways, in the traditional beehive shape or a simpler ball.

2 cups (1¹/₂ pounds) honey	3 cups all-purpose flour
1¹/₂ cups sugar	³/₄ teaspoon baking powder
1 cup boiling water	¹/₂ cup raisins (optional)
3 teabags	³/₄ teaspoon ground ginger
6 eggs	1 cup walnuts (optional)
1¹/₂ teaspoons vegetable oil	

Combine honey and sugar in a large stockpot, cover, and bring to a simmer over low heat while dough balls are prepared. Pour boiling water into a large mug over teabags; steep until dark and strong. Beat eggs and oil in a bowl with a mixer until light. Add flour and baking powder and mix well. Dough will be sticky.

For beehive shape, take a walnut-size ball of dough and roll into a long, thin pencil shape. Place two raisins between two fingers and wrap dough strip around raisins, continuing to twirl dough around you fingers in a downward spiral to form a beehive shape. Hives will be about 1¹/₂ inches long and 1 inch wide. Set hives aside on a floured surface, making sure they aren't touching.

For balls, pinch off a walnut-size ball of dough and insert raisins in the center, if desired. Roll into a smooth ball. Set aside on a floured surface, making sure balls aren't touching.

Raise flame under honey mixture and bring to a boil. Cook hives or balls by lowering into simmering honey mixture. Don't crowd the pan, and try not to let them touch, as they will expand as they cook. Bring mixture to a boil. Cover, lower heat and simmer for 20 to 30 minutes until golden brown, stirring to turn every 10 minutes with a slotted spoon.

Squeeze tea out of bags and pour tea into the honey mixture. Add ginger and nuts and mix well. Remove from heat. Pour into a heatproof bowl. Let cool, stirring occasionally. Cover with plastic wrap until serving time.

Makes 10 to 12 servings.

DELI ROLL

. . . .

Meat

"*This recipe is a favorite among kids and adults alike. My house is always full of kids on Shabbat, and I am convinced they come for the deli roll. I quadruple the recipe and make eight at a time because they freeze beautifully, so I am always ready. We also gave the option of including a potato center, which makes it like a hush puppy. When I serve it to adults, I plate two thin slices with a scoop of chopped liver between them and some coleslaw on the plate. It's like being at a deli!*"

1 (17.5-ounce) package frozen PEPPERIDGE FARM® Puff Pastry	8 ounces oven-prepared turkey, thinly sliced, divided
1/2 cup Dijon mustard or honey mustard, divided Potato Filling (optional) (see sidebar)	8 ounces pastrami, thinly sliced, divided
8 ounces smoked turkey, thinly sliced, divided	1 egg yolk
	1 tablespoon water Sesame seeds, poppy seeds (optional)

Preheat oven to 350 degrees. Roll out puff pastry on a floured surface to 1/8 inch thickness. Spread half the Dijon mustard in a thin layer over the pastry. Spread half the potato filling, starting 1 inch from the top, in a thin row horizontally across the pastry, leaving a 1/2 inch border.

Beneath potatoes, layer half the meat, starting with the turkey then pastrami. Roll up jelly roll-style, starting with the end nearest potatoes so that potatoes will be in the center. As you roll, stretch dough so that meat does not get pushed below pastry. Beat egg yolk and water and brush over the roll. Sprinkle with seeds, if you wish. Repeat with remaining ingredients. Place on a greased baking sheet. Bake for 45 to 60 minutes until golden brown. *Makes 4 to 6 servings.*

POTATO FILLING
Parve

Sauté 1 chopped small onion in 2 tablespoons oil in a medium saucepan for 8 to 10 minutes until golden brown. Remove from heat, add 1 cup water, 1/4 teaspoon salt, 1 tablespoon margarine, 1/3 cup soy milk or nondairy creamer and 1 cup instant mashed potato flakes and mix well.
Makes 16 servings.

SUKKOT

This fall holiday is a wonderful family-oriented celebration. Children decorate the sukkah, a temporary dwelling where all meals are eaten. Warm, hearty foods celebrating the bountiful harvest of autumn are traditional fare.

SHEMINI ATZERET/ SIMCHAT TORAH

These concluding days of Sukkot allow us to revel in the joy of concluding the last weekly portion of the Torah and beginning the yearlong cycle again. Extended family and friends come together to celebrate this unique holiday. With so many people on hand, a large buffet lunch or kiddush may be the order of the day.

TONGUE

Meat

If you prefer, buy a pickled, boiled tongue. Slice it, and then heat it in the sauce. Substitute water for the cooking liquid in the sauce.

1	(2- to 3- pound) beef tongue	1 (8-ounce) can tomato sauce
1	cup raisins	1/2 cup packed dark brown sugar
1 1/2	cups water	2 tablespoons all-purpose flour
1	teaspoon garlic powder	1/2 cup cold water
	Juice of 2 lemons	
1	tablespoon corn syrup	

Cover tongue with water in a large pot. Bring to a boil; drain. Refill with fresh boiling water and cook 2 1/2 to 3 hours until tender. Reserve 3 cups liquid. Peel tongue, cool completely and then slice.

Soften raisins in 1 1/2 cups water to cover in a large saucepan. Add reserved cooking liquid, garlic powder, lemon juice, corn syrup, tomato sauce and brown sugar.

Combine flour and 1/2 cup water in a small bowl and mix until smooth. Add to sauce mixture. Cook over low heat until thick. Add sliced tongue and cook until heated through. Serve hot. *Makes 5 to 7 servings.*

CABBAGE SOUP

Meat

This soup is better the second day!

1	pound flanken strips	3/4 cup uncooked rice
4	to 6 marrow bones	1/4 cup granulated sugar
1	(28-ounce) can crushed tomatoes	1/2 cup packed dark brown sugar
2	(48-ounce) cans tomato juice	2 McIntosh apples, peeled, cored and chopped
1	head cabbage, shredded	Juice of 2 lemons
2	onions, finely chopped	Salt and pepper to taste

Combine meat, bones and water to cover in a large stockpot. Bring to a boil, cover, and boil for 30 minutes. Skim soup. Add tomatoes, tomato juice and cabbage. Return to a boil and add remaining ingredients. Simmer 2 1/2 to 3 hours. Season to taste with salt and pepper. *Makes 6 servings.*

Sweet Noodle Kugel

Parve

1 *pound extra wide*	2 *teaspoons salt*
egg noodles	2 *teaspoons vanilla extract*
3/4 *cup (1 1/2 sticks)*	1 *quart nondairy creamer*
margarine	6 *eggs, lightly beaten*
1 1/2 *cups sugar*	

Preheat oven to 325 degrees. Boil noodles in salted water until tender. Drain and return to pot. Add margarine to hot noodles and toss to coat. Add remaining ingredients and mix until well combined. Pour into an ungreased 11×14-inch baking pan (or two 8×8-inch pans). Bake for 1 1/4 hours or until light brown. *Makes 6 to 8 servings.*

Potato Kugel Cholent

Meat

5 *pounds potatoes, quartered*
1 *large onion, peeled and quartered*
3 *eggs*
   Salt, pepper and garlic powder to taste
3 *pounds flanken, cut into chunks*
1 *pound kishke*
1 *cup water*

Preheat oven to 350 degrees. Process potatoes and onion in a food processor using the steel blade; pour into a bowl. Add eggs and salt, pepper and garlic powder to taste and mix well. Lay flanken in a single layer over the bottom of a large baking dish. Spread potato mixture over meat. Place whole kishke in the center, pushing in the center toward bottom. Bake uncovered for 1 hour. Add water and cover dish with foil. Lower oven temperature to 200 degrees and bake overnight for 18 to 24 hours. *Makes 8 to 10 servings.*

Shabbat

Friday night at sundown, Jews all over the world usher in the Shabbat. Concluding when the stars emerge Saturday night, the Shabbat is a time to reconnect, refocus, reflect, and re-energize. What better way to do that than to join around the Shabbat table surrounded by family and those you hold dear.

PLANNING PESACH MEALS

Bubbie's Fricassee 19

Chicken en Papillote 28

Colorful Fish Pâté 29

Seared Tuna and
Avocado Tartare 31

Avocado Dip 32

California Strawberry Salsa 33

Artichoke Soup 36

Purée of Carrot and Dill Soup 39

Roasted Cauliflower and
Dill Soup 42

Ratatouille Soup 43

Refreshing Summer Minted
Honeydew Soup 45

Garlic-Mushroom Soup 46

Exotic Mushroom Soup 48

Roasted Root Vegetable Soup
(omit garnish) 50

Sweet Potato and Leek Soup
with Pecan Garni 51

Garden Verde Soup 53

Zucchini and Spinach Soup 53

Avocado and Hearts of Palm
Salad 57

Chopped Greek Salad 59

Simply Delicious Beet Salad 64

Balsamic Chicken 83

Roasted Chicken with
Garlic Confit 87

Rosemary Chicken 94

Sun-Dried Tomato and
Artichoke Chicken 97

Squash and Apple-Stuffed
Turkey Breast 102

Apricot-Glazed Turkey 104

Pepper-Crusted Roast 111

Herbed Standing Rib Roast 114

Firecracker Rib-Eye Steaks 116

Passover is an eight-day holiday during which we remember and relive our forefathers' enslavement in Egypt and subsequent freedom. Passover seders evoke memories of our grandmothers' and great-grandmothers' homes. However, the restricted number of foods that can be served on Passover may prove daunting for even the most seasoned cooks. To help ease the menu-making process and facilitate an elegant but accessible meal, the following is a list of all Passover-appropriate recipes found in this cookbook. Please be sure to check all ingredients you use to make sure they bear proper Passover certification.

Sautéed Skirt Steak with
Caramelized Shallots 118

Rack of Lamb 125

Quick Lamb Chops 125

Cajun Veal Roast with
Mango Purée 126

Roasted Striped Bass with
Scallion Cream Sauce 133

Tangy Halibut 134

Cod Livornese 136

Oven-Roasted Whole Snapper
with Black Olives 137

Salmon with Tomatoes
and Shallots 139

Grilled Salmon Italiano 140

Rosemary Grilled Salmon and
Vegetables with Balsamic
Syrup (omit coriander) 141

Tilapia Fillets with
Pesto Butter 146

Roasted Eggplant and Bell
Pepper Terrine 178

Oven-Roasted Asparagus 190

Roasted Cauliflower 193

Bravas Potatoes 195

Herbed Mashed Potatoes 196

Scalloped Potatoes with
White Wine 196

Roasted Sweet Potatoes and
Mushrooms 198

Stuffed Zucchini 199

Fall Starburst 200

Portobello Mushroom Caps
Stuffed with Ratatouille 200

Mashed Sweet Potatoes
and Pears 213

Zingy Watermelon
with Mango 219

Strawberry Whip 225

Balsamic Glazed
Strawberries 227

Fresh Fruit Sorbet 227

Chocolate Roulade 242

Chocolate Chip Meringues 256

Almond Lattice Meringues 256

Lemon or Cream
Meringue Nests 257

Strawberry Meringues 258

Almond Coffee Squares 262

Fruity Applesauce 284

Where to start when the table features so many favorites? Clockwise from the top:
Individual Yerushalmi Kugel 211 • Deli Roll 279
Tomato Basil Angel Hair Pasta 158 • Sweet and Sour Meatballs 117
Mediterranean Chicken Salad 61 • Potato Kugel Cholent 281 • Colorful Fish Pâté 29.

Cool Marinated Salmon

Dairy

*T*his is a classic salmon dish. Many people grew up on salmon and cream sauce, and this recipe is it! It's easy to make and is the precise recipe of the classic you remember and love.

FISH
- 2 pounds salmon fillet, skin removed and cut into 2-inch strips
- 1/4 cup sugar
- 3 Spanish or Vidalia onions, cut into rounds
- Pinch of salt

SAUCE
- 1/2 cup mayonnaise
- 1/2 cup sugar
- 1/2 cup lemon juice
- 1/2 cup ketchup
- 1/2 cup water
- Dill weed for garnish

For the fish, combine salmon, sugar, onions and salt in a large skillet with a lid. Add enough water to cover the salmon. Cover and simmer for 15 minutes.

For the sauce, combine mayonnaise, sugar, lemon juice, ketchup and water in a bowl and mix well. Spread half the onions and half the sauce on the bottom of a large container or baking dish. Top with salmon, remaining sauce and remaining onions. Cover and marinate in the refrigerator 1 to 2 days. Garnish with dill weed to serve.
Makes 6 servings.

Fruity Applesauce

Parve

*T*his is a wonderful variation of plain applesauce and will be a nice complement to your latkes. It came from one of our grandparents, who said it is one of her grandchildren's favorites.

- 1 (16-ounce) package frozen rhubarb
- 1/2 cup water
- 1 (24-ounce) jar applesauce
- 2 (12-ounce) packages frozen sliced strawberries, thawed
- 2 boxes strawberry-flavored kosher gelatin

Combine rhubarb and water in a large saucepan over medium heat. Cook for about 20 minutes or until the rhubarb is very soft, stirring occasionally. Remove from heat. Add applesauce, strawberries and kosher gelatin and mix well. Refrigerate to chill.
Makes 8 to 10 servings.

Shavuot

The holiday of Shavuot celebrates the awe-inspiring time when the Jews received the Torah. Likewise, we celebrate the harvesting and bringing of the first ripe fruits of the seven species to the Temple. Traditionally, dairy foods are served on this festival. This provides the opportunity to explore and create with interesting varieties of fish, pasta and vegetables.

Chanukah

The defeat of the mighty Greeks at the hands of a small group of Jews called the Maccabees was the first miracle of Chanukah. The second miracle occurred when the small amount of oil the Maccabees used to relight the Temple Menorah lasted for eight long days. Thus was born the tradition of cooking all our favorite Chanukah foods in oil.

PASSOVER MATZOH MEAL-CRUSTED CHICKEN WITH VEGETABLES

Meat

2 eggs, lightly beaten
3 tablespoons water
1¹/₂ to 2 cups matzoh meal
 Salt, pepper and garlic
 powder to taste
1 chicken, cut into 8 pieces
3 to 4 tablespoons
 vegetable oil

1 large onion, chopped
3 ribs celery, chopped
8 ounces carrots, sliced
3 zucchini, peeled and
 chopped
2 cups MANISCHEWITZ®
 Chicken Broth

Preheat oven to 350 degrees. Combine eggs and water in a bowl and set aside. Combine matzoh with salt, pepper and garlic powder to taste on a plate or waxed paper. Dip chicken into egg mixture and then coat with matzoh meal mixture.

Heat oil in a large skillet over medium heat and brown chicken, then arrange in a roasting pan. You may need to do this in batches. Sauté the onions, celery, carrots and zucchini in the same skillet for 10 to 15 minutes until tender. Spread over chicken. Pour broth over vegetables and tightly cover the pan. Bake for 1¹/2 hours.
Makes 4 to 6 servings.

PASSOVER GEFILTE FISH PATTIES

Parve

FISH
1 (22-ounce) loaf frozen
 gefilte fish (sweetened),
 defrosted
¹/₃ cup matzoh meal plus
 additional for coating
 Canola oil for frying

HORSERADISH SAUCE
¹/₂ cup mayonnaise
¹/₄ cup white horseradish
 Splash of lemon juice

For the fish, combine fish and ¹/₃ cup matzoh and mix well. Wet hands and shape fish mixture into patties. Coat with additional matzoh meal. Heat oil in a large skillet over medium-high heat and fry fish on both sides until golden brown.

For the sauce, combine mayonnaise, horseradish and lemon juice in a small bowl and mix well. Serve sauce in scooped out lemon shells. *Makes 4 to 6 servings.*

PASSOVER CARROT PUDDING

Parve

  1 pound plus 2 carrots
     Raisins
$^1/_2$ cup crushed pineapple, drained
$^1/_2$ cup vegetable oil
$^1/_2$ cup sugar
  1 cup matzoh meal
  3 eggs, separated
     Pinch of salt

Preheat oven to 350 degrees. Boil carrots in water to cover in a saucepan for 15 minutes until just tender. Grate carrots into a bowl. Add pineapple, oil, sugar, matzoh meal, egg yolks and salt. Using an electric mixer, beat egg whites until stiff and then gently fold into carrot mixture. Spoon into a greased 2-quart glass baking dish and bake for about 1 hour or until brown. *Makes 6 servings.*

PASSOVER BROCCOLI CASSEROLE

Parve

  6 tablespoons vegetable oil
  1 cup chopped onion
$^1/_2$ cup chopped celery (about 3 ribs)
$1^1/_2$ cups grated carrots
$^3/_4$ cup matzoh meal
  3 eggs
$1^1/_2$ teaspoons salt
$^1/_8$ teaspoon pepper
  2 (10-ounce) packages frozen chopped broccoli, thawed and drained

Preheat oven to 350 degrees. Heat oil in skillet and sauté onion, celery and carrots for 10 minutes. Spoon into a bowl. Combine matzoh meal, eggs, salt and pepper in a bowl; add broccoli and mix well. Cool, and then add onion mixture and mix well. Spoon into a greased 9×13-inch baking dish and bake for 30 minutes. *Makes 6 to 8 servings.*

PASSOVER APPLE CRISP

Parve

12	McIntosh apples, peeled and chopped	1/2	cup sugar
1/4	cup lemon juice	3/4	cup (1 1/2 sticks) margarine
1	teaspoon ground cinnamon	1/2	cup chopped walnuts
		1	cup cake meal

Preheat oven to 350 degrees. Combine apples, lemon juice, cinnamon and sugar in a bowl and mix well. Combine margarine, walnuts and cake meal in a separate bowl until well blended. Press half the walnut mixture on the bottom of a 9×13-inch baking dish. Spread with apple mixture. Crumble remaining walnut mixture on top. Bake for 45 to 60 minutes. *Makes 12 to 14 servings.*

BUBBIE RAZIE'S PASSOVER BROWNIES

Parve

These brownies freeze well and make a frosty treat straight from the freezer.

4	eggs	1	cup vegetable oil
1/2	cup unsweetened baking cocoa	1	cup ground nuts
3/4	cup potato starch	1	(6-ounce) package chocolate chips
2	cups sugar		

Preheat oven to 350 degrees. Combine eggs, cocoa, potato starch, sugar, oil, nuts and chocolate chips in a large bowl with a fork. Spread in a greased 8×8-inch baking pan. Bake for 45 minutes. *Makes 9 squares.*

CHOCOLATE CHIP PASSOVER COOKIES

Parve

1	cup (2 sticks) margarine	1^1/$_3$	cups cake meal
1^1/$_4$	cups sugar	1	teaspoon baking soda
2	eggs	1	(6-ounce) package
1	teaspoon vanilla extract		chocolate chips
1	cup potato starch		

Preheat oven to 350 degrees. Beat margarine, sugar, eggs and vanilla in a large bowl until fluffy, using an electric mixer. Add potato starch, cake meal and baking soda and mix well. Fold in chocolate chips. Drop by teaspoonfuls onto a greased baking sheet. Bake for 8 to 10 minutes. *Makes 3 dozen.*

PASSOVER BLONDIE

Parve

4	eggs	1	cup vegetable oil
1	cup packed dark	1	cup potato starch
	brown sugar	1	cup finely ground nuts
3	teaspoons vanilla extract	1	(6-ounce) package
3	teaspoons baking powder		chocolate chips
1	cup granulated sugar		

Preheat oven to 350 degrees. Beat eggs, brown sugar, vanilla, baking powder, granulated sugar, oil, potato starch and nuts in a large bowl until well mixed, using an electric mixer. Spread batter in a greased 8×8-inch baking pan. Sprinkle chocolate chips on top. Poke holes in the batter. Bake for 50 to 60 minutes. *Makes 9 to 12 servings.*

PASSOVER MANDELBROT

Dairy or Parve

DOUGH

2³/4 cups matzoh cake meal, spooned in and leveled

3/4 cup potato starch, spooned in and leveled

1/2 teaspoon (scant) salt

1 cup (2 sticks) unsalted butter or margarine, slightly firm

1³/4 cups sugar

6 large eggs

6 ounces fine-quality bittersweet or semisweet chocolate, such as Lindt Bittersweet, coarsely chopped (optional)

1 cup toasted almonds, coarsely chopped

GLAZE AND TOPPING

1 large egg, beaten with 2 teaspoons water

1 teaspoon ground cinnamon

1 tablespoon sugar

Position the shelves in the upper and lower thirds of the oven. Heat the oven to 350 degrees. Butter or grease jelly roll pans. Strain together the matzoh cake meal, potato starch and salt. Set aside.

In the bowl of an electric mixer fitted with a paddle attachment, beat butter and 1³/4 cups sugar on medium speed for 2 to 3 minutes or until creamy and lightened in color. In a separate bowl, lightly beat 6 eggs. Add one-third at a time to the butter mixture and mix until well blended.

Reduce mixer speed to low and add the dry ingredients in three additions, mixing only to blend. Remove bowl from the mixer and, using a large rubber spatula, fold in chocolate and almonds.

Divide the dough into four equal parts, and with lightly oiled hands, shape each into a log 12 inches long and 2 inches wide. Place the logs 2 inches apart on the prepared baking sheets.

Brush the top of each log with some of the egg wash. Combine cinnamon and 1 tablespoon sugar and sprinkle over the logs. Bake logs for 35 to 40 minutes, then remove from the oven. To ensure even browning, toward the end of baking time rotate the baking sheets from top to bottom and front to back.

Reduce the oven temperature to 325 degrees. Slice logs into 1/2-inch pieces and place flat side down on the jelly roll pans. Return to the oven for 10 minutes, then turn slices over and bake for another 10 minutes or until the mandelbrot are crisp and the edges are light brown. Let cool on the pans. Store in an airtight container, layered between strips of wax paper, for up to three weeks. These cookies may be frozen. *Makes 84 cookies.*

Passover Chocolate Cake

Parve

8 eggs	1 1/4 cups vegetable oil
1 3/4 cups sugar	1/2 cup (heaping)
1 cup potato starch	unsweetened baking cocoa
3/4 teaspoon baking powder	2 teaspoons vanilla extract
3/4 teaspoon baking soda	

Preheat oven 350 degrees. Beat eggs and sugar in a bowl until light in color, using an electric mixer. Sift together potato starch, baking powder and baking soda in a separate bowl. Heat oil and cocoa in a saucepan or microwaveable bowl to boiling; let cool slightly. Add to egg mixture. Blend in dry ingredients and vanilla and mix well. Spoon into a greased 10-inch tube pan. Bake for 1 hour or until a tester inserted in the center comes out clean. Put pan on cooling rack and cover with a clean kitchen towel until cool. Remove from pan. *Makes 16 servings.*

Passover Substitutes

1 ounce baking (unsweetened) chocolate = 3 tablespoons unsweetened cocoa powder plus 1 tablespoon oil or melted margarine

6 ounces semisweet chocolate = 6 tablespoons unsweetened cocoa powder plus 1/4 cup oil and 7 tablespoons sugar

4 ounces sweet chocolate (German type) = 3 tablespoons unsweetened cocoa powder plus 2 2/3 tablespoons oil and 4 1/2 tablespoons sugar

1 cup confectioners' sugar = 1 cup minus 1 tablespoon sugar plus 1 tablespoon potato starch, pulsed in a food processor or blender

1 cup honey = 1 1/4 cups sugar plus 1/4 cup water

1 cup corn syrup = 1 1/4 cups sugar plus 1/4 cup water boiled until syrupy

1 cup vanilla sugar = 1 cup sugar with 1 split vanilla bean left for at least 24 hours in a tightly covered jar

1 tablespoon flour = 1/2 tablespoon potato starch

1 tablespoon cornstarch = 1 tablespoon potato starch

1 teaspoon baking powder = 1/4 teaspoon baking soda plus 1/2 teaspoon cream of tartar; if keeping for a while, add 1/4 teaspoon potato starch

1 cup graham cracker crumbs = 1 cup ground cookies or soup nuts plus 1 teaspoon cinnamon

1 cup bread crumbs = 1 cup matzoh meal

1 cup (8 ounces) cream cheese = 1 cup cottage cheese puréed with 1/2 stick (1/4 cup) butter or margarine

1 cup milk (for baking) = 1 cup water plus 2 tablespoons margarine, or 1/2 cup fruit juice plus 1/2 cup water, or 1 cup almond milk (blend 1/3 cup sliced blanched almonds with 1 cup water until smooth)

CHEESE BLINTZ LOAF WITH
BANANA BERRY TOPPING

Dairy

FILLING

16 ounces PHILADELPHIA
Cream Cheese, softened
2 (7-ounce) packages
farmer cheese
2 eggs, lightly beaten
1/4 cup sugar
1 tablespoon fresh
lemon juice
Pinch of salt

CRUST

1/2 cup (1 stick) unsalted
butter, softened
1/4 cup sugar
2 eggs, lightly beaten
3/4 cup milk
1 1/4 cups all-purpose flour
1 teaspoon baking powder
Pinch of salt

For the filling, preheat oven to 350 degrees. Grease a 5×9-inch loaf pan. Combine cream cheese, farmer cheese, eggs, sugar, lemon juice and salt in a bowl and set aside.

For the crust, beat butter and sugar in a bowl until fluffy, using an electric mixer. Add eggs, milk, flour, baking powder and salt, mixing well. Pour half the batter into the prepared pan. Spread filling on top, then cover with remaining batter. Bake for 45 minutes. Serve with Banana Berry Topping. *Makes 16 servings.*

BANANA BERRY TOPPING

Parve

2 ripe bananas, cut into chunks
1 pint strawberries, sliced
1 tablespoon sugar
1 tablespoon lemon juice

Toss bananas and berries with sugar and lemon juice.

Glossary of
Cooking Techniques
....

Blanch ....To immerse, usually vegetables or fruit, briefly into boiling water to inactivate enzymes, loosen skin, or soak away excess salt.

Braise ....To cook, especially meats, covered, in a small amount of liquid.

Caramelize ....To melt sugar in a heavy pan over low heat until golden brown, stirring constantly.

Clarify ....To remove impurities from melted butter or margarine by allowing the sediment to settle, then pouring off clear yellow liquid. Other fats may be clarified by straining.

Cream ....To blend shortening, butter, or margarine, which usually has been softened, or sometimes oil, with a granulated or crushed ingredient until the mixture is soft and creamy. Usually described in method as light and fluffy.

Deglaze ....To heat stock, wine, or other liquid in the pan in which meat has been cooked, mixing with pan juices and sediment to form a gravy or sauce base.

Dredge ....To coat completely with flour, bread crumbs, etc.

Fillet ....To remove bones from meat or fish. (Pieces of meat, fish, or poultry from which bones have been removed are called fillets.)

Fold in ....To blend a delicate frothy mixture into a heavier one so that none of the lightness or volume is lost. Using a rubber spatula, turn under and bring up and over, rotating bowl ¼ turn after each folding motion.

Infuse ....To steep herbs or other flavorings in a liquid until liquid absorbs flavor.

Julienne ....To cut vegetables, fruit, etc., into long thin strips.

Marinate ....To soak, usually in a highly seasoned oil-acid solution, to flavor and/or tenderize food.

Poach ....To cook in a small amount of gently simmering liquid.

Reduce ....To boil stock, gravy, or other liquid until volume is reduced, liquid is thickened, and flavor is intensified.

Sauté ....To cook quickly in a skillet containing a small amount of hot cooking oil. Sautéed foods should never be immersed in the cooking oil and should be stirred frequently.

Score ....To make shallow cuts diagonally in parallel lines, especially in meat.

Simmer ....To cook in or with a liquid at just below the boiling point.

Strain ....To pass through a strainer, sieve, or cheesecloth to break down or remove solids or impurities.

Truss ....To bind poultry legs and wings close to the body before cooking.

Wilt ....To apply heat to cause dehydration, color change, and a droopy appearance.

BASIC SUBSTITUTIONS

If the recipe calls for .... **You can substitute**

Flour

1 cup sifted all-purpose flour .... 1 cup less 2 tablespoons unsifted all-purpose flour

1 cup sifted cake flour .... 1 cup less 2 tablespoons sifted all-purpose flour

1 cup sifted self-rising flour .... 1 cup sifted all-purpose flour plus $1^1/_2$ teaspoons baking powder and a pinch of salt

Milk/Cream

1 cup buttermilk .... 1 cup plain yogurt, or 1 tablespoon lemon juice or vinegar plus enough milk to measure 1 cup—let stand for 5 minutes before using

1 cup whipping cream or half-and-half .... $7/_8$ cup whole milk plus $1^1/_2$ tablespoons butter

1 cup light cream .... $7/_8$ cup whole milk plus 3 tablespoons butter

1 cup sour cream .... 1 cup plain yogurt

1 cup sour milk .... 1 cup plain yogurt

1 cup whole milk .... 1 cup skim or nonfat milk plus 2 tablespoons butter or margarine

Seasonings

1 teaspoon allspice .... $1/_2$ teaspoon cinnamon plus $1/_8$ teaspoon cloves

1 cup ketchup .... 1 cup tomato sauce plus $1/_2$ cup sugar plus 2 tablespoons vinegar

1 teaspoon Italian spice .... $1/_4$ teaspoon each oregano, basil, thyme, rosemary plus dash of cayenne pepper

1 teaspoon lemon juice .... $1/_2$ teaspoon vinegar

Sugar

1 cup confectioners' sugar .... $1/_2$ cup plus 1 tablespoon granulated sugar

1 cup granulated sugar .... $1^3/_4$ cups confectioners' sugar, 1 cup packed light brown sugar, or $3/_4$ cup honey

Other

1 package active dry yeast .... $1/_2$ cake compressed yeast

1 teaspoon baking powder .... $1/_4$ teaspoon cream of tartar plus $1/_4$ teaspoon baking soda

1 cup dry bread crumbs .... $3/_4$ cup cracker crumbs, or 1 cup cornflake crumbs

1 cup (2 sticks) butter .... $7/_8$ cup vegetable oil, or 1 cup margarine

1 tablespoon cornstarch .... 2 tablespoons all-purpose flour

1 cup dark corn syrup .... $3/_4$ cup light corn syrup plus $1/_4$ cup light molasses

1 cup light corn syrup .... 1 cup maple syrup

$1^2/_3$ ounces semisweet chocolate .... 1 ounce unsweetened chocolate plus 4 teaspoons granulated sugar

1 ounce unsweetened chocolate .... 3 tablespoons unsweetened baking cocoa plus 1 tablespoon butter or margarine

1 (1-ounce) square chocolate .... $1/_4$ cup baking cocoa plus 1 teaspoon shortening

1 cup honey .... 1 to $1^1/_4$ cups sugar plus $1/_4$ cup liquid, or 1 cup corn syrup or molasses

currants .... raisins

1 egg .... $1/_4$ cup mayonnaise

1 tablespoon = 3 teaspoons   16 tablespoons = 1 cup

2 tablespoons = 1 ounce   1 cup = 8 ounces

4 tablespoons = $1/_4$ cup   2 cups = 1 pint

5 tablespoons + 1 teaspoons = $1/_3$ cup   4 cups = 1 quart

8 tablespoons = $1/_2$ cup   4 quarts = 1 gallon

12 tablespoons = $3/_4$ cup

METRIC CONVERSIONS

Weight equivalents

These are not exact weight equivalents, but have been rounded up or down slightly to make measuring easier.

American	Metric	American	Metric	American	Metric
1/4 ounce	7 grams	8 ounces (1/2 pound)	225 grams	16 ounces (1 pound)	450 grams
1/2 ounce	15 grams	9 ounces	250 grams	1 pound 2 ounces	500 grams
1 ounce	30 grams	10 ounces	300 grams	1 1/2 pounds	750 grams
2 ounces	60 grams	11 ounces	325 grams	2 pounds	900 grams
3 ounces	90 grams	12 ounces	350 grams	2 1/4 pounds	1 kilogram
4 ounces	115 grams	13 ounces	375 grams	3 pounds	1.4 kilograms
5 ounces	150 grams	14 ounces	400 grams	4 pounds	1.8 kilograms
6 ounces	175 grams	15 ounces	425 grams	4 1/2 pounds	2 kilograms
7 ounces	200 grams				

Volume equivalents

These are not exact volume equivalents, but have been rounded up or down slightly to make measuring easier.

American	Metric	Imperial
1/4 teaspoon	1.25 milliliters	
1/2 teaspoon	2.5 milliliters	
1 teaspoon	5 milliliters	
1/2 tablespoon (1 1/2 teaspoons)	7.5 milliliters	
1 tablespoon (3 teaspoons)	15 milliliters	
1/4 cup (4 tablespoons)	60 milliliters	2 fluid ounces
1/3 cup (5 tablespoons)	75 milliliters	2 1/2 fluid ounces
1/2 cup (8 tablespoons)	125 milliliters	4 fluid ounces
2/3 cup (10 tablespoons)	150 milliliters	5 fluid ounces (1/4 pint)
3/4 cup (12 tablespoons)	175 milliliters	6 fluid ounces (1/3 pint)
1 cup (16 tablespoons)	250 milliliters	8 fluid ounces
1 1/4 cups	300 milliliters	10 fluid ounces (1/2 pint)
1 1/2 cups	350 milliliters	12 fluid ounces
1 pint (2 cups)	500 milliliters	16 fluid ounces
2 1/2 cups	625 milliliters	20 fluid ounces (1 pint)
1 quart (4 cups)	1 litre	1 3/4 pints

Oven temperature equivalents

Oven	°Fahrenheit	°Celsius	Gas Mark
very cool	250-275	130-140	1/2-1
cool	300	150	2
warm	325	170	3
moderate	350	180	4
moderately hot	375	190	5
moderately hot	400	200	6
hot	425	220	7
very hot	450	230	8
very hot	475	250	9

American abbreviations

ounce	oz.
pound	lb.
teaspoon	t.
tablespoon	T.
cup	c.
pint	pt.
quart	qt.
gallon	gal.

INDEX

A

Almonds, Piquant 272

Appetizers (also see Dips; Pâtés)
Artichoke and Spinach Swirls 30
Barzargan (Cracked Bulgur Salad) 33
Bubbie's Fricassee 19
Chicken en Papillote 28
Chicken Spinach Rolls 26
Chopped Chicken with Dill en Croûte 27
Far Eastern Short Ribs 14
Glazed Garlic Chicken Wings 28
Lahamagine 18
Seared Tuna and Avocado Tartare 31
Sicilian Stuffed Rice Balls 16
Smoked Salmon Rolls 32
Spicy Turkey Wontons 24
Stuffed Wrappers with Meat and Rice 25
Todd's Merguez 15
Tortilla Shells with Meat Taco Filling 17
Yebra Sweet or Simple 22
Yebra with Chick-Peas 23

Apples
Apple Soufflé Omelet 170
Autumn Salad with Walnut Vinaigrette 60
Cabbage Soup 280
Fall Starburst 200
Fresh Fruit Trifle 218
Grandma's Apple Pie 226
Passover Apple Crisp 287
Pumpkin Apple Streusel Muffins 186
Snap-Crackle-Pop Apple Kugel 212
Squash and Apple-Stuffed Turkey Breast 102
Strawberry Rhubarb Crisp 225
Warm and Soothing Apple Crisp 219
Applesauce, Fruity 284
Apricot Pinwheels 262

Artichokes
Artichoke and Spinach Swirls 30
Artichoke, Fennel and Edamame Salad 56
Artichoke Soup 36
Chicken Salad with Roasted Garlic Mayonnaise . . 63
Grecian Chicken 82
Mediterranean Chicken Salad 61
Spinach Linguini with Tuna, Artichokes and
  Mushrooms 158
Sun-Dried Tomato and Artichoke Chicken 97
Tangy Halibut 134

Asparagus
Basmati Rice with Asparagus 209
Cream of Asparagus Soup 36
Grilled Luau Chicken 91
Oven-Roasted Asparagus with Orange Almond
  Vinaigrette 190
Rosemary Grilled Salmon and Vegetables with
  Balsamic Syrup 141
Spring Garden Penne with Asparagus 154
Vegetable Bundt Frittata 176

Autumn Salad with Walnut Vinaigrette 60

Avocados
Avocado and Hearts of Palm Salad with
  Pesto Vinaigrette 57
Avocado Dip 32
Avocado Spread 81
Baja Burritos 81
California Strawberry Salsa 33
Chilled Avocado Cucumber Soup 37
Deli Meat Salad 64
Mexican Salad 59
Seared Tuna and Avocado Tartare 31
Veggie Slaw 68

B

Banana Cake 237
Banana Berry Topping 291
Barley-Pine Nut Casserole 202
Barzargan (Cracked Bulgur Salad) 33

Beans (also see Green Beans)
Artichoke, Fennel and Edamame Salad 56
Baja Burritos 81
Black Bean and Quinoa Salad 58
Creamy White Bean Soup 38
Lentil Minestrone Soup 49
Mexican Salad 59
Spicy Bean Salad 58
Tortilla Shells with Meat Taco Filling 17

Beef (also see Ground Beef; Pastrami; Spareribs)
Bistro-Style Pasta Napolitana 124
Cabbage Soup 280
Cranberry California Roast with
  Portobello Mushrooms 112
Crusty Meat Loaf 124
Dutch Oven Brisket 109
Fillet Split with Port Glaze 113
Firecracker Rib-Eye Steaks 116
Herbed Standing Rib Roast 114
London Broil 113
Pepper-Crusted Roast 111
Potato Kugel Cholent 281
Sautéed Skirt Steak with Caramelized Shallots 118
Slow-Cooking Country-Style Stew 120
Sweet and Savory Brisket with Mushrooms and
  Caramelized Onions 110
Teriyaki Steak 115
Tongue 280
Top-of-the-Rib au Café 108

Beets
Green Bean, Watercress and Beet Salad 57
Mixed Vegetable Salad with Basil Vinaigrette 75
Simply Delicious Beet Salad 64

Blueberries
Berry Bundt Cake 237
Lemon Berry Bundt Cake 237
Very Berry Bread 187

Breads (also see Muffins)

Bread Machine Whole Wheat Challah 277
Chocolate French Toast with Raspberry Sauce 184
Cocosh 277
Crunchy Top Pumpkin Bread 207
Delicious Challah 276
Garlic Bread 40
Savory Olive Bread 40
Very Berry Bread 187

Broccoli

Broccoli Alfredo 154
Make Your Own Pizza 185
Passover Broccoli Casserole 286
Three-Cheese Baked Penne with Broccoli 155
to steam 48
Vegetable Bundt Frittata 176
Velvety Broccoli Soup 48

Brownies and Bars

Almond Coffee Squares 262
Bubbie Razie's Passover Brownies 287
Cappuccino Brownies 264
Double-Decker Confetti Brownies 265
Flavorful Krispie Treats 270
Heart-Shaped Brownies 264
Passover Blondie 288
Peanut Butter S'More Stacks 267
Quick Praline Bars 270
Strawberry Streusel Bars 268

Brunch

Apple Soufflé Omelet 170
Apricot Noodle Pudding 170
Cheese Blintz Loaf with Banana Berry Topping . . . 291
Cheese-Filled Portobello Mushrooms 177
Chocolate French Toast with Raspberry Sauce 184
Classic Spinach Casserole 173
Cranberry Orange Muffins with
    Cinnamon-Sugar Topping 187
Eggplant Rollitini 174
Leek and Brie Tart 172
Linguini, Basil and Mushroom Flan 181
Make Your Own Pizza 185
Mushroom Onion Torta 171
Polenta Lasagna 180
Pumpkin Apple Streusel Muffins 186
Roasted Eggplant and Bell Pepper Terrine 178
Salmon Breakfast Bake 173
Shiitake Mushroom and Herb Strata 179
Vegetable Bundt Frittata 176
Veggie Burgers 181
Very Berry Bread 187
Zucchini Frittata 176
Zucchini, Tomato and Mozzarella Tart 175

Burgers

Jay's Burgers 119
Salmon Burgers with Hoisin and Ginger 144
Tuna Steak Burgers with
    Ginger Mustard Spread 151
Turkey Burgers 103
Veggie Burgers 181
Burritos, Baja 81

C

Cakes (also see Cheesecakes)

Banana Cake 237
Berry Bundt Cake 237
Chocolate and Hazelnut Meringue Cake 241
Chocolate Roulade 242
Chocolate Sour Cream Pound Cake 247
Chocolate Torte 244
Crunchy Almond Confetti Cake 236
Decadent Creamy Pound Cakes 247
Decorated Black and White Cake 239
Orange Poppy Seed Cake 246
Passover Chocolate Cake 290
Pull-Apart Cake 249
Streusel Pound Cake 248
White Cake 239

Carrots

Bubbie's Fricassee 19
Cantonese Chicken Salad 62
Colorful Fish Pâté 29
Hearty Lentil Soup 44
Herb-Crusted Chicken Potpie 84–85
Mixed Vegetable Salad with Basil Vinaigrette 75
Passover Broccoli Casserole 286
Passover Carrot Pudding 286
Passover Matzoh Meal-Crusted Chicken with
    Vegetables 285
Purée of Carrot and Dill Soup 39
Roasted Cauliflower and Dill Soup 42
Roasted Root Vegetable Soup 50
Slow-Cooking Country-Style Stew 120
Sweet Potato and Leek Soup with Pecan Garni 51
Tomato and Spinach Bisque 52
Turkey Burgers 103
Vegetable Bundt Frittata 176
Veggie Slaw 68
Very Wild Basmati Salad 73

Cauliflower

Roasted Cauliflower 193
Roasted Cauliflower and Dill Soup 42
Cheese Blintz Loaf with Banana Berry Topping 291
Cheesecake Dessert 238

Cheesecakes

Chocolate Cheese Cupcakes 238
Classic Cheesecake 232
Espresso Cheesecake 233

Chicken

Baja Burritos 81
Balsamic Chicken 83
Beer Can-Roasted Chicken 80
Bubbie's Fricassee 19
Cantonese Chicken Salad 62
Chicken en Papillote 28
Chicken Kabobs 86
Chicken Monterey 92
Chicken Ruby 86
Chicken Salad with Roasted Garlic Mayonnaise 63
Chicken Spinach Rolls 26
Chopped Chicken with Dill en Croûte 27
Crumb-Coated Chicken 83
Georgian Pomegranate Chicken 95

Glazed Garlic Chicken Wings 28
Grecian Chicken 82
Grilled Luau Chicken 91
Hawaiian Schnitzel 90
Herb-Crusted Chicken Potpie 84–85
Honey-Ginger Chicken 91
Lacquered Chicken 87
Lemon-Pistachio Chicken Sliced over Greens 90
Linguini with Chicken, Leeks and Tomatoes 99
Making Your Own Stock 27
Mediterranean Chicken Salad 61
Mushroom-Stuffed Chicken Breasts 92
Oven-Glazed Chicken 82
Passover Matzoh Meal-Crusted Chicken and
    Vegetables 285
Roasted Chicken with Garlic Confit 87
Rolled Chicken Filled with Pastrami 93
Rosemary Chicken 94
Saucy Chicken Cutlets 90
Shiitake Ginger Chicken 96
Sun-Dried Tomato and Artichoke Chicken 97
Tomato and Wine-Infused Chicken 98

Chick-Peas

Mediterranean Chick-Pea Soup 43
Mixed Vegetable Salad with Basil Vinaigrette 75
Spicy Bean Salad 58
Summertime Couscous Salad 76
Veggie Burgers 181
Yebra with Chick-Peas 23

Chocolate

Almond Coffee Squares 262
Almond Crisps 250
Black Russian Frozen Dessert 228
Bubbie Razie's Passover Brownies 287
Cappuccino Brownies 264
Caramel Nut Tart 231
Chocolate and Hazelnut Meringue Cake 241
Chocolate Babka 240
Chocolate Cheese Cupcakes 238
Chocolate Chip Meringues 256
Chocolate Chip Passover Cookies 288
Chocolate Chip Peanut Butter Cookies 252
Chocolate Chocolate Chocolate Biscotti 263
Chocolate Cookie Glaze 250
Chocolate French Toast with Raspberry Sauce 184
Chocolate Frosting 239
Chocolate Peanut Butter Crunch 228
Chocolate Raisin Nut Clusters 271
Chocolate Roulade 242
Chocolate Sour Cream Pound Cake 247
Chocolate Toffee Pie 229
Chocolate Torte 244
Chocolate Turtle Pie 245
Crinkle Cookies 254
Crunchy Almond Confetti Cake 236
Decorated Black and White Cake 239
Double-Decker Confetti Brownies 265
Easy Chocolate Mousse 251
Espresso Cheesecake 233
Flavorful Krispie Treats 270
Fudge Sauce 230
Heart-Shaped Brownies 264
Marbleized Chocolate Chip Cookie Tart 230

My Mother's Mandelbread 266
Palmiers and Twists 261
Passover Blondie 288
Passover Chocolate Cake 290
Passover Mandelbrot 289
Peanut Butter S'More Stacks 267
Secret Recipe Chocolate Chip Cookies 251
Strawberries and Cream Pie 224
Warm Chocolate Soufflés 243
White Chocolate Pretzel Clusters 268
Whoopie Pies 269
Chocolate Garnishes 234, 244

Coffee

Almond Coffee Squares 262
Black Russian Frozen Dessert 228
Cafe Alexander 177
Cafe Benedictine 177
Cafe Caribe 177
Cafe Columbian 177
Cafe Dublin 177
Cafe Holland 177
Cafe Israel 177
Caffe Latte 173
Candied Pecans 271
Cappuccino 175
Cappuccino Brownies 264
Chocolate Roulade 242
Chocolate Toffee Pie 229
Espresso Cheesecake 233
Sweet and Savory Brisket with Mushrooms and
    Caramelized Onions 110
The Perfect Cup 171
Top-of-the-Rib au Café 108

Cookies (also see Brownies and Bars; Meringues)

Almond Crisps 250
Apricot Pinwheels 262
Apricot Rugelach 220
Butter Pecan Cookies 258
Chocolate Chip Passover Cookies 288
Chocolate Chip Peanut Butter Cookies 252
Chocolate Chocolate Chocolate Biscotti 263
Cinnamon Roll-Up Cookies 253
Classic Refrigerator Sprinkle Cookies 259
Cranberry Sticks 266
Crinkle Cookies 254
Ginger Cookie Press Cookies 255
Glazed Lemon Cookies 254
Marbleized Chocolate Chip Cookie Tart 230
My Mother's Mandelbread 266
Oatmeal (Coconut) Cookies 255
Palmiers and Twists 261
Passover Mandelbrot 289
Ruby Jewel Miniatures 260
Secret Recipe Chocolate Chip Cookies 251
Sinfully Delicious Cookies 264
Whoopie Pies 269

Corn

Asian Salad 74
Black Bean and Quinoa Salad 58
Mexican Salad 59
Roasted Corn Salad 61
Very Wild Basmati Salad 73

Cornish Hens, Tarragon-Stuffed 101

Couscous
Couscous Salad 58
Orange and Almond Couscous 203
Summertime Couscous Salad 76

Cranberries
Chicken Ruby 86
Cranberry California Roast with
Portobello Mushrooms 112
Cranberry Nut Pie 206
Cranberry Orange Muffins with
Cinnamon-Sugar Topping 187
Cranberry Sticks 266
Fall Starburst 200
Pear and Cranberry Crisp 203
Sweet-and-Sour Meatballs 117

Crisps
Passover Apple Crisp 287
Pear and Cranberry Crisp 203
Strawberry Rhubarb Crisp 225
Warm and Soothing Apple Crisp 219

Cucumbers
Chilled Avocado Cucumber Soup 37
Chopped Greek Salad 59
Cold Roasted Red Gazpacho with Tortilla Strips . . . 47
Garden Verde Soup 53
Smoked Salmon Rolls 32
Summertime Couscous Salad 76

D

Dips (also see Salsas)
Avocado Dip 32
Greek Garlic Dip 30

Desserts (see Brownies and Bars; Cakes; Cheesecakes;
Chocolate; Cookies; Meringues; Pies, Pastries and Tarts;
Sauces, Dessert)
Duck à l'Orange 100

E

Eggplant
Eggplant Rollitini 174
Ratatouille Soup 43
Ratatouille Tart 201
Roasted Eggplant and Bell Pepper Terrine 178
Rosemary Grilled Salmon and Vegetables with
Balsamic Syrup 141

Eggs (see Brunch)

F

Fennel
Artichoke, Fennel and Edamame Salad 56
Rice-Stuffed Trout 148

Fish (also see Salmon; Sea Bass; Snapper, Red; Trout; Tuna)
Carmela's Moroccan Fish 138
Cod Livornese 136
Colorful Fish Pâté 29
Crispy Fried Fish 134

One-Dish Wonder 196
Passover Gefilte Fish Patties 285
Roasted Striped Bass with
Scallion Cream Sauce 133
Sole with Orange Sauce 145
Tangy Halibut 134
Tilapia Fillets with Pesto Butter 146
French Toast, Chocolate with Raspberry Sauce 184
Fricassee, Bubbie's 19

Frittatas
Vegetable Bundt Frittata 176
Zucchini Frittata 176

Frostings and Icings
Chocolate Frosting 239
Vanilla Frosting 239
Fruit Tart, Rustic 222

G

Gazpacho, Cold Roasted Red with Tortilla Strips 47

Grains (also see Couscous)
Barley-Pine Nut Casserole 202
Barzargan (Cracked Bulgur Salad) 33
Black Bean and Quinoa Salad 58

Grape Leaves
Yebra Sweet or Simple 22
Yebra with Chick-Peas 23

Green Beans
Cold Green Beans with Dill and Pecan Sauce 191
Green Beans with Cremini Mushroom Sauce 192
Green Bean, Watercress and Beet Salad 57
Rosemary Grilled Salmon and Vegetables with
Balsamic Syrup 141
Salad Niçoise 69
Soy Sauce Green Beans 191

Ground Beef
Jay's Burgers 119
Lahamagine 18
Sicilian Stuffed Rice Balls 16
Stuffed Wrappers with Meat and Rice 25
Sweet-and-Sour Meatballs 117
Tortilla Shells with Meat Taco Filling 17

H

Hearts of Palm
Avocado and Hearts of Palm Salad with
Pesto Vinaigrette 57
Chicken Salad with Roasted Garlic
Mayonnaise 63
Deli Meat Salad 64
Honeydew Soup, Refreshing Summer Minted 45

K

Kugels
Potato Kugel Cholent 281
Snap-Crackle-Pop Apple Kugel 212
Sweet Noodle Kugel 281
Yerushalmi Kugel 211

INDEX • 298

L

Lahamagine 18

Lamb
Lamb Stew 129
Quick Lamb Chops 125
Rack of Lamb 125
Todd's Merguez 15

Lasagna, Polenta 180

Leeks
Artichoke Soup 36
Brown Rice with Leeks and Mushrooms 202
Garlic-Mushroom Soup 46
Grecian Chicken 82
Herb-Crusted Chicken Potpie 84–85
Leek and Brie Tart 172
Leek and Mushroom Stuffing 214
Linguini, Basil and Mushroom Flan 181
Linguini with Chicken, Leeks and Tomatoes 99
Squash and Apple-Stuffed Turkey Breast 102
Sweet Potato and Leek Soup with Pecan Garni 51

Lentils
Hearty Lentil Soup 44
Lentil Minestrone Soup 49
Lentil Rice (Engedrah) 207

M

Mangos
Cajun Veal Roast with Mango Purée 126
Fresh Fruit Sorbet 227
Mango Salsa 132
Mango Sauce 227
Zingy Watermelon and Mango 219

Marinades
Barbecue Marinade for Chicken 84
Chinese Marinade 93
Cutlet Marinade 95
Great Steak Marinade 122
Honey Mustard Marinade 92
Honey Soy Soak 122
Lemon Wine Marinade 95
Meat Marinade 122
Piquant Marinade 92
Slightly Thai Marinade 93
Sweet Marinade 122
Wonderfully Flavorful Marinade 122

Meat Loaf, Crusty 124

Meats (see Beef; Ground Beef; Lamb; Pastrami; Spareribs; Veal)

Meringues
Almond Lattice Meringues 256
Chocolate and Hazelnut Meringue Cake 241
Chocolate Chip Meringues 256
Lemon or Cream Meringue Nests 257
Meringues 256
Strawberry Meringues 258

Merguez, Todd's 15

Muffins
Coffee Cake Muffins 238
Corn Squash Muffins 211
Cranberry Orange Muffins with
  Cinnamon-Sugar Topping 187
Pumpkin Apple Streusel Muffins 186

Mushrooms
Asian Salad 74
Brown Rice with Leeks and Mushrooms 202
Cheese-Filled Portobello Mushrooms 177
Chicken Kabobs 86
Chicken Monterey 92
Chopped Chicken with Dill en Croûte 27
Cranberry California Roast with
  Portobello Mushrooms 112
Exotic Mushroom Soup 48
Farfalle with Shiitakes, Sweet Potatoes and Peas . . 159
Garlic-Mushroom Soup 46
Green Beans with Cremini Mushroom Sauce 192
Italian Portobello Mushrooms 194
Leek and Mushroom Stuffing 214
Linguini, Basil and Mushroom Flan 181
Linguini with Garlicky Marsala Mushrooms 156
Make Your Own Pizza 185
Marinated Portobello Mushrooms 194
Mushroom Onion Torta 171
Mushroom Roll-ups Florentine 164
Mushroom Salad 68
Mushroom-Stuffed Chicken Breasts 92
Orzo with Caramelized Onion and
  Mushroom Sauté 206
Portobello Mushroom Caps Stuffed with
  Ratatouille 200
Roasted Sweet Potatoes and Mushrooms 198
Rosemary Grilled Salmon and Vegetables with
  Balsamic Syrup 141
Saucy Chicken Cutlets 90
Shiitake Ginger Chicken 96
Shiitake Mushroom and Herb Strata 179
Sicilian Stuffed Rice Balls 16
Slow-Cooking Country-Style Stew 120
Spinach Linguini with Tuna, Artichokes and
  Mushrooms 158
Stuffed Zucchini 199
Sweet and Savory Brisket with Mushrooms and
  Caramelized Onions 110
Thin Spaghetti with Garlic Herb Sauce 160
Tomato and Wine-Infused Chicken 98
Traditional Chestnut Stuffing 215
Turkey Burgers 103
Wild Blend Rice Sauté 208
Zucchini and Mushroom Bake 200
Zucchini Frittata 176

N

Noodle Puddings
Apricot Noodle Pudding 170
Sweet Noodle Kugel 281
Yerushalmi Kugel 211

Nuts
Candied Pecans 271
Middle Eastern Spiced Nuts 71
Piquant Almonds 272
Spiced Nuts 272
Spiced Walnuts 71

O

Olive Butter 40

P

Palmiers and Twists 261
Parsley, Fried 85
Passover Recipes 285–290

Pasta

Apricot Noodle Pudding 170
Baked Ziti 165
Bistro-Style Pasta Napolitana 124
Broccoli Alfredo 154
Cheesy Fusilli Zucchini 167
Farfalle with Shiitakes, Sweet Potatoes and Peas . . 159
Greek Tortellini Salad 65
Homemade Rice and 'Roni 210
Lamb Stew 129
Lemon Garlic Pasta 155
Lentil Minestrone Soup 49
Linguini, Basil and Mushroom Flan 181
Linguini with Chicken, Leeks
    and Tomatoes 99
Linguini with Garlicky Marsala Mushrooms 156
Mediterranean Chicken Salad 61
Mediterranean Chick-Pea Soup 43
Mediterranean Pasta Shells 161
Modern Mac and Cheese—Not Just for Kids 157
Mushroom Roll-Ups Florentine 164
No-Bake Ziti 165
Orzo with Caramelized Onion and
    Mushroom Sauté 206
Roasted Garlic and Cherry Tomatoes 166
Roasted Root Vegetable Soup 50
Sesame Noodles 24
Spicy Tomato Olive Sauce à la Rigatoni 167
Spinach Linguini with Tuna, Artichokes and
    Mushrooms 158
Spring Garden Penne with Asparagus 154
Stuffed Shells 165
Sweet Noodle Kugel 281
Thin Spaghetti with Garlic Herb Sauce 160
Three-Cheese Baked Penne with Broccoli 155
Tomato Basil Angel Hair Pasta 158
Yerushalmi Kugel 211

Pastrami

Deli Meat Salad 64
Deli Roll 279
Rolled Chicken Filled with Pastrami 93
Slow-Cooking Country-Style Stew 120
Stuffed Breast of Veal 128

Pâtés

Colorful Fish Pâté 29
Veal Pâté 14

Pears

Mashed Sweet Potatoes and Pears 213
Pear, Arugula and Endive Salad with
    Spiced Walnuts 71
Pear and Cranberry Crisp 203
Pear Tarte Tatin 223
Rustic Fruit Tart 222

Peas

Asian Salad 74
Cantonese Chicken Salad 62
Farfalle with Shiitakes, Sweet Potatoes and Peas . . 159
Herb-Crusted Chicken Potpie 84–85
Peas with Spinach and Shallots 199
Very Wild Basmati Salad 73
Pecan Garni 51

Pesto

Classic Basil Pesto 162
Pesto Butter 146
Pesto Vinaigrette 57
Red Pesto 162
Spinach and Walnut Pesto 162

Pies, Pastries and Tarts

Chocolate Turtle Pie 245
Caramel Nut Tart 231
Chocolate Toffee Pie 229
Cranberry Nut Pie 206
Grandma's Apple Pie 226
Marbleized Chocolate Chip Cookie Tart 230
Pear Tarte Tatin 223
Raspberry Nut Tart 221
Rustic Fruit Tart 222
Strawberries and Cream Pie 224
Pineapple Rounds 213
Pizza, Make Your Own 185
Polenta Lasagna 180
Popcorn, Flavored 273

Potatoes

Artichoke Soup 36
Bravas Potatoes 195
Garlic-Mushroom Soup 46
Herbed Mashed Potatoes 196
Lamb Stew 129
Potato Filling (for Deli Roll) 279
Potato Kugel Cholent 281
Purée of Carrot and Dill Soup 39
Salad Niçoise 69
Scalloped Potatoes with White Wine 196
Slow-Cooking Country-Style Stew 120
Sweet Potato and Leek Soup with Pecan Garni 51
Zucchini and Spinach Soup 53

Poultry (see Chicken; Cornish Hens; Duck; Turkey)

Pumpkin

Crunchy Top Pumpkin Bread 207
Pumpkin Apple Streusel Muffins 186

R

Raspberries

Berry Bundt Cake 237
Berry Sauce 218
Fresh Fruit Sorbet 227
Lemon Berry Bundt Cake 237
Raspberry Nut Tart 221

Ratatouille

Portobello Mushroom Caps Stuffed with
    Ratatouille 200
Ratatouille Soup 43
Ratatouille Tart 201

Rhubarb

Fruity Applesauce 284
Strawberry and Rhubarb Sauce 225
Strawberry Rhubarb Crisp 225

Rice

Baked Veal Chops with Rice 121
Basmati Rice with Asparagus 209
Brown Rice with Leeks and Mushrooms 202
Cabbage Soup 280
Coriander Rice 209
Homemade Rice and 'Roni 210
Lamb Stew 129
Lentil Rice (Engedrah) 207
Rice-Stuffed Trout 148
Sicilian Stuffed Rice Balls 16
Spanish Rice 210
Stuffed Wrappers with Meat and Rice 25
Tarragon-Stuffed Cornish Hens 101
Tomato and Spinach Bisque 52
Veggie Burgers 181
Very Wild Basmati Salad 73
Wild Blend Rice Sauté 208
Yebra Sweet or Simple 22
Yebra with Chick-Peas 23
Rice Balls, Sicilian Stuffed 16
Root Vegetable Soup, Roasted 50

Rubs

Cajun Rub 122
Herb Rub 104

S

Salad Dressings (also see Vinaigrettes)

Basil Dressing 73
Creamy Sweet and Sour Dressing 62
Fiesta Dressing 64
Fresh Dill Dressing 69
Garlic Caesar Dressing 77
Garlic Herb Dressing 68
Lemon Cumin Dressing 76
Lemon Oregano Dressing 59
Parsley Dijon Dressing 71
Poppy Seed Dressing 72
Salsa Lime Dressing 59
Sesame Soy Dressing 62
Sweet & Sour Red Dressing 68
Tangy Dressing 64

Salads

Artichoke, Fennel and Edamame Salad 56
Asian Salad 74
Autumn Salad with Walnut Vinaigrette 60
Avocado and Hearts of Palm Salad with
   Pesto Vinaigrette 57
Barzargan (Cracked Bulgur Salad) 33
Black Bean and Quinoa Salad 58
Cantonese Chicken Salad 62
Chicken Salad with Roasted Garlic Mayonnaise 63
Chopped Greek Salad 59
Couscous Salad 58
Crunchy Nutty Salad 70
Deli Meat Salad 64
Greek Tortellini Salad 65
Green Bean, Watercress and Beet Salad 57
Mediterranean Chicken Salad 61
Mexican Salad 59
Mixed Vegetable Salad with Basil Vinaigrette 75
Mushroom Salad 68
Pear, Arugula and Endive Salad with Spiced Walnuts 71
Roasted Corn Salad 61
Salad Niçoise 69
Simply Delicious Beet Salad 64
Spicy Bean Salad 58
Strawberry Brie Salad with Poppy Seed Dressing . . 72
Summertime Couscous Salad 76
Turkey Caesar Salad 77
Veggie Slaw 68
Very Wild Basmati Salad 73
Watercress and Herb Salad 118

Salmon

Baked Salmon with Mustard and Tarragon 138
Colorful Fish Pâté 29
Cool Marinated Salmon 284
Grilled Salmon Italiano 140
Pepper-Crusted Marinated Salmon 139
Rosemary Grilled Salmon and Vegetables with
   Balsamic Syrup 141
Salmon Breakfast Bake 173
Salmon Burgers with Hoisin and Ginger 144
Salmon with Tomatoes and Shallots 139
Smoked Salmon Rolls 32
Zesty Slow-Roasted Salmon 144

Salsas

California Strawberry Salsa 33
Mango Salsa 132

Sauces, Dessert

Berry Sauce 218
Fudge Sauce 230
Mango Sauce 227
Raspberry Sauce 184
Strawberry and Rhubarb Sauce 225
Vanilla Sauce 223

Sauces, Savory

Béchamel Sauce 164
Chimichurri Sauce 122
Ginger Mustard Spread 151
Green Herb Mayonnaise 134
Horseradish Sauce 285
Orange Sauce (for fish) 145
Quick Mustard Sauce 14
Remoulade Sauce 150
Scallion Cream Sauce 133

Sea Bass

Crunchy Sea Bass with Mango Salsa 132
Roasted Sea Bass 135
Sesame Noodles 24
Slaw, Veggie 68

Side Dishes (also see individual listings) 188–215

Snacks (also see Popcorn)

Candied Pecans 271
Chocolate Raisin Nut Clusters 271
Piquant Almonds 272
Spiced Nuts 272
White Chocolate Pretzel Clusters 268

Snapper, Red
Oven-Roasted Whole Snapper with Black Olives . . 137
Red Snapper Algarve 135
Sorbet, Fresh Fruit 227
Soufflés, Warm Chocolate 243
Soup, Homemade Stock 27

Soups
Artichoke Soup 36
Cabbage Soup 280
Chilled Avocado Cucumber Soup 37
Cold Roasted Red Gazpacho with Tortilla Strips . . . 47
Cream of Asparagus Soup 36
Creamy White Bean Soup 38
Exotic Mushroom Soup 48
Garden Verde Soup 53
Garlic-Mushroom Soup 46
Hearty Lentil Soup 44
Lentil Minestrone Soup 49
Mediterranean Chick-Pea Soup 43
Purée of Carrot and Dill Soup 39
Ratatouille Soup 43
Refreshing Summer Minted Honeydew Soup 45
Roasted Cauliflower and Dill Soup 42
Roasted Root Vegetable Soup 50
Sweet Potato and Leek Soup with
    Pecan Garni 51
Tomato and Spinach Bisque 52
Velvety Broccoli Soup 48
Zucchini and Spinach Soup 53
Spaghetti with Garlic Herb Sauce, Thin 160

Spareribs
Citrus-Glazed Spareribs 116
Far Eastern Short Ribs 14
Succulent Spareribs 117

Spinach
Artichoke and Spinach Swirls 30
Asian Salad 74
Chicken en Papillote 28
Chicken Spinach Rolls 26
Classic Spinach Casserole 173
Colorful Fish Pâté 29
Creamed Spinach 193
Crunchy Nutty Salad 70
Make Your Own Pizza 185
Mushroom Roll-Ups Florentine 164
Peas with Spinach and Shallots 199
Polenta Lasagna 180
Roasted Root Vegetable Soup 50
Spinach and Walnut Pesto 162
Stuffed Shells 165
Stuffed Zucchini 199
Thin Spaghetti with Garlic Herb Sauce 160
Tomato and Spinach Bisque 52
Veal Pâté 14
Zucchini and Spinach Soup 53

Squash, Butternut
Corn Squash Muffins 211
Fall Starburst 200
Roasted Root Vegetable Soup 50
Squash and Apple-Stuffed Turkey Breast 102

Stews
Lamb Stew 129
Slow-Cooking Country-Style Stew 120

Strawberries
Balsamic-Glazed Strawberries 227
Banana Berry Topping 291
Berry Sauce 218
California Strawberry Salsa 33
Fresh Fruit Sorbet 227
Fruity Applesauce 284
Strawberries and Cream Pie 224
Strawberry and Rhubarb Sauce 225
Strawberry Brie Salad with Poppy Seed Dressing . . 72
Strawberry Meringues 258
Strawberry Rhubarb Crisp 225
Strawberry Streusel Bars 268
Strawberry Whip 225
Very Berry Bread 187

Stuffings
Leek and Mushroom Stuffing 214
Traditional Chestnut Stuffing 215

Sweet Potatoes
Farfalle with Shiitakes, Sweet Potatoes and Peas . . 159
Mashed Sweet Potatoes and Pears 213
Roasted Root Vegetable Soup 50
Roasted Sweet Potatoes and Mushrooms 198
Sweet Potato and Leek Soup with Pecan Garni 51
Sweet Potato Purée with Almond Streusel 197

T

Taiglach 278

Tarts, Savory
Leek and Brie Tart 172
Mushroom Onion Torta 171
Ratatouille Tart 201
Zucchini, Tomato and Mozzarella Tart 175

Tarts, Sweet (see Pies, Pastries and Tarts)

Tomatoes
Avocado and Hearts of Palm Salad with
    Pesto Vinaigrette 57
Baja Burritos 81
Cabbage Soup 280
Carmela's Moroccan Fish 138
Cheese-Filled Portobello Mushrooms 177
Chicken en Papillote 28
Chopped Greek Salad 59
Cod Livornese 136
Cold Roasted Red Gazpacho with Tortilla Strips . . . 47
Deli Meat Salad 64
Grilled Salmon Italiano 140
Hearty Lentil Soup 44
Italian Portobello Mushrooms 194
Lamb Stew 129
Lentil Minestrone Soup 49
Linguini with Chicken, Leeks and Tomatoes 99
Make Your Own Pizza 185
Mediterranean Chicken Salad 61
Mediterranean Chick-Pea Soup 43
Mediterranean Pasta Shells 161

Mexican Salad 59
Mixed Vegetable Salad with Basil Vinaigrette 75
Modern Mac and Cheese—Not Just for Kids 157
Mushroom Salad 68
Ratatouille Soup 43
Ratatouille Tart 201
Red Pesto 162
Roasted Garlic and Cherry Tomatoes 166
Rosemary Chicken 94
Salad Niçoise 69
Salmon with Tomatoes and Shallots 139
Spanish Rice 210
Spicy Tomato Olive Sauce à la Rigatoni 167
Spinach Linguini with Tuna, Artichokes and
    Mushrooms 158
Summertime Couscous Salad 76
Sun-Dried Tomato and Artichoke Chicken 97
Tangy Halibut 134
Tomato and Spinach Bisque 52
Tomato and Wine-Infused Chicken 98
Tomato Basil Angel Hair Pasta 158
Tortilla Shells with Meat Taco Filling 17
Tuna Steak Burgers with
    Ginger Mustard Spread 151
Veggie Burgers 181
Zucchini, Tomato and Mozzarella Tart 175

Tortillas
Baja Burritos 81
Tortilla Shells with Meat Taco Filling 17
Tortilla Slices 59
Tortilla Strips 47
Trifle, Fresh Fruit 218

Traditional 274–291

Trout
Rice-Stuffed Trout 148
Trout with Hazelnuts, Lemon and Parsley
    Brown Butter 147
Walnut-Crusted Trout Fillets 146

Tuna
Grilled Tuna with Herbed Aïoli 150
Salad Niçoise 69
Seared Tuna and Avocado Tartare 31
Seared Tuna Steaks with Wasabi Mayonnaise 149
Spinach Linguini with Tuna, Artichokes and
    Mushrooms 158
Tuna Steak Burgers with
    Ginger Mustard Spread 151

Turkey
Apricot-Glazed Turkey 104
Deli Meat Salad 64
Deli Roll 279
Spicy Turkey Wontons 24
Squash and Apple-Stuffed Turkey Breast 102
Stuffed Wrappers with Meat and Rice 25
Tangy Turkey Breast 103
Turkey Burgers 103
Turkey Caesar Salad 77
Turkey Preparation 105

V

Veal
Baked Veal Chops with Rice 121
Cajun Veal Roast with Mango Purée 126
Pan-Seared Veal Chops with
    Mustard Sage Sauce 127
Stuffed Breast of Veal 128
Veal Pâté 14
Veggie Burgers 181

Vinaigrettes
Basil Balsamic Vinaigrette 75
Citrus Vinaigrette 70
Creamy Mustard Vinaigrette 63
Fresh Tarragon Vinaigrette 61
Honey Mustard Vinaigrette 63
Lemonade Vinaigrette 70
Lime Balsamic Vinaigrette 58
Mint Vinaigrette 65
Our Favorite Vinaigrette 68
Pesto Vinaigrette 57
Raspberry Vinaigrette 62
Rice Vinaigrette 70
Tamari Vinaigrette 74
Walnut Dijon Vinaigrette 57
Walnut Vinaigrette 60

W

Watercress
Autumn Salad with Walnut Vinaigrette 60
Green Bean, Watercress and Beet Salad 57
Watercress and Herb Salad 118
Watermelon and Mango, Zingy 219

Wontons
Spicy Turkey Wontons 24
Stuffed Wrappers with Meat and Rice 25

Y

Yebra
Yebra Sweet or Simple 22
Yebra with Chick-Peas 23

Z

Zucchini
Cheesy Fusilli Zucchini 167
Garden Verde Soup 53
Passover Matzoh Meal-Crusted Chicken with
    Vegetables 285
Ratatouille Soup 43
Ratatouille Tart 201
Rosemary Grilled Salmon and Vegetables with
    Balsamic Syrup 141
Stuffed Zucchini 199
Turkey Burgers 103
Zucchini, Tomato and Mozzarella Tart 175
Zucchini and Mushroom Bake 200
Zucchini and Spinach Soup 53
Zucchini Frittata 176

The Kosher Palette II
Coming Home

c/o Joseph Kusher Hebrew Academy/Rae Kushner Yeshiva High School
110 South Orange Avenue • Livingston, New Jersey 07039
(973) 597-1115 ext. 1197 • www.thekosherpalette.org

Please send me:

The Kosher Palette II cookbook	@ $29.95 each	Quantity_____	$ _____
Postage & Handling for first book	@ $ 6.00		$ _____
Each additional book to same address *(U.S. only)*	@ $ 2.00		$ _____
Sales Tax *(New Jersey residents only add 6%)*	@ $ 1.80		$ _____
		Total Enclosed	$ _____

Ship to:

Name _____

Address _____

City _____ State_____ Zip Code _____

Phone Number _____ Email Address *(optional)* _____

Make checks payable to The Kosher Palette II.

Charge to *(circle one)*   Visa   MasterCard   Signature _____

Account number _____Expiration Date _____

All proceeds from The Kosher Palette II: Coming Home will benefit the educational needs
of the students of the Joseph Kushner Hebrew Academy and Rae Kushner Yeshiva High School.

Thank you for your order.

- -

The Kosher Palette II
Coming Home

c/o Joseph Kusher Hebrew Academy/Rae Kushner Yeshiva High School
110 South Orange Avenue • Livingston, New Jersey 07039
(973) 597-1115 ext. 1197 • www.thekosherpalette.org

Please send me:

The Kosher Palette II cookbook	@ $29.95 each	Quantity_____	$ _____
Postage & Handling for first book	@ $ 6.00		$ _____
Each additional book to same address *(U.S. only)*	@ $ 2.00		$ _____
Sales Tax *(New Jersey residents only add 6%)*	@ $ 1.80		$ _____
		Total Enclosed	$ _____

Ship to:

Name _____

Address _____

City _____ State_____ Zip Code _____

Phone Number _____ Email Address *(optional)* _____

Make checks payable to The Kosher Palette II.

Charge to *(circle one)*   Visa   MasterCard   Signature _____

Account number _____Expiration Date _____

All proceeds from The Kosher Palette II: Coming Home will benefit the educational needs
of the students of the Joseph Kushner Hebrew Academy and Rae Kushner Yeshiva High School.

Thank you for your order.